Republican Tradition in Europe.

First Published in 1911

To

A. LAWRENCE LOWELL

PRESIDENT OF HARVARD UNIVERSITY

DEAR PRESIDENT LOWELL,

This book is the fruit of a course of lectures delivered at the Lowell Institute in the first year of your College Presidency. Will you allow me to dedicate it to you as a token of sincere admiration and friendship, and with every hope that the great University of Harvard may go from strength to strength under your vigorous and enlightened rule ?

Though there have been a few alterations and additions, this little volume substantially represents my lectures as they were written for delivery, nor have I attempted to convert a series of discourses intended for a general audience into a complete or systematic treatise. The subject is large, and I do not profess to supply more than a bare outline of the course of Republican thought and action from the downfall of the Roman Empire to the present day. But the matter is comparatively unfamiliar, and, save for Emilio Castelar's "Historia del Movimiento Republicano," a characteristic monument of Andalusian exuberance, I am not aware that it has been made the subject of a book. To an American audience, nurtured

v

in the Republican tradition of the New World, it may
be interesting to learn at what epochs, and within
what limits, and with what results a political idea
similar to their own has been an operative force in
European politics.   For even in the Old World there
have been moments when some have dreamt the dream
of Abraham Lincoln : " Friend, the Lord prefers
common-looking people ; that is why He made so
many of them."   And so I venture to transgress the
very sound maxim which reminds us that what will
do well enough in a lecture-room is very seldom fit
for the society on a book-shelf.

Yours sincerely,

HERBERT A. L. FISHER

NEW COLLEGE, OXFORD
    January 1911

CONTENTS

CHAP.   PAGE

I. MEDIEVAL THOUGHT AND ANCIENT TRADITION .   I

The Monarchical Faith in Europe—Bossuet on Louis XIV. and the Qualities of Monarchy—Eclipse of the Republican Tradition under the Roman Empire—The Barbarian Monarchies—Monarchy in Early Medieval Literature—The Commonwealth of Iceland, 930-1264 —Medieval Theory of Politics—Papacy and Empire— Monarchy the Most Perfect Form—Absence of Systematic Democratic Thought in the Middle Ages—John Wyclif, d. 1384.

II. VENICE AND FLORENCE   13

The Roman Republic, 1155-1354—The Italian Conception of Liberty—The Rise of the Despots—Tyrannicide—Influence of the Classic Spirit—Political Revolutions in Florence, 1494-1530—Venice and Florence— Reputation of Venice—Donato Giannotti, 1492-1572 —His Views on the Republican Experiments in Florence —The End of the Republic in Florence—The Catholic Reaction in Italy—Estimates of Popular Government— Niccolo Machiavelli, 1469-1530 — Francesco Guicciardini, 1482-1540.

III. THE PROTESTANT SPIRIT   34

Protestant Leaders and Political Obedience— Political Speculations of the Huguenots—Rise of the Dutch Republic, 1568-1581—Its Influence on Political Speculation—Triumph of Monarchy in the Seventeenth Century—Resistance to the Crown in England, 1603-45 —The Democratic Party—The Opportunists—Oliver Cromwell is offered the Crown, 1657—Aristocratic Character of the Commonwealth—Sir James Harrington, 1611-1677—Milton's "Ready and Easy Way"—Algernon Sidney, 1622-83—Republicanism and Classical Literature—Republicanism and the Protestant Spirit.

IV. The Rise of the French Republic   .   .   53

Enlightened Despotism — Philosophic View of
Monarchy—Idea of the Republic in the Writings of the
Philosophers—Turgot (1727-81) on Republics—Influence
of America—especially in France—Practical Character of
the Cahiers of 1789 Monarchical Professions, 1789-91
—Intellectual Influences making for Republicanism—
Polemical Advantage of Extreme Opinions—First Signs
of a Republican Party—Influence of the King's Character—Mistakes of the Court—The Flight to Varennes
—The Interregnum—Growth of Republican Literature
—Condorcet's Argument—Royalist Reaction, July-
September 1791—The Legislative Assembly, September
1791 to September 1792—The Capture of the Tuileries,
August 10, 1792—Psychology of the Terror—Hesitations
of the Assembly—The Invasion of France—Elections to
the Convention, September 1792—The Republic proclaimed—Character of the French Monarchy—Influence
of the War—The Guns at Valmy, September 20, 1792—
Influence of Cicero and Plutarch on the French Revolution—Classical Character of French Education—J. J.
Rousseau, 1712-78.

V. The Revolutionary State   81

Unique Character of the French Republic—Its
Sanguine Psychology—Centralization of Government—
Its Anticlericalism—Growth of Scepticism in France—
The Civil Constitution of the Clergy—Erastian Char-
acter of the Settlement—Civil Marriage and Divorce—
Schism and Separation—September 1794—Propagan-
dist Character of the French Republic—Defiance of
Treaty Rights—Traditional Ambitions—The Rhine
Frontier — The Humanitarian Strain — Condorcet,
1748-94—The First Republican Constitution, 1793—
The Machinery of the Terror—The Eclipse of Freedom
—Reversal of Early Principles—The Royalist Cause
—Beginnings of Reaction—The Constitution of 1795
—Government of the Directory — The Crime of
Fructidor — The Last Two Years, 1797-99 — The
Fructidorians—Phenomena of Revolution—Work of the
Jacobins.

VI. The Sower and the Seed   12

Germany and the French Revolution—Discredit
attaching to the Republican Idea—The Work of
Napoleon—Italy on the Eve of the Revolution—The
Risorgimento—Influence of France—Bonaparte and

CONTENTS

Italy—The Cisalpine Republic. The Dynastic Tradition broken. Flight of the Bourbons from Naples. The Parthenopean Republic. Its Constitution. Conquerors of the French. Fall of the Republic. Permanent Influence of the Napoleonic Policy. Course of Political Opinion in England, 1789-1792. Essential Conservatism of the English People. The Revolution Societies. Constitutional Character of the Agitation. English Republicans. Thomas Paine, 1737-1809. William Godwin, 1756-1836. Robert Southey, 1774-1843. Samuel Taylor Coleridge, 1772-1834. Walter Savage Landor, 1775-1864—William Wordsworth, 1770-1850

VII. AUTOCRACY AND ITS CRITICS 150

The Reaction, 1815-49. Special Influence of the Revolution in the Latin Zone. The Restoration in France. Antithesis between Social and Political Institutions. Insecurity of the Monarchy. Coalition of Republicans and Bonapartists. Liberals and Ultras. Charles X., 1824-1830. Godefroy Cavaignac (1801-45) and the Revolution of 1830. The Duke of Orleans reaps the Fruit. Jeremy Bentham, 1748-1832. Bentham on Monarchy. Current Administration of America, 1800-1840. The Belgian Revolution, 1830. Dutch Errors. And Belgian Protests. The National Congress. Arguments for Monarchy

VIII. THE SECOND REPUBLIC IN FRANCE 171

The Revolution in Retrospect. The Napoleonic Legend. Growth of Socialist Ideas. St. Simon, 1760-1825. Influence of Socialist Writers. C. Fourier, 1772-1837. Louis Blanc, 1811-82. Growth of a Socialist Party. Defects of the July Monarchy, 1830-48. Agitation against the Government. The Paris Revolution, February 1848. Resignation of the King. The Birth of the Republic. Extraordinary Enthusiasm. Work of Lamartine's Government. The National Workshops. Paris and the Provinces. The Days of June. The "Red Spectre". The Constitutional Committee. The Presidential System—Permanent Effects of the Second Republic.

IX. ITALY 191

Europe in 1848—Policy of Metternich, 1815-1848. The Carbonari. The Austrian Dead Weight. Giuseppe Mazzini, 1808-72—His Distrust of Piedmont—

Source of his Power—His Political Ideal—Scope and Limits of his Influence—The Disunion of the Patriots —Italian Union impossible in 1848—The Venetian Republic—Flight of Pio Nono from Rome, November 24, 1848—Declaration of the Roman Republic— Garibaldi, 1807-82—The Siege of Rome—The Retreat of Garibaldi—Effects of the Republican Resistance.

X. THE GERMAN REVOLUTION . . . .

Condition of Germany, 1815-48—American Influence —Influence of the Polish Dispersion—Radical Movement in Switzerland—Action of France on Germany— Karl Marx (1814-83) on the '48—Confusion of Political Ideals in Germany—The Republicans—The Baden Rising—The Frankfort Parliament and the Danish Question—The Last Republican Rally, April-May 1849— The Republican Federalists—The Unitarians—A Story of the Revolution.

XI. THE THIRD REPUBLIC . . . . .

Early Popularity of Napoleon III.—And Subsequent Discredit—The Autocratic *régime*—The Period of Concessions—Ollivier and Liberalism—The Liberal Empire, 1870—The Republican Opposition—The *Internationale* and the Doctrine of Class War—The Individualist Republicans and Léon Gambetta—Fall of the Empire, September 3, 1870—Origin and Character of the Third Republic — The Assembly of Bordeaux — Adolphe Thiers, 1797-1877—His Opposition to the Second Empire — The *Pacte de Bordeaux* — Outbreak of the Commune—Communard Philosophy — The Achievement of Thiers—Royalism's Last Chance—The Republican Solution, 30th January 1875—Orleanist Defections—Gambetta (1838-82) and the Third Republic— Gambetta's Fundamental Beliefs—The Latin Schism.

XII. AN EXPERIMENT IN SPAIN . . . .

Charles Bradlaugh (1833-91) in Spain—Undercurrent of Republican Feeling in England—R. Carlile, 1790-1843 —The Spanish Republic—Effects of Peninsular War in Spain—Working of the Constitutional System—The Revolution of 1868—Forced Resignation of Amadeo of Savoy—The Federalists—Federalist Philosophy—The Federal Republic and the Cantonal Insurrection—Emilio Castelar, 1832-99—Fate of the Republic, 1874—The Federal Cause.

CONTENTS

XIII. THE REPUBLICAN CAUSE . . . .

Improvement in the Position of European Monarchies since 1848. This Improvement specially evident in England. Causes of the Popularity of Monarchy. Expansion of Popular Liberty found to be consistent with the Retention of Monarchy. Diversion of Interest to Social Problems. The Success of Bismarck. Influence of Imperialism. Dynastic Alliances. The Instance of Norway, 1905. Reasons for preferring a Monarchy to a Republic. Influence of Historical Memories in Norway. Permanence of the Republican Idea in the Consciousness of Europe.

NOTES . . . . .

INDEX .

NOTE

I cannot allow this little book to go out without acknowledgi
the valuable help which I have received from my friend a
colleague, Mr Leopold Wickam-Legg, who has been kind enou
to read the sheets as they passed through the Press.

THE REPUBLICAN TRADITION
IN EUROPE

CHAPTER I

MEDIEVAL THOUGHT AND ANCIENT TRADITION

Moribus antiquis res stat Romana virisque.—ENNIUS

Let this moment be the beginning of an epoch of austere morality and of immaculate justice.—FIRST MANIFESTO OF THE PORTUGUESE REPUBLIC, Oct. 5, 1910

AMONG the political records of Europe there are few documents more instructive than those austere and noble pieces of pedagogic literature which were composed for the only son of Louis XIV, by the greatest Catholic Bishop of the seventeenth century. Of the moral elevation and literary splendour of Bossuet's spacious treatises, of the "Discours sur l'Histoire Universelle," which first inspired the ambition of the youthful Napoleon, and "La Politique tirée de l'Ecriture Sainte," it is needless to speak in this connexion; they have been appraised by many qualified judges. But some words may be said about the political creed which is expressed with so patient and systematic an intellectual procedure and in terms of such tranquil and unfaltering conviction. It is the creed of Catholic and Monarchical Europe formulated by a mind which saw in the resplendent triumphs of the French Monarchy fresh

argument for the design of Providence to bring m
under the yoke of Christian and Catholic Kings.

"After St Louis," writes Bossuet to Innocent X
to whom he renders an account of his stewardsh
" we exhibit to Monseigneur the actions of Lo
the Great and that living history which passes befi
our eyes : the state strengthened by good law
the finances well ordered ; the grand discoveri
military discipline established with equal pruder
and authority ; the magazines ; the new mea
of besieging towns and keeping armies in the fi
at all seasons of the year ; the invincible coura
of our soldiers ; the natural impetuosity of the nati
sustained by extraordinary qualities of firmness a
constancy ; the firm belief common to all Frenchm
that nothing is impossible to them under so great
King ; and lastly the King himself, who alone is wor
a grand army : the force, the concatenation, t
impenetrable secret of his councils ; the hidden sprir
whose artifice is disclosed by an unending ser
of surprises ; our enemies panic-stricken and co
founded ; our allies faithfully defended ; pea
given to Europe on equitable conditions after
assured victory ; lastly, that incredible attachme
to the defence and promotion of religion, combin
with a continual effort to attain to all that is grand
and best in life. These are the qualities which
remark in the father, and these are the qualities whi
we commend to the imitation of the son." [1]

To Bossuet the monarchical form of governme
seemed to be commended alike by the circumstan
of human history and by the texts of Divine Scriptu
Surveying the political plan of Europe, he descri
indeed a few republics—the United Provinces, Veni

the Swiss Confederation, the free cities of Germany;
but of these he remarks that since they had previously
been subject to hereditary monarchies, and since
the greater part of the world was still, as it had been
from the beginning, governed by monarchs, it was
clear that monarchy was the form most natural to
man. Hereditary monarchy had three principal
advantages, and was characterized by four essential
qualities. Its advantages are that it is natural,
dignified, calculated to sustain an identity of interest
between ruler and ruled; its essential qualities,
that it is sacred, paternal, absolute, and submitted
to reason. If, as an additional precaution against
insecurity, females be excluded from the succession,
the State attains perfection and realises the declared
purpose of God. "And so France, where the succession
is regulated according to these maxims, may boast
of having the best constitution possible and the one
most conformable to that which God Himself has
established; all of which shows the wisdom of our
ancestors and the special protection which God
extends to this Kingdom." [1]

The course of European history gave some sanction
to the sublime but near-sighted confidence of the
patriotic divine. Ever since the fall of the Roman
Republic the main political tradition of Europe had
been monarchical.

That an ideal which inspired some of the noblest
literature of antiquity was obscured for many
centuries is a matter which ceases to cause surprise
when we remember the two great facts of the Roman
Empire and the Christian Church. The triumphs
of the Empire prepared the durable domination of
Roman Law and secured the survival of an Imperial

tradition which coloured the whole political thinkin
of Europe until the Reformation. The fact th
the Founder of Christianity was born in the reig
of Augustus was assumed to be an indication th
the Roman Empire was the political receptac
preordained by God for the manifestation and t
workings of the true religion, and when Christiani
was adopted as the Court religion under Constantin
it became a dominant purpose of Christian poli
to support and to control the secular authorit
The old republican traditions of the world, wheth
presented in the romantic rhetoric of Livy, or i
mild and humane beauty of the parallel lives
Plutarch, or in the abounding eloquence of Cicer
or in Lucan's passionate verse, or in the bitt
aristocratic irony of Tacitus, became obscured,
years went on, by the increasing interest attachi
to religious controversy and by the diminishi
interest attaching to the criticism of an instituti
which seemed to be as firmly rooted in the nature
things as the stars of heaven or the sins of me
" Render unto Cæsar the things that are Cæsar's
said the Church. " Quod Principi placuit leg
habet vigorem " said the State. Against such pote
maxims of absolutism the memories and aspiratio
connected with the Republic were academic a
shadowy. Human history was conceived in a ret
spect as a succession of great empires, and t
wonderful story of Hellenic liberty was contract
to an insignificant point in the development of ma
Indeed, but for the fact that the Hellenic world form
part of the Empire of Alexander, it would hard
have left a mark upon medieval chronicles. Throu
the most troubled centuries of human history, wl

creed was battling with creed, and the old world was crumbling away, and the old culture was ebbing, and a new society was being founded, one thing remained constant, the political faith of the Mediterranean nations. Virgil, the poet and prophet of the young Empire, guides the steps of Dante in his visionary pilgrimage.[3]

The barbarian world was full of freedom and anarchy. Tacitus, who wrote his account of Germany from full knowledge, remarks that many of the tribes were kingless, and that where Kings existed their powers were strictly limited. The affairs of the tribe were governed by the assemblage of freemen ; the dooms were popular ; the system of cultivation common and extensive, and exhibiting a sharp contrast to the intense several cultivation of the Italian olive yard or fruit-garden. But as these Teutonic tribes found their way into the Roman Empire and established themselves in the Roman shell, their polities, partly from the needs of the situation, but partly from conscious reflection of the Roman model, assumed more and more the monarchical form and divested themselves more and more of their democratic character. The successful chieftain becomes a King, and sometimes claims titles drawn from the magnificent vocabulary of Byzantium. Goths and Vandals, Franks and Saxons practise their clumsy monarchies before the broken mirror of the Roman Empire.

Great as was the influence of Rome, it combined with instincts and traditions derived from dim Teutonic antiquity. The Anglo-Saxon alliterative verse, the old German epics, the *chansons de geste*, depict an heroic age of which fighting is the main business, and are full of that spirit of hero-worship

which is the stuff out of which the early monarchie
were made. In the nomadic age of Teutonic histor
and even long afterwards, when feudal conditior
were thoroughly established in Europe, the hero:
poem made no attempt at historical fidelit\
Attila and Theodoric, Charlemagne and Roland a\
dim, gigantic figures represented without any attem\
at psychological consistency or political perspectiv
and indeed for the most part with a curiously comple
oblivion of the actual circumstances of their live
It is sufficient that in the common consciousness
the Teutonic race these names stood for greatne
and power. Legend clustered round them, a\
unexpected miracles were worked with their names.

There is indeed one people and one literature whi\
escapes the common tendency of Europe to find
monarchy the principle of progress. The civilizati\
of Iceland dates from a migration of Norse chieftai\
who, to escape the tyranny of Harold the Fair Hair\
turned their prows to the west and landed up
the shores of that solitary and distant island. He
among glaciers and morasses, mountain torrents a
geysers, the settlers formed a commonwealth upor
social compact. It was a republic, but unlike a
other republic that had ever existed. There w\
neither taxes nor police, nor an army, nor an admi
strative officer, nor a foreign policy, nor indeed a
joint means of coercion; only the heads of \
scattered settlements—settlements divided one fr\
another by snow mountains and lava fields and be
of black volcanic sand and pebbles—met toget\
once a year in a common assembly and agreed to ol
and enforce a common law. It was a society wh
realised the conditions of the heroic age, save tha\

was devoid of the ideal of monarchy—a commonwealth rudimentary, robust, and quite unique in its lack of political cohesion and in its preservation in a clear and self-conscious form of its own splendid tradition of aristocratic anarchy. And the prose literature of Iceland is as unique as the story which it relates with so much plain and human circumstance. But in 1264 the commonwealth of Iceland came to an end. It had been founded in 930, some fifty years after the first Norse settlement, and was therefore coeval with the foundation of the strong monarchical tradition of medieval Europe. But upon the general march of European ideas the literature and politics of this remote and singular community exerted no influence whatever.[4]

The political conditions of the Middle Ages were unfavourable to the growth of republican sentiment. War was chronic, communication difficult, and social inequality engrained in the necessary institution of feudalism. The countries which were best ordered were those the extent of whose territory did not exceed the powers of a medieval monarchy to control, such as Aragon, Sicily, England; and the advance of monarchy was a sure indication of national progress. Clerk and burgess looked to the King for protection against the rapacity of the noble, and the whole influence of the Roman Church was enlisted in the support of an institution from which she received and expected material benefits, and which she believed to be founded on the impregnable rock of Scripture. The political theory of the early Middle Ages, forged in the stress of the conflict between the Empire and the Papacy, bears witness to this general belief in the necessity and divinity of Kingship.

The Papalist controversialists of the twelfth cer
tury neither contested the God-ordained characte
of the Roman Empire nor questioned its duration
Still less did they propound republican ideals. I
was a sufficient step for them to assert that monarch
was an office founded upon a contract, and that
the contract were violated by the sovereign he coul
be lawfully deposed. In England, constitution
growth was sure and wholesome, and though th
Barons' War was stoutly contested, the song of Lew
which proclaims the theory of the opposition to th
Crown does not belong to the category of democrat
documents. It proclaims no republic, sketch
no scheme of natural rights. The remedy for th
ills of the harassed nation is that Henry III., who
" gentle soul " flits through Dante's " Purgatory
should govern with the consent of his baronage.[4]

Political thought is for the most part the produ
and not the cause of political conditions. Me
describe what they find around them and throw in
the form of a deductive philosophy what is in reali
the result of their own partial observations. In t
centuries of faith, when religion determined t
policy of Kings, and every remarkable incident w
liable to be regarded as a miracle ; when the Chur
was the sole receptacle of culture, and imposed
canons of belief upon a rude, passionate, and credulo
society, political thought was dominated by
idealism which was both dictated and circumscrib
by scriptural texts and analogies. It was believ
that the world would for ever be controlled by the tw
forces of Papacy and Empire, though it was a mat·
of keen dispute whether or not the temporal w
or was not subject to the spiritual power. Studei

of history remarked that the world had passed under a succession of empires—Assyrian, Median, Persian, Macedonian, Roman—and in a sequence so constantly attested it was an instinct of theology to discover evidence of a polity plotted by God for the well-being of man. As late as the age of Shakespeare a Calabrian monk, arguing from the premise that a universal monarchy was essential to the existence of society and the salvation of souls, contended that the mantle of Rome had fallen upon the shoulders of the Spaniard, whose dominion should accordingly spread over the earth. Having driven the Moors into Africa and exterminated the sectaries of the Low Countries, the new Cyrus would destroy the Ottoman Empire and purge England and France of heresy. So persistent was the belief that the monarchical constitution of the Church Catholic should be reflected in the institution of the world empire.

The greatest of the Gentile philosophers supported a tenet which was believed to be a part of the divine providence by the doctors of the Catholic Church. Aristotle maintained that of all forms of government the most perfect was the rule of one good man, and the Christian teacher saw in the government of God both the pattern of the perfect monarchy and the exemplar expressly divined for the imitation of His human subjects. A curious instance of the power of this belief is afforded by Savonarola's "Treatise upon the rule and government of States," written in 1494 for the guidance of the city of Florence. It was the object of this remarkable discourse to explain that the people of Florence, being at once the most intellectual and spirited community in Italy, were unsuited to a monarchical or aristocratical govern-

ment. A monarchy might do well enough for the
Northern races, who were robust but unintellectual
or again it might be adapted to Orientals, whose
activity of mind was balanced by physical languor
but wherever intellect and high spirit were combined
some form of popular government (*Governo civile*
must be established. Yet this conclusion is prefaced
by an elaborate profession of belief in monarchy
as the ideal form of government, not only because
concentrated power was stronger than dispersed
power, but also because monarchy was more like God
" The government of the world," argues the Dominican
preacher, " is by nature the best government ; and
since Art follows nature, the more closely the govern
ment of human things resembles the government
of the world and of nature, the more perfect it is
Since, then, the world is governed by a single Person
who is God, and since all natural things in whom
some government is seen are governed by One, as
the bees by a king and the powers of the soul by reason
and the members of the body by the heart, and
similarly with other things which have government
it follows that that government of human things
which is administered by a single governor, is of its
nature the best of all governments. Whence our
Saviour, wishing to give to His Church the best gover
nor, made Peter head of all the faithful, and in every
diocese, nay, in every parish and ministry, wished that
the government should be through a single person
and that finally all the lesser heads should be under
one head, His Vicar." [7]

It is true that from time to time the physical
miseries of an uncomfortable age produced a crop
of speculations which went far beyond the orbit

respectable thought. The right of the Church to possess wealth, or of the State to exercise coercive power, was questioned in the thirteenth century by the sectaries of Southern France, for whose chastisement was invented the terrible weapon of the Inquisition. But such anti-social vagaries were rigidly suppressed. The heresies of the early Middle Ages contained a mixture of wild fancy and obdurate realism, exactly calculated to secure the discomfiture of those who held them. They were in the main the beliefs of the poor and oppressed, of men who felt the full force of the ironic contrast between the promises of the gospel and the performance of the world; who questioned doctrine where it seemed to conflict with the patent evidence of the senses; and finding the world full of evils, cried out against the fundamental principles upon which it was arranged. Such a spirit of wholesale revolt is common to every age and clime. In the Middle Ages, when the State was loosely jointed, and the dominant evil was to be found rather in the deficiency than in the excess of governance, the spirit of democratic protest was sporadic and unorganized. No comprehensive political programmes were drawn up; no revolutionary philosophy of the State was formulated. Disciplined minds avoided original speculations, which in that theological atmosphere might easily glide into heresy; and to the sectary of the mountain valleys the science of political architecture was as hidden as the anatomy of the body or the vast continent on the other side of the Atlantic Ocean.

There can be no clearer proof of the strict limitations which the character of the medieval polity imposed upon political speculation than the case

of John Wyclif. In the whole course of mediev
history few thinkers were bolder or were driven
the consecutive employment of a powerful und
standing to more original conclusions. Wyc
attacked pilgrimages and relics, the doctrine
purgatory, and even the central mystery of transt
stantiation. He anticipated all the main positic
of Protestantism a century before Luther was bc
and a generation before the summoning of the fi
General Council for the reform of the Papacy. Y
his speculations were curiously circumscribed
the character of the society in which he lived. Holdi
the audacious doctrine that dominion was found
on grace, or, as we should now phrase it, that virt
alone could give a valid title to power and proper
Wyclif still conceived of the world as organised ir
feudal hierarchy. The King held of God upon
tenure of grace, and forfeited his office upon faili
to conform to the conditions of the tenement.
every generation good men have been perplexed
the paradoxical relation between moral and econor
values. Wyclif dreamed of a society in which wea
and power would be strictly determined by mc
qualities ; but while he denied that a commun
organized on any other principle could possess
adequate moral sanction, he made no propos
for a political revolution, and cannot be included
the roll of European republicans.

CHAPTER II

E facil cosa è conoscere donde nasca ne' Popoli questa affezione del vivere libero ; si vede per esperienza le cittadini non aver mai ampliato nè di dominio nè di ricchezza, se non mentre sono state in libertà.—MACHIAVELLI, "Discorsi"

The free cities of Italy, now delivered from the German yoke, began to enjoy and to abuse the blessings of wealth and liberty. The most trifling incident was sufficient to produce a conspiracy, a tumult, and a revolution. Among these troubles the dark, insidious, vindictive spirit of the Italians was gradually formed.— GIBBON, "Miscellaneous Works"

IN Italy alone the political conditions helped to sustain the memories of the classical age. Here was a land of ancient cities and splendid monuments, a development of civic life so vivid and powerful that it absorbed the Lombard aristocracy and successfully affronted the power of the German Emperors. The Lombard towns regarded themselves as part of the Roman Empire, but as enjoying guaranteed rights of substantial independence under it. Venice slowly and by degrees shook itself free of Byzantine control, and vied with Genoa in imperial enterprise. But the spirit and memory of the ancient Republic were most clearly exhibited in the chequered and violent history of medieval Rome. Here, in the middle of the twelfth and again in the middle of the fourteenth century, attempts were made to revive the ancient Respublica Romanorum. The leaders

of these forlorn movements. Arnold of Bresci
Cola di Rienzo, are among the most pictū
figures in history, but they had as little ꞏ
statesmanship in their composition as Shel
Victor Hugo. Arnold held the ascetic do
of ecclesiastical poverty; the mystic Rienzo che
the ideal of a federation of Italian republics
a Latin Emperor elected by the people of
Neither of them understood the practical con
of the hour; yet each made some ineffectual
to glorify the politics of a grasping age by
of justice, piety and patriotism. The ꞏt
fate of these medieval tribunes of the ꞏl
Republic—Arnold, executed by the Emperor, I
torn to pieces by a city mob—illustrates the
enmity of these classical memories amid the
feuds of Guelph and Ghibelline. The oath
of Petrarch was aroused by the sanguine
of Rienzo, "the tribune of Freedom, Peace, J
and the Liberator of the Holy Roman Rep
and the rise of the Roman Republic was hail
letter, and celebrated in an ode from the pen
first humanist in Europe. For a while the
feuds of medieval Rome were quelled by the clo
of a common notary, the son of a washerwom
a wine-seller. The barons were cowed into subm
the country roads were cleared of bandits;
blasphemy, and concubinage fell into sudden dis
Rienzo dreamed that the union of Italy migh
out of the concord of Rome. He declared tha
Italian was a member of the Roman Republic, j
summoned the Emperor and Electors to subm
claims to the sovereign city, and in a full parli
attended by deputies from the Tuscan cities, ꞏ

that no Emperor, King, Prince or Marquis might set foot on Italian soil without licence of the Pope and the Roman people. The fantastic revival of this impracticable polity lasted no more than seven months; and Rienzo, driven into retirement by a few Neapolitan lances, became in turns a hermit, a Ghibelline, and a Guelph. Returning to Italy in 1353, after seven years' absence, he was enabled, through the aid of the great Cardinal Albornoz, in whose suite he was voyaging, to regain his authority in Rome. But the spare and mystic tribune of Italian independence had now grown into the corpulent officer of a French Pope. He surrounded himself with a bodyguard, exhibited in the quality of his rule the principal attributes of a classical tyranny, and met the doom which is appointed for city tyrants. Some four hundred years afterwards Montesquieu made the just observation that the republics of Italy had done less to secure human liberty than the constitutional monarchy of England.[1]

Not dissimilar was the judgment of a great political observer in the opening decades of the sixteenth century. "It is better," writes Guicciardini, "to be the subject of a prince than of a republic, for a republic keeps its subjects under, and gives no share of its greatness save to its own citizens; a prince is common to all, one man is as much his subject as another, therefore everyone can hope to be favoured or employed."[2] Liberty was the grandest and most living ideal in the political consciousness of the Italian race, but it was difficult to harmonize with the spirit of the Guelph and Ghibelline, or with that hard treatment of subject communities, which was everywhere in Italy attendant on the spread of civic dominion.

The cynical maxim of Lorenzo de' Medici, that [...]
must be held down by famine, Pistoia by [...]
and Volterra by a fortress, would not have [...]
repudiated by the firmest Florentine admirer [...]
Harmodius and Aristogeiton. Liberty in the s[...]
of political independence and class privilege was b[...]
understood than liberty in the sense of poli[...]
toleration; and so ingrained was the spirit of privi[...]
in the morals of the nation, that an Italian pat[...]
of the sixteenth century congratulated himself [...]
the political disunion of his country, being un[...]
to separate in his mind the idea of a su[...]
Italian republic from the oppressive rule of a [...]
oligarchy [2]

It is to this spirit of jealous exclusion, operat[...]
alike against rival factions, dependent cities, and [...]
humblest elements of society, that we trace the [...]
of the Italian despotisms. The free cities of [...]
early Middle Ages owe the loss of their liberties [...]
much to the violence of their own inner discords [...]
to the crimes or ambitions of the successful usurp[...]
Nor is it possible to assert that the Italian ge[...]
flourished more abundantly in the fierce air [...]
republican freedom than under the shelter of prince[...]
rule.[4] But though Italian despotism had its rea[...]
for existence and discharged a function in the discipl[...]
and development of the race, it was by its very nat[...]
associated with frightful evils. The crimes and c[...]
rices of the despots of Italy from Eccelin da Roma[...]
the viceregent of Frederick II., to Alessandro [...]
Medici, the contemporary of Sir Thomas More, fo[...]
one of the darkest and least credible pages in hum[...]
history. We read of whole populations barbarous[...]
mutilated, of the butchery of all the members of [...]

and of torture erected into a fine art and
as an established diversion.

as natural that the evils of tyranny should
a standard theme with the moralist and
acher, and that with the growth of a passionate
t in the authors of antiquity the ethics of
icide should be founded on classical example.
and Cassius, whom Dante the imperialist
in an age which had lost the knowledge of
ch's Lives) consigned with Judas Iscariot to
west abyss of the Inferno, were heroes to the
mporaries of the Visconti and the Borgia.[5]
a tyrant was regarded as a necessary art and
passport to immortality. Now the murderer
draw inspiration from the Catilinarians of Cicero,
from the lives of Brutus or Timoleon. When
Pagolo Boscoli was condemned to death in
for an attempt on the lives of Giuliano and
zo de' Medici, he prayed that Christ might
ce Brutus from his soul, and was comforted
is confessor's assurance that St Thomas had
essly sanctioned conspiracies against usurping
ts. In 1536 Lorenzo de' Medici, a youth notorious
is profligate ways, decoyed his kinsman, Duke
andro, into a private house by the lure of a
aceful amour, and slew him at night with the
tance of a professional cut-throat. The brutal
was applauded by all the victims of the Medicean
ion, and Giannotti, the leading publicist of
ence, commended the "glorious deed" of this
ad Brutus, as "a most noble theme" for the
t of a contemporary poet. The historian Varchi,
recounts the story of the murder in all its cruel
umstance, refuses to pronounce upon the moral

purity of the deed, but asserts that if it were indeed
true, as Lorenzo affirmed, that he was solely desirous
of liberating his country, then no praise or reward
could be adequate to his merits. To an uneasy
youth burning with a desire for immortality no
path was so short or certain as tyrannicide, provided
only that the slayer might survive the slain and defend
his motives to an admiring audience. The puny
Lorenzacchio, as he was contemptuously called,
lived to write a formal apology for his act, which
presents a curious illustration of the moral code of
that age. He assumes that it is universally allowed
that popular government is better than tyranny,
and undertakes to demonstrate that Alessandro was
a tyrant more impious than Nero, more flagitious
than Caligula, and more cruel than Phalaris. Critics
had objected that it was dishonourable to murder a
man to whom the slayer was bound by ties of obligation,
trust, and kinship. Even if these facts were so, tyrants,
however slain, were best dead. Lorenzacchio, however,
takes pains to deny the allegation that he had failed
to observe the polite statutes of social honour. He
was not in any true sense the kinsman of the
murdered bastard, but even if he were, did not Timoleon earn a deathless name by killing his brother
in the cause of liberty ? He was under no obligation
to a man from whom he had not even received the
privilege of exemption from the taxes. He was
unfaithful to no trust, for Alessandro was incapable
of confidence, and drawn to his doom by the mere
force of his own libidinous appetites. His motive
had been simple, the liberation of his native city from
an intolerable yoke. If the end had not been reached,
if one tyrant had been succeeded by another,

that was not his fault. So far as one man might
serve liberty, he, at the risk of life, had served the
liberties of Florence.[6]

Here, as in every other department of Italian thought
and feeling in the age of the Renaissance, it is difficult
to overestimate the authority of classical tradition.
We who are removed by many generations from the
twilight of the Middle Ages can afford ourselves the
luxury of sentimental sympathy for a social state
whose meanness and narrowness of view, whose
cruelties, vices, and discomforts we are not called
upon to share, and can only with the greatest stretch
of historical imagination imperfectly represent to our
minds. But the men of the Renaissance were but
just emerging from the darkness, the incongruity,
the discomfort. That which is distant and gracious
to us, was near and sordid to them. That which
is an insensible part of our abundance, was to them
an imperious necessity and a toilsome conquest.
We enjoy a great modern literature, informed alike by
the classical and the Christian spirit ; for them the
liberating and rational influences could only be won
by a devout interrogation of the classical texts themselves. The black clouds still hung about the sky
in stark relief against the brilliant illumination shed
from the retrimmed lamps of ancient learning. And
the more that ancient world was studied the more
did it appear to be a world of giants. The best
medieval chronicler, compared with a Polybius, a
Livy, or a Tacitus, was childish, empty, and pedestrian.
The most powerful modern State sank into insignificance when measured against the imposing fabric of the
Roman Empire. For the men of the Renaissance
ancient wisdom was the supreme wisdom, ancient

poetry the consummate art, ancient eloquence the rich and most exquisite music of persuasion.' When a Florentine historian wishes to praise a Capponi or a Ferrucci, he says that he deserves to be compared rather with the ancients than with the moderns, regarding ancient virtue as something austere and heroic, grander in scale and purpose, more decorative and more dignified than the humble and retiring graces of the Christian soul. And as the course of Roman history provided the sovereign body of precepts by which communities might prosper to the highest point of affluence and glory, so in 'the whole field of political prudence everything worth saying had been said by the Greeks and the Romans. Aristotle had praised the mixed state, in which the monarchical, aristocratic, and popular elements were combined in due proportion, and every Italian thinker of the Renaissance followed in his train. He had condemned democracy, and they agreed that popular government was full of dangers. He had recommended the exclusion of tradesmen and artisans from the privilege of citizenship; and even Varchi, the most democratic of Florentine historians, acknowledges that a commercial republic is an anomaly, and argues that the greatness of Florence, a city in which, to the horror of the polite Venetian, silk-mercers were politicians and politicians were silk-mercers, implied an extraordinary degree of merit in its inhabitants, since it was an acknowledged axiom of philosophy that no polity of shop-keepers was ever well ordered.[7]

The revival of classical studies, coinciding with an epoch of political revolution, produced in Florence, then the intellectual capital of Europe, an illustrious generation of historians and publicists. Political thought flourishes most vigorously in an epoch of change, and at the turn of the fifteenth century the political system of Italy was violently deranged by the invasion of Charles VIII. and by the expulsion of the Medici from Florence. That a city so famous for its intelligence should suddenly throw off a despotism and adopt a popular constitution was not only in itself an arresting and impressive fact, but the exciting cause of political speculations which Europe had never entirely consented to neglect. For six and thirty years after the revolution of 1494, the political fate of Florence was in the cauldron. The stormy republic of Savonarola and Soderini was supplanted in 1512 by a Medicean restoration, and this in turn, after fifteen restless and unquiet years, by a brief, unsteady gust of liberty. Finally, in 1530 the Second Florentine Republic succumbed to the overwhelming power of the Imperial arms, after a defence of eleven months so gallantly and tenaciously conducted as to throw a final ray of glory upon a blemished and a bankrupt cause. After that catastrophe, which was followed by a tale of savage proscriptions, the Medici ruled the State for some two hundred years, upon a system which lasted till the French Revolution, and if the verdict of history is to count for anything, it proves that the Medicean system rather than the Republic was best suited to Florentine conditions.

Rare repubbliche popolare si vede essere state diuturne—" popular republics are rarely found to be lasting "—was the judgment of a Venetian who visited Florence in the last year of its liberty, and predicted the approaching doom of freedom in a State "fuller of factions than all the other cities of Italy." [8] Yet it is only just to remember that the experiment of a free commonwealth was tried at a crisis of overwhelming difficulty, and only overthrown by an unscrupulous league of Emperor and Pope.

The reasons why the republican form of government flourished in some parts of Italy and not in others furnished matter for speculation as soon as the Humanists of the Renaissance turned the lamp of inquiry on to the field of politics. Machiavelli argued that if the Republic throve in Tuscany and Venice and not in Naples, Lombardy, or the Romagna, the explanation was to be found in the texture of society. A free commonwealth could not consist with a feudal class, and must be established upon the foundation of social equality. When these conditions did not exist, failure could only attend upon a republican experiment, unless indeed it were prefaced by a massacre of nobles. Of this the brief and distracted chronicle of the Ambrosian Republic in Milan (1447-1450) was sufficient evidence. Venice, it is true, was both a republic and the classic city of Italian aristocracy, but the noblemen of Venice were noblemen only in name. They drew no large revenue from lands, they owned no castles, exercised no feudal authority, and such wealth as they possessed existed in the form of merchandise and chattels. Venice therefore constituted no real exception to the rule that social equality was necessary to free government. And yet Venice and Florence, however much they might be forced into the same political category, stood out in the Italian imagination as sharply contrasted types—Venice as the model of permanence and stability, Florence of that sick and fevered unrest which Dante has denounced in the sixth canto of the " Purgatory." To the political philosopher of the sixteenth and seventeenth centuries Venice seemed to have solved the great riddle of statecraft. She was admired with the same sincerity with which the ancients admired Lacedemon, and largely for the same reasons. No State was so well-informed either as to its own resources or as to the resources of its neighbours. No State was better served or more generous to its servants or supported by so high and constant a temper of patriotism in its citizens. Dynasties rose and fell, city after city was racked by faction and civil war; Venice alone of all the Italian States preserved her polity uninjured through every vicissitude.[9]

To the mind of Machiavelli and his contemporaries such stability was a sign not of weakness but of vigour and health. The notion that continuous change is a part of improvement, or that States must be always adjusting themselves to conditions which are in turn continually altering, was entirely foreign to that age. History indeed was witness to a constant series of changes which no student of past politics could ignore, but those changes were cyclical, not progressive. The secret of political happiness was not to promote change but to discover and maintain a condition of wholesome equilibrium. And tried by whatever tests were available in that age, Venice seemed to have attained that desirable equipoise. Very rarely had the even current of her life been perplexed by conspiracy. No clusters of embittered exiles menaced her peace or spread the poison of their spited hopes broadcast through Italy. She had won a great empire in land and sea, had fought with

German Hungarian and Turk on even terms. Her arsenal was one of the famous sights of Europe, her canals were sweet, her police strict, her justice renowned for competence and equity, and so greatly had she triumphed over the Church within her gates that there was a moment when ardent Protestants, doubting whether so high a spirit of political independence could consist with a loyal devotion to the Papal See, believed that the Republic of St Mark could be drawn into the circle of the Reformed Communities.

To a Florentine who had lived through the first Medicean restoration and the second republic, who had seen the execution of Savonarola, the sack of Prato, the plottings and counter-plottings, the battles and sieges, the executions and proscriptions, and all the unmistakable accessories of a revolutionary period, the tranquil course of Venetian history must have seemed to be full of instruction. Why was it that Venice succeeded where Florence failed? What was the inner secret of that marvellous durability which made it possible to compare Republican Venice to its own advantage even with so famous a structure as Republican Rome?

Among the exiles of Florentine liberty, who were cast out after the events of 1530, was a certain Donato Giannotti, born of humble or at least not of illustrious parentage, who was driven by the circumstances of his life to undertake this enquiry in a serious spirit and from whom we may learn something of the quality of Florentine republicanism, as that creed was held by serious and honourable men. Of Giannotti's outward life little need be said here. He was born in 1492, received the best classical education which

Florence could provide, and opened his literary career in a delicate shower of Latin verse and light Italian comedy. The first Medicean restoration, coming as it did when he was twenty years of age, and shattering all the brilliant expectations which had been framed out of the triumph of liberty by men of his class and set, forced the central problems of statecraft upon his mind. To think of statecraft was to think of Venice, the supreme mistress of political wisdom. Giannotti visited the city of the lagoons, and in a graceful dialogue, composed in 1526 but not published till 1540, explained the anatomy of the Venetian State and expressed his admiration for its manifold virtues. Using a simile which quickly passed into the general currency of thought, he likened the Venetian constitution to a pyramid of which the base was formed by the Gran Consiglio, the apex by the Doge, and the intervening stages by the Collegio and the more numerous Consiglio de' Pregati. Such a union of the many, the few, and the one seemed to him to be the true political compound, conformable alike to the prescriptions of Aristotle and to the natural postulates of political stability. The young Florentine, whose own city had fallen back into the control of a despot, looked with eyes of envy upon the aristocratic republic which had contrived for so many centuries to occupy and inspire the patriotism of its members. Nothing, he asserts, is more calculated to elevate the human soul than the task of government, nothing more certain to debase it than exclusion from public affairs. To live under a tyranny is to live " without high thought," a life " worse than the animals," for what is tyranny but a government framed with the express object of making men " so base and vile that

they do not know whether they are awake or asleep
in the world " ? There is a fine manly ring in these
outbursts of republican sentiment. Giannotti spoke
not from books but from a full heart. He knew the
grim realities of Italian caprice and had witnessed
the pollution of public virtue which comes from the
violence of tyrannical lusts.

The idea of a free Florentine Republic, which
more than any beauty of art or literature, kindled
Giannotti's enthusiasm, was within a measurable
distance of being realised during the three years
which elapsed between the second expulsion of the
Medici and their final restoration. That was the golden
period of Giannotti's life,—the years that he would
have loved to chronicle,—when he was Secretary to
the Council of Ten, filling the office recently held by
Niccolo Machiavelli and himself taking an active
part in the drama of public affairs. It was a shining
interval of liberty, but so brief that the actors of the
Republic had hardly settled down to their parts
before a new company of players forced their way
upon the stage with a dark and hateful tragedy
To Giannotti, pondering afterwards upon the catastrophe which overtook the free Commonwealth of
Florence, it seemed that the lesson was one of misused
opportunity. The foundations of the true Republic
had been laid ; the soil was sound and holding, the
materials all ready to hand and of the proper consistency, and yet the building had never been made
proof against the weather, but came toppling over at
the first big storm. What were the flaws and how
could they be corrected ? That was a question upon
which Giannotti had written a memorandum when
he was an official of the Republic, and which occupied

his mind during the ample leisure of exile. In a treatise upon the Florentine constitution, composed in 1531, the defects of the two unfortunate republican experiments are examined, and a recipe prescribed for a durable and pacific policy in case the Medicean tyranny should for the third time be happily overthrown. There must be a General Council to fulfil the desire for liberty in the common people, a senate to gratify the appetite for honour in the middle class, a Collegio or Cabinet, and at the head of the State a prince or Gonfalonier of Justice, holding office for life. The secret of a good polity lies in the fact that it gratifies every class of society, the people whose cry is liberty, the middle class who thirst for liberty and honour, the nobles who being brought up in the pride and pomp of wealth must find some element of grandeur in the state. No free government could really be based on an aristocracy alone. 'A city in which the nobles obtain their desire, is nothing else but a company of masters and slaves ordered to the satisfaction of the avarice and dishonest wishes of the ruling class.' In Florence, however, social conditions clearly pointed to a republic. The proscriptions of Cosimo de' Medici had levelled the nobility; there was a large and powerful middle class equal in strength and influence to the united force of nobles and people; and if the destiny of Florence had not been fulfilled it was owing to assignable and removable causes, such as the refusal to make the Gonfalonierate a life-office, the presence of faction, and the unhappy influence of the Convent of St Mark upon the deliberations of the State and the temper of the people.[11]

"The pencil of the Holy Ghost," says Bacon,

"hath laboured more in describing the afflictic
of Job than the felicities of Solomon," and the fu
agonies of the Florentine Republic have receiv
more attention from contemporary historians th
any period of equal length in the prosperous rei
of Lorenzo de' Medici. The city, which was c
fended by the genius of Michael Angelo, stood c
as the last bulwark of Italian liberty against Span
dominion. Deserted by all its allies, torment
by plague, faction and hunger, it affronted the wra
of Pope and Emperor and the famous profession
infantry of the Prince of Orange. To defend th
liberty from the hated rule of the Medici t
republicans of Florence fired the luxurious vill
which glistened among the olives and cypresses
their girdling hills, sacrificing a treasury of luxu
and art to the military needs of the moment. Su
fanaticism in a desperate cause seemed to conter
poraries marvellous and half-insane. Guicciardin
an opponent of the Republic, cites it in his Ricor
as an example of the power of faith working in
population naturally superstitious and fevered l
confident prophecies of a holy triumph. Vare
ranks it with the defence of Saguntum as one of tl
most memorable sieges in history. Yet neith
to contemporaries nor to posterity is the last essa
in Florentine Republicanism free from severe reproac
Its legislation was hectic, ill-considered and ofte
unjust. Despite the honourable efforts of Nicco
Capponi, its first Gonfalonier, it so failed to exorci
the demon of faction that its course was stain
by mock trials and cruel executions. To Varcl
who recounts the story of the struggles for libert
with eloquent enthusiasm, the ultimate cause c

failure was rooted in the defects of the Florentine temperament. No good man could rise to eminence without becoming the mark of envy and persecution. No reputation was ever stable. The air was full of mocking wit and fierce jealousy and the quick incessant flash of party spite. "O ingenia magis acria quam matura!"—Guicciardini who looked on at the play with eyes of distaste confirms in his secret notebook Petrarch's famous comment on the Florentine temperament.[12]

The Medicean restoration in 1530 ushers in the Spanish period of Italian history. We pass from an age of freedom and grandeur to an epoch of servility and exhaustion marked by the revived power of the Papacy with its Jesuit Order and its Spanish legions. The spirit of republican liberty which had flamed out in the sermons of Savonarola and the speeches of Carducci was henceforth ruthlessly suppressed and the virtues of the antique world were placed upon the Index as only less dangerous than the philosophy of Machiavelli. In 1548 Francesco Burlamacchi, a noble Lucchese, dreamed of a league of Tuscan Republics and of a Church reduced to apostolic poverty; but such imaginings were of no practical account in this age of schooled compliance and lost ideals. Art swiftly declined; literature became feeble and sickly. The spirit of manliness and hope passed out of politics. A great Latin scholar struggling day after day with ignorant ecclesiastics for leave to teach Tacitus to his Roman class is a little fact emblematic of the new world of clerical obscurantism into which the most brilliant and creative race in Europe had so suddenly passed. Venice indeed preserved her aristocratic autonomy, and the ancient Republic of San Marino which survives to this day serves to remind us that several civic communities were sheltered by insignificance or timely compliance from the ruin which overtook the aspiring Republic of Florence. Such survivals did not alter the main facts of the political situation. The barbarian was master of Italy and the Pope was his accomplice.[13]

The two great political thinkers who lived in this heroic age were both opposed to popular government. Machiavelli indeed served the Republic of Savonarola, as Secretary to the Council of Ten, but thirteen months after the Republic had been destroyed is found cringing to the Medici. The "Prince," his most famous treatise, is dedicated to the grandson of the great Lorenzo, who is recommended to free Italy from the barbarians by a policy compounded of force and fraud. To the staunch Florentine republican no counsel seemed more flagitious, but Machiavelli could find nothing in Italian Republicanism but certain disunion. The case was different with Germany and Switzerland, countries which had little communication with their neighbours and had not learnt corruption from France, Italy and Spain, the three polluting nations of the world. In the city republics of these simple races liberty was still sustained by a reverence for law and by a wholesome lack of territorial ambition; but in Italy Machiavelli despaired of self-government. He found his countrymen, uneasy, factious, tormented by ambition and yet enervated by the long use of mercenary troops and accustomed to luxurious ways of living. A drastic medicine was needed to expel an inveterate malady. The young Lorenzo was invited to take a lesson from

Cesare Borgia, the master-adventurer who in a swift and thrilling sequence of plot, battle, siege and murder had built up a short-lived state out of the jarring atoms of the fierce Romagna.

Francesco Guicciardini was the younger contemporary of Machiavelli and lived to see the end of the second Florentine Republic and the final restoration of the Medicean power. Like Machiavelli his life was passed in affairs, and he gained, as men of affairs are apt to do, a shrewd, circumspect habit of mind and a distrust, though not altogether an unsympathetic distrust, of enthusiasm. He had learnt his politics in a bad school, at the court of Ferdinand of Aragon, whose duplicity was a byword through Europe, and for many years of his life was employed in various administrative capacities by the Papal Curia. Being a man of full, minute powers of observation, but deficient on the side of poetic imagination and abstract thought, he was very conscious of the puzzling play of human motive, of the diverse talents, conflicting interests and uneasy humours of the body politic. He thought government a very difficult business, shockingly conducted by tyrants but liable to be terribly mismanaged if the common folk were given a voice in affairs. "Who says people, says a mad animal, prone to a thousand errors, a thousand confusions, without taste, without delight, without stability." But facts were facts, and a city which had once tasted liberty could not be treated as if the appetite for liberty did not exist or had never been gratified. Guicciardini was neither the victim of phrases nor a builder of theories. More than once he compares the function of the political inquirer to that of the grave and expert doctor who

is called in to diagnose a malady and to prescrib
according to the requisites of the case. There wa
no curative power in catch-words. "The fruit o
liberty," he says, "is not that everyone shoul
govern, but that the fit should govern." The ever
lasting talk about the ancient Romans sickened him
As well compare the Florentines with the Romans a
expect an ass to run like a horse. Some thing
Florence could not be. She could not be ancien
Rome; and equality was too deep in her marrow
for her ever to acquiesce in the rule of a clos
aristocracy. The Medicean government had man
faults; so too had the first Republic, thoug
Guicciardini seems willing to admit that the valu
of the experiment could not be properly judged b
the rough and confused beginnings of popular rul
The problem was to find some form of well-ordere
polity, sufficiently popular to satisfy the Florentin
spirit and yet avoiding the evils inherent in demo
cratic rule—the irresolution, confusion and dela
of popular deliberation, the liability of democracie
to be sparing of money when it was necessary to b
lavish, open when it was essential to be secret, neutra
when the one rule of safety was to take side
Guicciardini the aristocrat ends like Giannotti th
republican as the prophet of mixed governmen
ha can imagine the sort of constitution he woul
subs framed, a grand council of discreet, well bor
asked ntial citizens speaking only when they wer
fit to for their opinion and electing no one but th
senate, ffices of state, a patriotic and circumspe
long ter a Doge or Gonfalonier chosen for life or
and equi of years. His taxes would have been ligh
able, with no unfair discrimination again

political enemies, his civil justice uncorrupt and
accessible to all, and the poor and weak would have
been protected by the whole force of the state against
the oppression of the strong. Critics accused him
of avarice and pride, and the astonishing record of
his secret thoughts shows that he was schooled in the
art of self-repression. He was a little cold, a little
cowardly and only faintly touched by that great
overflow of heart and spirit which swept through the
rapt congregations of the Duomo and made Florence
for the time a city of penitential ecstasy; but no
Italian of that age had a stronger grasp of those first
essentials of public welfare, failing which a state,
whether monarchy or republic, can never content
its members.[14]

CHAPTER III

THE PROTESTANT SPIRIT

A Popular Assembly without a Senate cannot be wise
A Senate without a Popular Assembly will not be honest
The reasons why the Nations that have Commonwealths use
them so well and cherish them so much, and yet that so few nations
have Commonwealths, is that in using a Commonwealth it is not
necessary that it should be understood, but in making a Commonwealth that it should be understood is of absolute necessity.
HARRINGTON (1611-77), " Political Aphorisms "

THE Protestant Reformation of the sixteenth
century was the great dissolvent of European
conservatism. A religion which had been accepted
with little question for twelve hundred years, which
had dominated European thought, moulded European
customs, shaped no small part of private law and
public policy and delighted the world with exquisite
fabrics in stone, glowing altar pieces, and solemn
music, was suddenly and sharply questioned in all
the progressive communities of the West.

Yet the leaders of this great and comprehensive
revolt were careful to mark their respect for the
secular authority. Their followers might lampoon
the Pope and asperse the barbarous monk with a
sharp shower of ridicule, but of Princes, rulers and
magistrates no evil word must be spoken. Martyrdom
was better than Civil War ; the tyranny of the heretic
prince should be passively borne by the godly subject.
Luther, who railed against the rebellious peasantry,

34

was as peremptory in his defence of political obedience
as Calvin who dedicated his " Institutes " to Francis I.,
or William Tyndale who wrote the " Obedience of
the Christian Man." There was indeed one exception.
Spurred by the persecutions of Queen Mary the fiery
Knox broke away from the tenets which were enjoined
in Geneva and from his own earlier doctrine and
openly supported the assassination of a heretic Prince.
But this was an exceptional and temporary lapse :
Salmasius was justified in his assertion that John
Milton's " Defence of Regicide " found no support
from the captains of Protestant theology. If European
democracy owes much to the Protestant reformation
it owes nothing whatever to the direct teaching of
the Protestant leaders.

So deeply rooted was the reverence for monarchy
that even the wars of religion in France and
the Netherlands produced no distinctive republican
doctrine. The massacre of St Bartholomew created
a feeling of fierce and passionate distrust for the
government of Catherine de' Medici, and Huguenot
pamphleteers dipped their pens in gall to denounce
the Italian poison with which Machiavelli was alleged
to have infected the policy of the French state. The
old arguments were furbished up with some improvements and with the note of asperity which belongs
to a period of bitter struggles. That monarchy was
not an hereditament but an office, that it was conferred by the people and could be withdrawn by its
accredited magistrates, that a tyrant who had violated
his compact either with God or the people could
be lawfully resisted, not indeed by private individuals,
but by lawfully appointed magistrates—such was
the substance of the *Vindiciæ contra tyrannos*, a famous

pamphlet used in turn to justify the revolt of the
United Provinces and the execution of Charles I.
But this marks the extreme boundary of Huguenot
license. The "religion" possessed a candidate for
the French throne and saw in the ultimate triumph
of Henry of Navarre a prospect of established security.
To demand that the States-general should be summoned was a counsel of prudence, to oppose the
principle of monarchy would have been madness.
Every prominent member of the Huguenot party
accepted monarchical government.[1]

One new republic emerged from the religious
conflicts of the sixteenth century. The Dutch threw
off the Spanish yoke after a struggle perhaps un-
paralleled in history for its proud and desperate
tenacity. They founded a new nation, broke away
from the most powerful monarchy in Europe, and
out of the nation grew an empire beyond the seas.
Incredible material success followed the triumph
of liberty, success which stood out in brilliant colours
against the growing shadows which were creeping
over the older lustre of Spain. A generation had
hardly elapsed after the close of the war of Independence before the Dutch had made themselves
the first commercial power in Europe. They carried
the sea-borne harvests of the Baltic plains, mastered
the spice-trade, and gave Europe its first discipline
in the principles of banking and modern commerce.
It was a great republican advertisement. Thomas
Hobbes, who did not like republics, attributed some
part of the English revolution to the admiration which
London and other English trading towns had conceived for the prosperity of the Low Countries.
Voltaire, writing about a century afterwards on the

benefits of political liberty, took the Dutch Republic
as his text. " The registers of the accounts of the
Low countries," he writes, " which are now at Lille,
show that Philip II. did not draw 80,000 crowns
from the seven United Provinces. An account of
the revenues of the single produce of Holland made
in 1700 shows a revenue of 22,241,339 florins or in
French money 46,706,811 livres 18 sous—about
the revenue of the King of Spain at the beginning of
this century." [2]

Yet neither in its opening nor in its concluding
stages was the war of Dutch Independence a conscious effort to found a republic. The Dutch leader
William of Orange had been brought up at the Spanish
Court and had served the Spanish throne in diplomacy
and in war. He was the most conservative of men
and he led the most conservative of races. For a
long time he maintained the fiction that he was
contending for the King of Spain against his evil
advisers. He inscribed upon his banner the words,
Pro rege, grege, lege, for the King, for the people,
for the law, and at any moment it might have
been open to the monarchy of Spain to recover the
allegiance of the revolting provinces by the withdrawal of the Spanish troops and by politic concessions
to the spirit of religious and constitutional liberty.
Those concessions were not made, and ultimately
in 1581 the Spanish allegiance was cast off in a solemn
act of abjuration. But so far were the Dutch from
desiring to found a Republic that while Holland and
Zealand insisted upon placing themselves under
William of Orange, the remaining provinces invited
the Duke of Anjou to step into the place of the King
of Spain. The sovereignty of the Dutch provinces

was offered in turn to the Hapsburg, the Valois ¿
the Tudor Houses; and in the institution of
Stadholderate the Dutch found a means of gratify
something of that monarchical instinct which
tyranny of Spain had been unavailing to destroy.

No great revolution in affairs has had so li
foundation or support in revolutionary the
Johannes Althusius, a Syndic of the town of Em
published his " Politicæ methodiæ Digesta " in
final and expanded form in 1610, with a dedica
to the Estates of Frisia. In his preface he all
with admiration to the laudable conduct of
Confederate Provinces, who by casting off the y
of a powerful King had recognised that sovereig
was no inseparable property of the prince but belon
to the united multitude and people of the diffe
provinces. But while allowing in most dist
terms the sovereignty of the general will, the Ger
burgess has nothing but contempt for the pe
through whom that will is made manifest.
masses are credulous, envious, fierce, turbid, sediti
inconstant. There is, luckily it would seem,
modern example of the democratic republic, and
a description of such a polity the philosopher n
go back to Aristotle. Althusius has been descri
as a Radical, and it is true that the fundame
principles of Rousseau's Social Contract are to
found in this scholastic treatise written under the f
impression of the great Dutch triumph. Althu
like Rousseau, bases sovereignty upon contract,
sees that all forms of government ultimately
on popular consent, but in his practical rec
mendations he goes no further than the author of
Vindiciæ. Government should be shared betv

the supreme magistrate and the ephors whose duty
it is to watch and if necessary to depose the executive
head of the State. The merits and demerits of
hereditary monarchy are nowhere discussed.[3]

The religious convulsions caused by the Protestant
Reformation were, so far as the continent of Europe
was concerned, appeased by the middle of the
seventeenth century. The Treaty of Westphalia
acknowledged the independence of the Dutch and
the Swiss Confederations, and settled the perplexed
confessional frontiers of Germany. In the course
of the struggle which led up to the settlement some
important ideas were generated or revived; that
the religious might be disengaged from the civil
power, that toleration was a necessity, that resistance
to tyranny was lawful, that sovereignty was based
on contract. But as yet these ideas were on their
trial. The Catholic powers were not inclined lightly
to surrender the ideal of orthodox unity which had
guided Latin Christianity through the long agonies
of the Middle Ages. The disruptive forces of
Protestantism were met by a challenging effort of
concentration not in the Catholic world alone. Absolute monarchy, its praises heralded by Bodin
and Bacon, seemed to many minds to be the true
guarantee of material force and progress. Men
whose grandfathers told them of the glorious days
of Queen Elizabeth, and who themselves witnessed
the triumphs of Louis Quatorze, may well have thought
that Kingship could not be too strong or power too
absolute. It was a common belief that the world
was settling down to an age of despotism, and that the
superiority of monarchies over republics had been
patently exhibited in the course of history.

a right to it; wherever it was useful, it should
respected. To those who argued that monarc
was destined to disappear from the face of the ear
Ireton replied that he was confident that if ever
power of monarchy were destroyed it would not
by the hand of man but by " the breaking fo:
of the power of God among men to make su
forms needless." The debates in the army w
rough and obstinate, but finally the moderate pa:
triumphed.[4] The Instrument of Government lodg
the executive power in the hands of a single pers(
and took good care that the franchise should 1
fall into the hands of Cavalier ploughmen. Oli'
Cromwell was King in all but name and a party ar(
which demanded that, wielding as he did the substar
of power, he should also assume the title.

There was much to be said in favour of such
course. The whole machinery of English law assun
the existence of the monarchy. The writs ran in
name of the King. The Statutes were enacted
the King with the advice of the Lords and the ass(
of his faithful Commons. The King was the fount
of justice, prosecuted criminals, named the judg
touched for the King's evil. The assumption of
royal title by the Protector would solve ma
difficulties and quiet many scrupulous conscien(
Oliver hesitated and refused. He consented
restore the second Chamber and acquiesced in
petition that he should name his successor; but
would not take the crown. The son of the Hunting(
brewer who had proved himself the first soldier ;
the first statesman in England, who had made Engl;
the greatest military power in Europe, who, for
first time, had gathered the British Islands int(

legislative union, who had wrested Jamaica from Spain and humbled the navies of the Dutch, would not take the crown of Elizabeth. Again and again in the spring of 1657 he resisted the pressure not only of a majority in Parliament but of his own solid conviction that "something with monarchical power in it would be most effectual for the settlement of the nation." In a dim way he felt that to assume the Crown of England would be an act of treachery to a devoted following, and with this loyal scruple there was mingled a shrewd suspicion that he could not estrange one half of the Party which had made him Protector without weakening the foundations of his rule.[5]

The Commonwealth then remained, growing in the lineaments of its outward structure more and more like the ancient monarchy and less and less like the radical ideal of the army. In no sense could it be called a Democratic Republic. Sir Henry Vane, who led the Parliamentary Republicans, doubted if it could be called a republic at all. The parliamentary franchise was limited to men of substantial fortune, and the Protector's actual powers were far in excess of those which had been wielded by Charles I. To John Milton, the official Apologist of the Commonwealth, the image of the Republic came in the splendid garb in which it had been invested by the historians of "the old and elegant humanity of Greece." He defended the deposition of the tyrant, argued in his "Defence of the English People" against Salmasius that Hereditary Government was contrary to the law of nature, since no man had a right to exercise Kingship unless he exceeded all others in wisdom and courage ; but his ideal republic was no more democratic than the actual commonwealth which was arousing the impatient disgust of Lilburne and Vane. His " Defensio Secunda " reveals alike his aversion from the rule of a single person and contempt for the principle of popular sovereignty. How could he trust " the besotted and degenerate baseness " which upon the appearance of the Eikon Basilike was " ready to fall flat and give adoration to the image and memory of this man who hath offered at more cunning fetches to undermine our liberties and put tyranny into an art than any British king before him " ? But the course of history clearly showed that the days of the aristocratic classical republic were over.

Among those who held republican opinions at this period there was none more ingenious than Sir James Harrington, the founder and leading spirit of the Rota Club, a society of gentlemen, who, while Parliament was sitting, would meet every night in the New Palace Yard at Westminster to discuss constitutional problems. In an effort to account for the origin of the Civil War Harrington had made a discovery of some importance : it was due, he thought, to a change in the balance of property. Formerly the balance of property had been with the Crown and nobility ; gradually, owing to the policy of the Tudor Kings, it had passed from the aristocracy to the Commons. The balance of power in other words depends upon the balance of property ; and consequently if a State is to be stable, it must repose upon an equal distribution of wealth. Now a monarchical restoration would in Harrington's view be inadvisable, because a King trying to govern in England by Parliament would find the nobility of no effect at all; but a Parliament where the nobility· is of no effect at all is a mere popular Council, and such a Council will never receive law from a King. A republic, therefore, England must have, but a republic based upon principles which were not to be found in the Cromwellian Protectorate. That was a Government based upon a system of exclusions ; Oceana—the ideal Commonwealth—must comprehend all parties in the State. The Protectorate began with a single chamber ; Oceana must have a Senate as well as a popular assembly. A popular assembly without a Senate cannot be wise ; a Senate without a popular assembly cannot be honest. The one body could not be too small ; the other could not be too numerous. Harrington in other words rejected both that type of republican opinion which found its ideal in the Long Parliament and that which looked back with regret upon the rule of an elect Council of Saints. Two special pieces of mechanism would secure the continuity and stability of his ideal State, a rota and an " Agrarian." By the system of the rota which Harrington was the first to recommend, a third of the Senate and Popular Assembly was to retire every year and their places to be filled by the ballot. By the " Agrarian " the land of Oceana was divided into five thousand lots yielding an income of £2000 apiece, primogeniture abolished and equal division at death enjoined by law. It was a fanciful polity drawn largely from the example of Venice, a state which Harrington preferred to all other governments in the world. Such speculations were too fantastic for practical politics, and were forgotten in the wild joy which heralded the Restoration.

One more treatise of enduring interest belongs to that short period of political uncertainty which lies

between the death of Cromwell and the return of
Charles II. In 1659 and again in the spring of 1660
Milton published his "Ready and Easy way to establish
a Free Commonwealth." The Royalist banners were
advancing, the line of the Puritan defence was clearly
shaken, and a blast of the old trumpet was needed
to rally the wavering courage of the godly host.
The thoughts of the thoughtless were turning to
Kingship, "a government burdensome, expensive,
useless and dangerous." "Where," asks Milton,
"is this godly tower of Commonwealth, which the
English boasted they would build to overshadow
Kings and be another Rome in the West?" Was
England to lose "in a strange after game of folly"
all the battles she had won, all the treasure she had
spent? Was she to prove herself inferior to "our
neighbours of the United Provinces, to us inferior
in all outward advantages, who notwithstanding
in the midst of greater difficulties courageously,
wisely, constantly went through the same work
and are settled in all the happy enjoyments of a
potent and flourishing 'Republic' to this day?"
Was she to renounce that free Commonwealth "not
only held by wisest men in all ages the noblest, the
manliest, the equallest, the justest government,
the most agreeable to all due liberties and pro-
portionate equality, both humane, civil and Christian,
most cherishing to virtue and true religion, but also
(I may say it with greatest probability) plainly
commended or rather enjoined by our Saviour Himself
to all Christians not without remarkable disallowance
and the hand of Providence upon Kingship?" He
could not doubt that all "ingenious and knowing men"
would easily agree with him that "a free Common-

wealth without single person or house of Lords"
was by far the best government that could be had.
But the free Commonwealth of Milton's dream
would be governed neither by the mob nor even by
short Parliaments but by a permanent Council of
" ablest men chosen by the people." An imagination
nourished on the heroic figures of Plutarch could
never rest in the flat and equal levels of democratic
arithmetic. " The enjoyment of civil rights," he
says, " would be best and soonest obtained if every
county in the land were made a little Commonwealth
and their chief town a city, where the nobility and
chief gentry may build houses or palaces befitting
their quality, may bear part in the government,
make their own judicial laws and execute them by
their elected judicatures without appeal in all things
of civil government between man and man." In
this, as in other passages, the feeling for aristocracy
is shown to be as essential a part of Milton's political
enthusiasm as his fierce ardour for political and civil
liberty. The shires of England might be " little
Commonwealths," but never, if Milton were to have
his way, " little democracies." He conceived them to
be controlled by the " nobility and chief gentry "
of the county, expert horsemen, fine and catholic
scholars, fashioned in that elaborate mould of poly-
glot learning and finished courtesy which he depicts
in his essay on education, and living in " houses or
palaces befitting their quality " at the seat of government, with no less of pride and power than the long-
descended rulers of Genoa or Venice.

In striking contrast to these two writers, in whose
dreams there was little that could possibly be applied
in the public temper which then prevailed, is the

Provinces of the Low Countries afforded "an example of such steadiness in practice and principle as is hardly to be paralleled in the world." The Swiss Cantons, despite every defect which could be imagined in the constitution of their Federation, had, " ever since they cast off the insupportable yoke of the Earls of Hapsburg, enjoyed more peace than any other state in Europe, and from the most inconsiderable people are grown to such a power that the greatest monarchs do most solicitously seek their friendship." But there was an example nearer home still—Sidney cast his eyes back upon the Commonwealth of which he had been the servant. " We need no other proof . . . than what we have seen in our own country, where in a few years good discipline and a just encouragement given to those who did well, produced more examples of pure, compleat, incorruptible and invincible virtue than Rome or Greece could ever boast." [7]

There is a famous lament in Hobbes' " Leviathan " to the effect that the civil troubles of England in the seventeenth century were due to the study of the Greek and Latin classics. Aubrey traces Milton's Republicanism to "his being so conversant with Livy and the Roman Authors," and in the writings of Harrington and Sidney we may equally trace the influence of classical tradition. Sidney's examples of popular government are taken from Rome, Athens, and Sparta. He decides on the testimony of the classical authors that an aristocratical republic is better than one in which " the democratical part " is supreme. The " best and wisest of the Ancients " are still for him the supreme guides in political prudence. And this liberal influence of the Greek and Roman classics was not confined to professed republicans and revolutionaries. No two men were more unlike Algernon Sidney in their outlook on life and in the colour of their convictions than Montaigne and Dryden, the one an exquisite epicurean, the other a Tory Roman Catholic. Yet both felt the force of that ancient literature of political freedom which is one of the precious heirlooms of the modern world. "When we hear this author speaking," writes Dryden of Polybius, "we think ourselves engaged in a conversation with Cato the Censor, with Lælius, with Massinissa and with the two Scipios; that is with the greatest heroes and most prudent men of the greatest age in the Roman Commonwealth. This sets me so on fire when I am reading here or in any ancient author their lives and actions, that I cannot hold from breaking out with Montaigne into this expression: "It is just," says he, "for every honest man to be content with the government and laws of his native country, without endeavouring to alter or subvert them; but if I were to choose where I would have been born, it should have been in a Commonwealth." [8]

To glorify liberty is one thing, to prompt revolution, another. The republics of the sixteenth and seventeenth centuries rose out of practical grievances and were the work of men steering to no certain goal, but driven onward by the stress of unexpected tides. Geneva throws off the yoke of Charles III. of Savoy just in time to become the republican capital of the Calvinist faith; the Dutch Republic is the reluctant answer of an oppressed people to the cruelties of a persecuting Church and an alien army; the English Commonwealth the protest of a contentious, conservative, and divided nation against innovations, making for tyranny, in Church and State. Wherever we find it to flourish, the tree of liberty grows from the root of injured interests. Nor was it in the countries of Latin speech and of the classical tradition that the principle of monarchy was first openly repudiated. European Republicanism, which, ever since the French Revolution, has been in the main a phenomenon of the Latin races, was a creature of Teutonic civilization in the age of the sea-beggars and the Roundheads. It is true that the absolute monarchies of Spain and France were severely tested in the seventeenth century. Portugal broke away from Spain, revolution blazed out in Catalonia and Naples, and for five years the French monarchy was paralyzed by the troubles of the Fronde. The word republic was timidly whispered in Lisbon, lightly spoken in Paris. Yet through all the wars and turmoils which followed in the wake of the Reformation, the monarchical faith of the Romance nations was firmly maintained. The only partial exception was the half-Latin city of Geneva, the source of that stream of democratic opinion in Church and State which, flowing to England under Queen Elizabeth, was repelled by persecution to Holland and thence directed to the continent of North America. There, out of the original principle of religious independency, men of the English race built up free communities whose history and example have ever since been of account in the fortunes of Europe.[9]

CHAPTER IV

THE RISE OF THE FRENCH REPUBLIC

Le Républicain en France est un être classique. —MICHELET

THE eighteenth century has rightly been regarded as the age of enlightened despotism. In almost every quarter of Europe, from the Ural mountains to the Lusitanian coast, from Stockholm to Naples, from Vienna to Berlin, it was possible at one time or another to admire the operations of a vigorous and progressive monarchy. In Russia there was Peter the Great, and after an interval Catherine II.; in Naples and Spain Charles III.; in the Austrian dominions, Maria Theresa, Joseph II., and Leopold; in Prussia, Frederick the Great; in Sweden, Gustavus III. In each of these different countries the problems to be attacked, the abuses to be swept away had their own peculiar character, but one feature was common to the general malady. The evils of European society were rooted in feudalism and entrenched in privilege. It followed from this that the power of the monarchy to cure the disease varied in direct proportion to the inability of the aristocracy to arrest its operations. Where the monarchy was absolute, where it was unfettered by the opposition of privileged corporations or estates, a campaign could be planned on a comprehensive design and pressed to a victorious and efficient conclusion. But in proportion as these conditions were unrealized, the struggle was likely to be long, arduous, and perplexed. Nowhere was progress so swift and palpable as in Russia, where the Tsar united in his own person the supreme and absolute authority both in Church and State ; nowhere so slow as in France, where the royal will was impeded by a powerful judicial corporation and by the great and opulent interests of a numerous and privileged aristocracy and a mundane and privileged Church.

There are two tests which may be applied to any Government, the test of efficiency and the test of education. The philosophers of the eighteenth century, impressed as they naturally were with the achievements of monarchy in their own age, and holding as they did that politics was a deductive science, a series of immutable principles discoverable by reason, valid for all time and place, and containing infinite potentiality of happiness for the human race, primarily regarded the test of efficiency. They did not care to ask themselves what form of government was likely to enlist the greatest amount of civic energy or to impart to the members of the State the most valuable political education. Their principal concern was to discover the most efficient instrument for the rapid diffusion of rational ideas, and with few exceptions they recommended monarchy. In his beautiful life of Turgot, Condorcet describes the views of the great French reformer in the following terms : " The equal right of contributing to the formation of laws is doubtless an essential, inalienable, and imprescriptible right which belongs to all proprietors. But in the actual state of society the exercise of this right would be almost illusory for the greater part of the people, and the free and assured enjoyment

of the other rights of society has a much more extensive
influence on almost all citizens.   Besides, this right
has no longer the same importance, if laws be regarded
not as the expression of the arbitrary will of the
majority, but as truths deduced by reason from
principles of natural law and adopted as such by
the majority.   The sole difference then is that the
consent to these truths is tacit in one constitution,
while in another it is public and subjected to legal
and   regular   forms."   Pursuing   this   general   line
of reasoning, Turgot concludes that monarchies are
peculiarly adapted to promote the general happiness
of mankind, since the monarch has not and cannot
have any interest in making bad laws, since he can
often act in pursuance of enlightened opinion without
waiting upon the slow march of the common mind,
and since there was reason to hope that bad laws
could   be   attacked   to   best   advantage   under   an
unfettered monarchy.[1]

It was no part of the philosophical programme of
the eighteenth century to regenerate humanity by
hoisting   the   republican   flag   over   the   capitals   of
Europe.   The philosopher still drew his ideas of
the republic from the writings of the ancients, and
after   distributing   some   academic   commendations,
proceeded   to   enunciate   the   traditional   warnings
against the opposite evils of the demagogue and the
despot.   The republic, according to Montesquieu,
postulated a large supply of public virtue, a small
territôry, and an absence of luxury and large fortunes.
If small, it was liable to destruction at the hands of
a foreign power; if great, it was inevitably corroded
by internal decay.   Federation alone could preserve
the existence of so delicate and precarious an organism :

and federation, as exemplified in Holland, in German and in the Swiss Leagues, had undoubtedly succeed in giving stability to many republican polities whi would otherwise have succumbed to the dange incidental to their constitution. Rousseau w not, like Montesquieu, a professor of the doctrine relativity. His prescriptions were made up f humanity at large in royal independence of time an space; but he agreed with the witty author of th "Esprit des Lois," in thinking that democrac could only properly belong to small and poor State With this opinion, much as he despised Rousseau political masterpiece, Voltaire is in substantial agre ment. Premising that there has never been a perfe democracy, because men have passions, he hol that the people are likely to receive more attentio and to enjoy more prosperity in a small than in large republic. It is easier, he observes, to get peopl to listen to reason in an assembly of a thousand tha in an assembly of forty thousand. Such an observa tion shows clearly that Voltaire's mind was pre occupied by the city republics of ancient or o medieval times. When he thinks of a republic, hi mind naturally conjures up the image of a market place crowded with enfranchised citizens or of a podestà summoned in to adjust the griefs of the Montagues and Capulets. He will allow to such a government certain merits; and when shaking himsel free from these associations, he turns to the green and thriving pastures of Switzerland or to the busy marts of the Netherlands and contrasts them with the Roman Campagna, once crowded with glittering marble villas and now, under the desolating paralysis of papal rule, so solitary and plague-stricken that you may voyage a whole day without seeing man or beast, he acknowledges the triumphs of political liberty. But the modern republic lacks grandeur : it is no seminary of statesmen. It can show no Oxenstiern or Sully or Burleigh on its civic rolls. To the monarchy, aided by the wisdom of the wise, Voltaire looked for the regeneration of France.[2]

Turgot used often to say that he had never known a really republican constitution. The communities which boasted of the name of republic, turned out, upon a close examination of their political anatomy, to be no better than vicious aristocracies. He had never known a community in which the proprietors had an equal right of contributing to the formation of laws and of regulating the public institutions of the State. If the life of that noble reformer had been prolonged for eleven years, he would have witnessed the formation of a great democratic polity on the other side of the Atlantic. He would have seen the principles of the true republic fixed and embodied in living institutions, and he would have realised that it is possible for communities of free men to form diplomatic alliances, to carry on war, to frame the terms of a triumphant peace, and finally to construct a state upon original lines suited to their own peculiar needs and proclivities, without the support of an aristocracy or the shelter of a crown.[3]

The foundation of the United States of America was a fact the magnitude and import of which was at once perceived in Europe. It proved that a great modern State could adopt the republican form ; it showed that a pure democracy was capable of avoiding the follies and dangers which were considered to be peculiar to democratic government. The

example given by the New World might be copied in
the obsolescent states of Europe. In the New World
a whole continent, stretching from the Atlantic to
the shore of the Pacific, would in the inevitable march
of time be brought into one great democratic federation. A whole continent would be rescued from the
barbarism of dynastic wars by the simple expedient
of having no dynasties. The principle which in
America secured the everlasting peace of a great
section of the globe, by establishing a system of
federated republics, might eventually be extended to
Europe. If Kings could be made to vanish, with
their absurd family ambitions, their costly armies
and their intriguing diplomats; if every State in
Europe could be governed by the popular voice, it
was reasonable to expect that the gravest obstacles
to international union would disappear. It was
argued that States with homogeneous constitutions
must themselves be homogeneous ; that the interests
of democracies are essentially identical; and that
communities regulated upon the principles of natural
justice would find their ethical satisfaction in the
sentiment of human fraternity.[4]

No country in Europe was so quick as France in
appropriating morals from the American Revolution
The war of American independence had been waged
against England, the enemy of many centuries, and
seemed in the eyes of patriotic Frenchmen to be
the retribution of Providence for the British conquest
of Canada, and a triumph of natural right over force
and fraud. A French army had helped to procure
the American triumph, and returned to its native
land saturated with republican spirit. The French
navy had recaptured some of its lost prestige. By

an ironic coincidence the last military triumph of
the old dynasty was combined with the first practical
demonstration of those principles of natural right
which, passing from the writings of the French
philosophers into the common mind of France, with
all the splendid corroboration of the Peace of
Versailles and the American Constitution, helped to
undermine the fabric of the monarchy.

We must not, however, overrate the influence
of philosophy upon the generation which preceded
the great awakening of the French Revolution. Even
now, if account be held of the general mass of men,
philosophers claim a small audience, and their
audience was far smaller in the eighteenth century.
There was no system of compulsory education; there
were few public libraries; a book was still something
of a luxury. It is questionable whether Voltaire
in his long lifetime numbered as many readers for
his seventy volumes as a successful American novel
would find in the course of a single season. The vast
mass of the French population was still illiterate,
and of the people who read books only a small proportion was interested in politics. Madame Roland
was a literary lady of the middle class. She read
Shakespeare, and Plutarch's "Lives," and Thomson's
"Seasons," besides assisting a prosaic husband in
the compilation of a "Dictionary of Arts and Crafts";
yet in the whole course of her correspondence, which
has recently been published, there is no single allusion
to public affairs before the summoning of the States
General. The Revolution seems to cut a clean chasm
across her mental life. Before it she knows nothing
about politics, and after it she lives for nothing else.[*]
We shall not therefore be surprised to find that when,

in 1789, all France was invited to formulate its grievances, those grievances took a very practical shape.
The *cahiers* of 1789, in so far as they reveal the mind
of France, and the revelation is certainly authentic
and comprehensive within the sphere of public policy,
are very realistic documents. The men who compile
them do not argue from first principles. They do not
say, " We must have Equality, Liberty, Fraternity ! "
They do not demand a republic or make any profession of principle inconsistent with the continuance
of the French monarchy. They nowhere demand
the abolition of the nobility or clergy as separate
orders of the State. Most of the *cahiers* express a
wish that the Catholic religion should remain the State
religion. " France," says M. Champion, who has read
more of the *cahiers* than anyone else, " remains so
profoundly Catholic that she has much difficulty
in ridding herself of her ancient intolerance." It
is not only the Church which ten years after the death
of Voltaire with difficulty resigns itself to the edict
in favour of the protestants and wishes that " the
national religion should preserve all its privileges as
the State religion " ; this view is shared by a great
portion of the Third Estate. In general, while admitting that protestants should obtain civil rights and
that they should be qualified to hold certain appoint-
ments, it refuses them any place in the judicial
administration, in educational work, or in the police.
They are to have no churches, no public assemblies
or ceremonies ; they must keep silence on religious
questions. There is indeed a whole revolution
contained in the *cahiers*, but it is not a republican
revolution. France desires a better administration,
a better judicial system, the abolition of privilege,

of feudal dues, of the militia service, the elimination
of caprice from the system of government. The
republic is so little in the mind of the country that
the peasants fire the castles and destroy the muniments
in the belief that their actions are countenanced by
the King.[6]

How then did the French Republic come to be
established four years later, seeing that republicanism
had never been recommended by the philosophers
and was no part of the general creed or tradition
of the country? The Constituent Assembly was
profoundly monarchist, and left as the final monument
of its labours a constitution which preserved the
monarchy though with diminished and diluted powers.
The Church of course was monarchical, the aristocracy was monarchical, the peasantry monarchical.
Mirabeau, who was certainly one of the most impressive
figures in the early history of the revolution, not only
by reason of his sonorous and powerful eloquence,
but also by reason of the fact that he had grasped
the transcendent necessity of plucking privilege
out by the roots without surrendering the country
to anarchy, urged again and again on the Constituent
Assembly the doctrine that the King was the direct
representative of the people and that it was to the
interest of the people that his power should be strong.
The man who had written the classical treatise against
the *Lettres de Cachet*, who had championed the claims
of the Third Estate against the Clergy and the Nobles,
and has told the King's usher that the National
Assembly would not disperse save at the point of
the bayonet, claimed that the King should possess
an absolute veto on legislation, that he should be
empowered to declare war, and to make peace, and that

his ministers should have a place in the Legislativ
Assembly.

To give a complete account of the causes whic
secured the triumph of the Republican princip
in France would involve the whole story of the earl
stages of the revolution. Some of them belong t
the intellectual tissue of the age ; others were grounde
in human character ; others again proceeded fror
political developments which were beyond the scop
of abstract philosophy or common prudence to foretel
So far as the moral and intellectual causes wer
concerned it may be sufficient to note that the me
who wrote for the newspapers in Paris and th
summoning of the States General was the signal for
sudden and altogether unprecedented output o
newspapers and pamphlets—the men who orate
to the mob in the gardens of the Palais Royal, wh
harangued at the street corners, and in the club
and who howled down the moderate speakers i
the Assembly, were possessed by a fierce hatred fc
privilege and by a passion for social equality. The
had taken from Rousseau either at first, or at secon
or at third hand, the doctrine that the General Wi
is sovereign, that man is by nature free but everywhe
in chains, equal but everywhere affronted by distinc
tions of caste, and that it was the one and only functio
of government to restore the lost code of Natur
in all its simple harmonies. From Voltaire, whos
influence was assisted by the intolerance of the Church
the literary class of Paris had long learnt to despis
the priests and to discount the alleged religiou
sanctions of the French monarchy. They believe
nothing in a tradition, which was the legacy of pre
judice, or in a history which was the record of crime

Holding 'that man was infinitely perfectible, and believing that it was in the power of law to effect vast and immediate improvements in human nature and society, they were impatient of any arguments based upon grounds of national temperament, or vested interest. Society was rotten at the core, and it was the duty of France to effect a thorough revolution. They had an array of first principles which would do the business, but if the principles were rigidly applied there would be no place for an hereditary monarchy in France.

The first French democrats started with an advantage which in any deliberative assembly is more precious than numbers. Accepting the premises which the majority of French intellectual men accepted, the premises about the Rights of Man and the sovereignty of the People and so forth, they drew a strict conclusion against which there was no logical defence, if once it were admitted that tradition was to count for nothing and logic for everything in the control of human affairs. In England extreme opinions are seldom listened to because English deliberative assemblies are too stupid or too prudent to believe that the world is helped forward by strict logical deductions. But in the Constituent Assembly, the more extreme an opinion the more logical it was likely to be and therefore the more cogent. This might indeed have been otherwise had the founders of the first revolutionary constitution of France been privileged to deliberate with shut doors and in the tranquil atmosphere of the Philadelphia Convention. Had such been their good fortune they would not indeed have given France a second Chamber, for they regarded the noble with some

justice as the great culprit of French history and were
not prepared to create for him a fortified position
from which he might carry devastation over the wide
fields of democratic reform ; but they would have
left the monarchy a real instead of an illusory force
in the constitution.   Unfortunately they were never
free agents.   Their business was conducted to a
running accompaniment of savage and excited com-
mentary from benches crowded with as violent a
mob as any city in Europe could produce.   They
could not record a vote without the certain chance
of being held up to execration if it were given on the
unpopular side ; and, being in no ways above the
general level of human courage but probably somewhat below it, they permitted themselves to be carried
further than their own cool judgment would have
allowed down the path which led to the republic.

M. Aulard, who has investigated so closely the
development of political opinion in France during
the French Revolution, finds the first traces of an
avowed republican party in the autumn of 1790.
There was a certain Mme. Robert, wife of a Jacobin
advocate from Liège, who held a political salon in
Paris, and inspired the politics of a newspaper called
the *Mercure national*.   On October 1, 1790, the
Mercure declared for the Republic, and the ball was
set rolling.   It was a fine theme for debate.   In
December M. Robert himself entered the lists with
a pamphlet entitled *Le Républicanisme adapté à la
France*, but the republicans were neither numerous
nor influential.   There was still an immense reserve
force in the French monarchy if only the King knew
how to use it.[7]

There are some occasions in history in which every-

thing seêms to depend upon the character of an
individual. The continuance of the monarchy in
France depended on the character of Louis XVI.
That it would have been in his power to avert a comprehensive economic and administrative revolution
is scarcely credible ; the great part of the nation
demanded it with passionate unanimity. But a man
of strength and clearness of vision, a man whose
character, bearing, and intellect would have appealed
to the imagination of France as of one who was
resolyed to control the storm rather than to be
driven hither and thither by every gust, would have
certainly saved a throne which was rooted in some of
the deepest instincts of the nation. The unfortunate
Louis committed almost every error which it was
possible for him to commit. Having invited the
whole population to formulate its grievances, and
having thus aroused through the length and breadth
of the country a consciousness of the evils which
it suffered only less profound than its resolve that
these evils must forthwith be cured, he summoned
the States General to Versailles without having
framed in advance a scheme of reform or a plan of
concessions. When the financial needs of the realm
had been made known to the three orders, the King
withdrew and left them to their own devices. His
mother was a Saxon and he possessed his full share
of Teutonic phlegm. He preferred the chase in the
fine spring air to weary lucubrations in the Cabinet.
It never occurred to him that by putting himself at
the head of a constitutional movement he might
control the assembly and hold the citadel of his
ancestors. So he let things glide on ; hunted while
the Third Estate wrangled with nobles and clergy ;

5

hunted while they declared themselves the National Assembly of France; and then tardily and maladroitly intervened with a scheme of constitutional reform which on May 5, 1789, would have been saluted as a splendid gift, and on June 23 was viewed as a grudging and insufficient concession.

But this was only part of his error or misfortune. It would perhaps have required a great man and a hard man to shake himself free from the aristocratic influences which had hitherto surrounded him and to make it clear to the world that neither the Queen nor the court camarilla had any part in shaping his course. Louis was not capable of such a determination. He could not clear himself from the meshes in which he was fatally implicated, by showing a frank, continuous and unreserved goodwill to the cause of reasonable constitutional reform. The Queen was his more determined half, and she hated the assembly with a hate which was not dissembled from the world. On July 12, 1789, she obtained a victory over her husband. Necker, the popular Swiss minister, was dismissed, and troops were massed under the Marshal de Broglie to overawe the Paris mob. A really effective display of force would at this time have secured great benefits to France, but Louis was not the man to impress upon his subordinate officers the supreme necessity for vigour. The troops were slackly handled, the Paris mob was allowed to storm the Bastille, and, overwhelmed by popular clamour and disturbance, the unfortunate King recalled Necker to his counsels. He now appeared in the eyes of the club politicians of the capital as the centre of a military conspiracy against the principles of the revolution. That conspiracy had been foiled, thanks to the heroes of the Bastille, but so long as Louis was in Versailles, Paris might again be imperilled. In October a mob marched upon the palace of Versailles and brought the King and Queen helpless captives to the Tuileries. Already the Princes of the blood, followed by a crowd of nobles, had taken wing for the frontiers. Paris, filled with starving workmen and indifferently policed by Lafayette's national guard, was no place for quiet men. In a memoir submitted to the Count of Provence on October 16, Mirabeau, clearly perceiving that, unless the Assembly were removed from the surrounding sea of anarchy, ill work would be made of the Constitution, recommended the King to escape to Rouen and thence to publish a manifesto declaring his adhesion to the principles of the revolution and summoning the Assembly to assist him in converting them into law. In view of the prevailing disturbance of the country districts and of the suspicious temper of the Assembly itself, it is doubtful whether this, or any other of the numerous plans devised by Mirabeau for the rescue of the monarchy, would have met with success. But in truth there were only two courses open to the King. He must either enforce law and order in the capital or he must escape.

The election which he made and how it prospered is the most famous and dramatic episode of the French Revolution. Mirabeau was dead; and the warning voice against a flight to the frontier died with him. The position of the King in Paris was steadily made more difficult and intolerable. He had been forced against the promptings of his conscience, August 24, 1790, to sign the Civil Constitution of the clergy, and was informed that none

save constitutional priests would be permitted to
administer the sacrament to him in his private chapel.
To satisfy a scrupulous conscience he made an attempt
to spend Easter at St Cloud, and was driven by the
Paris mob into the Tuileries.   Finding that a public
departure was impossible, he and the Queen determined to put into practice a scheme, which had long
been before their minds, of escaping to Metz, where
they would find a loyal army, and whence they might
use the instrument of a military demonstration to
bring Paris to its senses.   On the night of June
20-1, 1791, the King and Queen made their escape,
the King leaving behind him a criticism of the Constitution and a formal retractation of the measures
which he had been forced to pass in his captivity.
Five days later the fugitives were brought back to
Paris.   A great multitude was in the streets.   " Every
citizen kept his hat on his head as by a common
understanding."

When the intelligence was first spread about in
Paris that the King had escaped there was a feeling,
first of stupor, then of indignation, then of panic.
France had never been without a King and imagined
that every conceivable form of horror might ensue
from the lack of one.   The country would be invaded
by foreign armies ; the nation dissolved in unspeak-
able anarchy.   Accordingly when King and Queen were
recovered a great relief spread through the country
as if it had recovered a familiar talisman against
misfortune.   And yet the flight to Varennes may
almost be described as the first provisional stage
of the French Republic.   When the news of the
King's escape was received the executive authority
devolved upon the Assembly.   The Assembly declared

itself *en permanence*, sent representatives through the departments, notified its accession to foreign powers, gave orders to the ministers, insisted on hearing the diplomatic correspondence, and caused the name of the King to be omitted from the civil oath. The King returned, but the Assembly did not abdicate. It decreed that the King should be given a guard, or in other words that he should be held in strict captivity. And the King was suspended from his functions. It was, as 290 deputies of the right protested, " a republican Interim."

The sudden interruption of a long-established convention has an effect quite out of proportion to its duration in time. France woke up to find itself without a King and realised that the earth still revolved in its accustomed orbit. A letter from Paris written on June 24, 1791, says, " The wise measures taken by the Assembly make even the poor people believe that they can get on without a King, and everywhere I found people saying, ' We have no need of a King : the Assembly and its ministers are good enough for us. Why should we have an executive power which costs 25 millions when the work can be done for 2 or 3 ? ' " The extreme newspapers break out into open professions of republican faith. " Louis XVI. has broken his own crown," says the *Patriote Français*, the organ of Brissot, " After such an act of perjury the King cannot be made to harmonize with the constitution." The *Révolutions de Paris*, the *Annales Patriotiques*, the *Bouche de Fer* pronounced against monarchy. The Cordeliers petitioned the Assembly to establish a Republic. About a fifth of the Jacobin Club concurred. " No King, or a King with an elective or removable Council, such in two words is my pro-

fession of faith," wrote Brissot in the *Patriòte Français*. Republican pamphlets were scattered abroad
*l'Acéphalocratie ou Louis XVI. roi des Français détrône
par lui-même*. A special Republican paper was
started, *Le Républicain*, with Thomas Paine and
Condorcet for principal editors. A controversy was
engaged between Sieyès and Tom Paine in the
Moniteur. Sieyès defended monarchy. "A monarchical government finished in a point, a republican
in a superficies, and the monarchical triangle was
better adapted to that division of powers which was
the real bulwark of public liberty than the flat surface of the republic." On July 8, 1791, there was a
meeting of the Federal Assembly of the Friends
of Truth addressed by Condorcet, who pointed out
that this unexpected event had freed France from
any obligations to the King and that they could
therefore consider whether monarchy was essential
to liberty. He proceeds to refute the current
objections brought against a Republic. The size
was no obstacle ; on the contrary a recommendation
as it prevented the idol of the capital from becoming
the tyrant of the Nation. It had been argued that
a republic would lead to tyranny, but, given the
freedom of the press and the division of powers, how
could tyranny arise ? It was said that a King was
necessary to prevent the usurpations of the Legislature ; but if the Legislature was frequently renewed
and the constitution revised at stated intervals by
a National Convention, how could these usurpations
be conducted ? To those who argued that it was
better to have one master than many, Condorcet
replied that there was no necessity to have a master
at all. It was alleged that without a king the

executive power could not receive the necessary degree of force. In the days when powerful associations could resist the laws, the executive power did undoubtedly require to be very strong, and even despotism was not strong enough. But now that the corporations were abolished, that equality reigned, very little force would be required to induce obedience to the law. The force of the executive would in fact be strengthened rather than weakened by the abolition of the hereditary monarchy, since a King necessarily excites against himself the suspicions of the friends of liberty. Lastly it had been argued that a Republic would lead to a military dictatorship. In a passage memorable for its lack of foresight Condorcet addresses himself to the refutation of this favourite thesis. "What conquered provinces," he asks, "will a French general despoil to buy our votes? Will an ambitious man propose to us, as an ambitious man once proposed to the Athenians, that we should levy tributes on our allies, that we may raise temples or give festivals? Will he promise our soldiers the pillage of Spain or Syria? Surely no, and it is because we cannot be a people-king that we should remain a free people." [8]

How it might have been for France, if, after the return from Varennes, a republic had been proclaimed, it is idle to guess; there are some who think that such a course would have saved the country from great disaster. As it was, the Republic was proclaimed in the midst of a desperate war, and was therefore from its origin associated with all the passions and evils which war brings in its train. But opinion would never have sanctioned the deposition of Louis in the summer of 1791. Gravely as the Constituent Assembly had disapproved of his action, and ignominious as were the restrictions which it proceeded to place upon his liberty, it was not prepared to alter the foundations of the work upon which it had been so actively engaged. Four-fifths at least of the Jacobin club were still monarchist and, though there were no means of actually probing the opinion of the provinces, there was no reason to imagine that the common man had faltered in his allegiance to the crown. A republican demonstration in the Champ de Mars was put down with a display of force which for the moment drove the violent spirits into hiding and produced a marked reaction in the tone of the panic-stricken press. When in September 1791 the Constituent Assembly concluded its labours and the King formally accepted the Constitution, he enjoyed a brief St Martin's summer of popularity. Condorcet, who did not wane in his belief that a republic was preferable to a monarchy, confessed that France did not seem to like the prospect, that it preferred to make trial of the new constitution, and that the new constitution made adequate provision for liberty.

There is perhaps no more crucial episode in the annals of modern Europe than the history of the Legislative Assembly which met in September 1791 and for the space of one year governed the destinies of France. It was this Assembly which declared war upon Austria and thus began that great duel between the French Revolution and the dynasts of Europe, which received its final settlement in the field of Waterloo. It was this Assembly which by its decrees against the *émigrés* and the priests drove the King into a position in which he was bound to sacrifice either the last shreds of his honour or the last shreds of his popularity. While this Assembly was deliberating in Paris, and not a little as the result of its deliberations, the storm arose which uprooted the ancient trunk of the Bourbon monarchy. A decree was passed ordaining the formation of a camp of twenty thousand *fédérés* in the outskirts of Paris. Louis vetoed it. In Marseilles, where republican spirit ran high, a body of five hundred patriots marched on the capital, disregarding the royal veto, and chaunting a war song written for the army of the Rhine and destined to be the baptismal hymn of the young Republic. They found Paris aglow with the passion and tremor of war, volunteers tramping off to the frontier, the forty-eight sections *en permanence*, and a central committee of the sections plotting insurrection at the Hôtel de Ville. As they marched in by the Quartier St Antoine they were received with acclamations and brigaded with the forces of revolution. The plotters were men of action, not visionaries. They had no scheme for the government of France, they had drafted no plan of a Republic, but they argued with a rough and true instinct that no war can be conducted to a successful issue if the head of the executive sympathizes with the enemy. That this was the case with Louis was a matter which had long been established to the satisfaction of Danton and his followers. Had he not designed to stifle the revolution at its birth by throwing Broglie's army into Paris ? Had he not attempted to escape to the frontier ? Had he not repudiated the constitution and openly advertised his alliance with the enemies of the nation by vetoing the punitive decrees against the *émigrés* and the priests ? Such arguments ran through Paris and, since the Assembly was too timid to act, the Directory of Insurrection resolved to act for it. On August 10, 1792, an assault was made on the Tuileries. The King, taking refuge with the Assembly, ordered the Swiss troops, who, if left to themselves, might have saved the palace and cowed the riot, to retire to their barracks, and by this final act of clemency or cowardice signed the doom of a dynasty which had reigned over France for more than eight hundred years. Surprised and frightened by the violence of the streets, the members of the Legislature strained their ears for tidings of the conflict. But when the issue was assured, when it was known that the last loyal regiment of the monarchy was hacked to pieces in its desperate and forlorn retirement, that an insurrectionary commune flushed with victory was established at the Hôtel de Ville, and that the mob was pillaging the treasures of the Tuileries, the Legislature of France affixed its seal to the event. They decided that the chief of the executive power should be provisionally suspended, and that a National Convention should be summoned to take such measures as might secure the sovereignty of the people and the reign of liberty and equality. The Commune demanded that Louis and his wife should be imprisoned within the grim walls of the Temple, and, as the Commune was master of Paris, its will was done.

It is a matter of common observation that a crowd is more than the sum of the individuals who compose it. The collective body thinks and acts in ways which the component units thinking and acting for themselves would never sanction and would often reprobate. In general the action of the crowd is more emotional and less intellectual than the action of an individual. The nerve counts for more, the brain for less. Waves of sentiment or cruelty pass through the collective body with a force which the individuals who compose it find it difficult to comprehend, when they are removed from the contagion of their neighbours, and can rehearse the emotion in solitude. Conduct then seems silly, or wicked, or incomprehensible, which in the excitement of collective action was so instinctive and immediate as to fall outside the area of self-consciousness altogether. Empty phrases and maxims exert a power which the individual in a cool hour of reflection finds it impossible to explain ; and what is there which a crowd will not do when a panic strikes it or when the poison of suspicion is in the air ? " We were cowards "—" *Nous étions des lâches* "—said Barère in simple but adequate explanation of the Terror.

It must not therefore be assumed that the Legislative Assembly was republican because the whole course of its policy was directly calculated to destroy the monarchy. Such a supposition would be the reverse of the truth. The Assembly contained some avowed republicans, and a large number of men whose political principles would more easily harmonize with a republic than with a monarchy, but at no time previous to the 10th August did it record any distinct affirmation of the republican principle. Strong language was used by democratic rhetoricians, but even the most violent orator did not propose a constitutional revolution. The most eloquent orator of the Legislature was Vergniaud. " From this window," he cried on March 10, 1792, " we see the palace where the King is misled by perfidious

counsels. Terror and fear have often issued from
yon palace: let them return to-day in the name of
the law, and let all those who inhabit that palace
know that the King is alone inviolable, that the law
will strike down the guilty without respect of persons,
and that there is not a guilty head which can escape
its sword."

Yet on July 20 the author of those vague and
pompous threats joins with Guadet and Gensonné
in a petition to the King to form a Jacobin ministry,
and even on August 10 the Assembly does not
definitely dethrone the King. It votes for provisional
suspension; it contemplates a governor for the
Dauphin, and it became a matter of accusation
against the Girondins that by voting for suspension
rather than deposition they had aimed at preserving
the monarchy.

Forty-two days elapsed between the capture of
the Tuileries and the gathering of the National Convention. The Assembly upon whom the government
of France now devolved entrusted the executive
power to a committee of ministers and marked its
acquiescence in the latest popular revolution by
giving to Danton the portfolio of Justice. The word
Republic was not pronounced, but a kingless government conducting a national war is a republic in fact
if not in deed. In the life and death wrestle which was
now beginning there was not much time to spin
theories. The Austrians and Prussians crossed the
frontier on August 19 and opened their campaign
with a series of easy and alarming victories. On
August 20 the Duke of Brunswick invested Longwy;
on September 2 he took Verdun; on September 6
his army was in leaguer before Thionville, and as

the enemy advanced, the character of the struggle in which France was engaged became more and more apparent. The new democracy was pitted against the old dynasties of Europe, an experiment against a tradition, an aspiration against an instinct, a reason against a romance, a theory of human equality against the stubborn fact of human deference. Catching the general spirit in the air, the Assembly voted that the seal of State should bear a figure of Liberty, the cap of freedom on her head and a pike in her hand with the legend, " In the name of the French nation." Then on September 4, in a moment of excitement, it took a step which was even more decisive. Rising to their feet the members swore that they would fight to the death Kings and Kingship. " Their oath," says a newspaper, " was repeated by the spectators, and with cries of *Vive la Liberté*. It is graven in the heart of all Frenchmen and they will keep it."

Meanwhile France was in the throes of a general election. The Legislative had been elected upon a restricted franchise : it decided that restrictions upon the franchise were inconsistent with the true spirit of democracy. The Convention was to be elected upon a scheme of universal suffrage (universal save for the exclusion of domestic servants) and by the indirect methods of electoral councils. It is idle to consider what sort of an Assembly France would have returned but for the pressure of the war and the clubs. M. Aulard, whose learned history is composed with a strong revolutionary bias, maintains that the Convention was as freely elected as any French Assembly down to 1848. That may or may not be so ; the fact remains that the elections were dominated by the clubs and that but a small portion of the

voting power of France went to the polls.   An instance
which M. Aulard quotes in favour of freedom is, in
reality, a complete demonstration of the pressure
which was applied from Jacobin headquarters.   Ir
a number of the *Annales* published on September 1
and freely distributed among the electoral assemblies
Carra, a man who had previously suggested that
the Duke of York might be invited to take the crowr
of France, declared that any future deputy whc
should propose to re-establish the monarchy shoulc
be buried alive.   Upon the strength of this civilizec
proposition Carra was elected in eight departments
He stood above the philosopher Condorcet who wa:
elected in five departments, above Tom Paine whc
was elected in four, above Brissot who was electec
in three, above Cloots who was elected in two.   Thi
obscure journalist, who had proposed burying aliv
as the proper treatment for monarchical deputies
was, if these September elections are to be taken a
reflecting the real voice of the country, the mos
popular man in France.   The inference is irresistible
The elections represented not the country but th
violent group who had captured the electoral machine
According to one calculation the Convention whic
proclaimed the French Republic was elected on th
mandate of about 6 per cent. of the electors of France

The first session of the Convention was held o
September 20, 1792, a date twice memorable in th
annals of France since it was also the day of Valm;
Out of 749 members only 371 had arrived in Par
on the day of opening, and the attendance is hardl
likely to have been greatly increased on the followir
day.   Yet, despite the fact that its numbers wer
incomplete and that it was only in the second da

of its session, the Convention unanimously decreed the abolition of monarchy. " Kings," said Grégoire, " are in morality what monsters are in the world of nature." When the decree was passed, " cries of joy," said the *Gazette de France*, " filled the hall, and all arms were raised to heaven, as if to thank it for having delivered the land of France from the greatest curse which had affected it." On the next day it was resolved that all acts of State should henceforth bear the date, " The first year of the French Republic." But there were no fireworks or solemn promulgation. Some of the papers fail to mention these important decrees. " It seems," writes M. Aulard, " that the French Republic was introduced furtively into history, as if the Convention were saying to the nation, ' There is no other course possible.' " To quiet a very prevalent apprehension that a republic must be either a small city or a loose federation, the Convention, upon the motion of Danton, passed, on September 25, 1792, the famous resolution that the Republic is one and indivisible. But no one of these important decrees, neither the decree abolishing the monarchy, nor that establishing a Republic, nor that which declared against the federal solution, was submitted to a *plébiscite* of the French nation.

In a private letter, written after the outbreak of the war, a democratic monarchist, who had taken a large share in the making of the first revolutionary constitution, declared that the Constituent Assembly had made a mistake in not at once dethroning Louis XVI. and transferring the crown to another dynasty. The development of events taught Sieyès a lesson in history—a department of knowledge which he affected to despise. A monarch is the creature of a tradition and the symbol of a faith. The tradition may be absurd, the faith may be injurious to the dignity of man; but there they are and you must reckon with them. The French monarchy had not suffered the salutary interruptions which had secured the liberties of England. It was not the gift of a Parliament or the result of a contract. It had not been limited by a Magna Carta or a Bill of Rights. It was a monarchy claiming to be based upon divine right, and deriving its credentials from an unbroken record of service dating back to a distant and barbaric age. It was closely associated with the Catholic Church, and, since the decline of Spain, had been the most powerful promoter of its interests. No royal house was so national, if long association with a nation's history deserves the epithet, and no royal house was so international. The Bourbons ruled in Madrid, in Naples, in Parma. The two brothers of Louis XVI. were married to Savoyard princesses. The King himself had taken a bride from Vienna as a symbol of that Austrian alliance which, despite all the disasters it entailed, was still the corner-stone of French diplomacy. Situated thus, Louis XVI. could not be, in any genuine sense, the King of a revolution which regarded the monarch as the agent, not of God but of the people, which despoiled the Church of its property, and violated the Catholic conscience by abruptly severing the connexion with Rome. Even if the King himself could show the requisite degree of elasticity, there was his wife, there were his brothers, there was the tradition of the family recommended from the allied thrones and certain to be one of the most powerful ingredients in the education of the infant Dauphin. These incompatibilities were indeed evident from the first, but it needed the stern stress of war to strain them to a rupture.

The war out of which the French Republic arose was not entirely the result of dynastic interests. The annexation of Avignon, the abolition of the feudal dues in Alsace despite express treaty stipulations that the German princes who held land in that quarter should be protected in all their sovereign rights and privileges, the open encouragement given to a rebellion in the Austrian Netherlands, the wild language used against crowned heads, the pronouncement of subversive principles of public law—all these acts and symptoms created a feeling of acute tension which might have led to difficulties even if the royal house in France had not been closely connected with the Imperial family. But the treatment of the French royal family was the main grievance which weighed with Austria and the other courts of Europe. The Emperor Leopold, faced as he was with the difficult problems bequeathed to him by the injudicious administration of his quixotic brother, had no wish to draw the sword; but he could not turn a deaf ear to the entreaties of his sister. It was her belief that some sharp external pressure would school the strange impudence of the French Democrats and restore the throne to its former position. Leopold acquiesced. He issued a circular to the monarchs of Europe calling them to free the King from the restraints of the Paris mob; and then, meeting the King of Prussia at Pillnitz, in August 1791, concerted a demonstration intended to impose upon the fears of the French. The two monarchs addressed an invitation to all the powers of Europe, calling upon

6

them to aid in the restoration of the French King
to his lawful position; and subjoined an undertaking
to mobilize their forces in the event of such aid being
given by all the Powers.

No nation is so lost to pride as to submit the
conduct of its internal affairs to the arbitrament of
foreign powers. To the proud and sensitive democracy of France the declaration of Pillnitz was not a
discipline, but an irritant : and so far from mending
the position of the royal family it only helped to
make it worse. At the same moment elections were
held all over France to the Legislative Assembly.
The men who were returned had no acquaintance
with the subtle and complicated undercurrents of
European policy. They were not aware that nothing
was further from the wishes or designs of the Emperor
than a war with France, and that he would anxiously
clutch at the King's acceptance of the Constitution
to wash his hands of a troublesome business. They
only knew that France had been insulted by two
crowned heads and that there was no reason in the
ultimate nature of things, seeing that all men were
free and equal, why crowned heads should exist at all.
The collection of armed bodies of *émigrés* in the
electorates of Trier-Mainz gave a pretext for a quarrel,
which Francis, who succeeded the pacific Leopold
in March 1792, was not anxious to avoid. In Paris
war was eagerly desired partly by the royalists who
thought that a military success might retrieve the
fortunes of the Crown, partly by the Girondins who
argued that at the call of revolutionary France the
peoples of Europe would throw off their chains.
Both expectations were falsified in the event. Europe
declined to accept the new gospel from France, and

inexorable sequence of cause and effect the war
 the deposition of Louis XVI. and the pro-
 ion of the French Republic.
 he morning of that twentieth day of September
 ch the members of the Convention held their
 ssion in the riding school at Paris, the Duke
 nswick, whose advance from the frontier had
 series of uninterrupted successes, came into
 n with the army of Dumouriez and Kellermann.
 ench gunners, posted on the heights of Valmy,
 so handled that Brunswick, failing to silence
 with his own batteries, refused to permit his
 o attempt a frontal attack upon the position.
 sses on either side were slight, since the forces
 never closely engaged, and the credit of the
 belongs, not to the volunteers of the revolu-
 ut to the batteries formed under the *ancien*
 ; yet Goethe, who saw the engagement,
 ly divined in it the beginning of a new epoch.
 tionary France had given a check to the famous
 of Prussia, showing that the new democracy
 ot merely a thing made up of frothy speeches
 ewspaper articles, of mad and extravagant
 which could leave no durable print upon the
 of history. As the last wreath of smoke
 ed in the September air a new France revealed
 to the discerning eye of the German poet, a
 neither self-enveloped in a cloud of amiable
 ations nor so hopelessly divided by the fury
 tion as to present a passive resistance to her
 out hard, warlike, patriotic. In France the
 of the victory was decisive. In the first thrill
 amphant excitement the Republic was pro-
 d, and, to those who cherished the Republican

tradition during the reaction which followed the
downfall of the Empire, the Republic was indelibly
associated with victorious patriotism, with the defence
of the nation's frontiers, and the humiliation of foreign
kings.

" the fair
And fierce Republic with the feet of fire."

The oratory and journalism of the French Revolution
are greatly influenced by the work of three writers,
of whom two belong to the ancient and one to the
modern world. Cicero died in 43 B.C.; Plutarch
flourished at the end of the first, Rousseau in the
middle of the eighteenth, century. The first was the
oracle of the dying Roman Republic; the second
was a Greek who wrote when the Roman Empire was
in its fresh and splendid youth, and while yet the
memory of Freedom remained alive and fragrant
in the world; the third was the son of a French
watchmaker and was born in the free city of Geneva.
In the Middle Ages the works of Cicero were the
favourite quarry for the grammarian and the school-
master, and it was only by slow degrees that he reconquered his fame as the supreme master of Latin
eloquence. Once established, his ascendancy was as
unchallenged in the sphere of prose style as that of
Aristotle in the sphere of thought. Preachers formed
themselves on Cicero; advocates studied his methods
as part of their professional education; his literary
work was found to contain a whole discipline in
philosophy and politics. Mirabeau denounces the
Court in a speech modelled on the second " Catiline ";
Robespierre replies to Louvet in the manner of the
" Pro Sulla." And hardly less influential in another
way were the " Parallel Lives of Plutarch," a bio-

graphical work which, more than any other single
book, has nourished the passion for the public virtues
among the nations of the West. To imitate ancient
heroism, as it was revealed in grand and simple
outlines by the Greek biographer, became a governing passion. Politicians would adopt ancient names
and be half persuaded that they had recaptured the
grand gesture of antiquity. Brissot was the younger
Brutus, Roland the younger Cato, Mme. Roland
was Marcia, and Vergniaud was Cicero. "Since
the Romans," exclaimed St Just, "the world has been
empty." The fatal pall of monarchy had fallen over
Europe. And it was for the Revolution to continue
the work which had been begun by the expulsion
of the Tarquins and was broken by the usurpation
of Julius Cæsar.⁹

That the authors of antiquity should have exerted
so great an influence in the later half of the eighteenth
century need cause no surprise when we remember
not only that the education of boys then ran almost
exclusively in the old classical groove, but that the
knowledge of the current politics of the world was
the privilege of a small aristocracy of birth and office.
A boy at school, who knew nothing of the civil and
military history of his own country, would be familiar
with Marathon and Cannae, the Gerousia and the
Senate ; and in a secretive despotism there was no
common and obvious means of redressing the balance.
There was neither a free press, nor a formed habit
of political discussion, nor indeed any method, short
of official employment itself, by which the ordinary
citizen could become acquainted with the springs
of government. Men grew old and grey in this strange,
and to us almost inconceivable, ignorance, carrying

about with them through life, as their principal casket of political knowledge, the recollection of the Greek and Roman history which they had learnt at school. The French Revolution burst upon a generation of young people who had received this, and little else, for intellectual food, and the learning of the schoolroom foamed out into the street. The young advocate who threw himself into the maelstrom of politics naturally found his standards and analogies in the only literature of public life with which he was acquainted. A legislator must be a Lycurgus or a Minos, a King a Nero or a Caligula, a patriot a Pericles or a Brutus. The writings of the Ancients were " nearer to nature." To be as they were was to be free, to breathe the air of liberty flowing straight and fresh from the far blue mountains of Hellas.

This pose or vanity of Classicism was associated with a fiery democratic sentiment derived, so far as its origin is to be sought elsewhere than in the stress of outward circumstance, from the political teaching of Rousseau. A style so clear, passionate and musical, has never been placed at the service of a body of doctrine at once so coherent with itself and so congruous with the sentiments and appetites of the age. Rousseau was the prophet of Nature. From the complicated artifice of civilized life, he appealed to the simpler conditions of the natural state, preaching, for instance, that Education must follow the instinctive proclivities of the child, that the God of Nature can be worshipped without the formal and obscuring mechanism of theologies, and that the wholesome State must be founded on the natural rights of the individual. Equality, liberty, the sovereignty of the general will, the three cardinal premises* of a democratic civilization, acquired for the first time in Rousseau's teaching a coercive power over the thought of a whole nation. Consciously or unconsciously everyone in politics used his language and debated his ideas. His thoughts, his catchwords, his sentiment, permeated the atmosphere ; and so far as the creation of the Republic can be referred to any one intellectual influence, it may be traced to the mind of the shiftless, brilliant and corrupt adventurer who had carefully explained that the Republican form of government is only perfectly adapted to a small State.

CHAPTER V

THE REVOLUTIONARY STATE

By the soul
Only the nations shall be great and free.—WORDSWORTH

La France est le pays du monde le plus orthodoxe, car c'est le
pays du monde le moins religieux.—RENAN

THE French Republic was a new phenomenon
in the history of the world. The republics
hitherto known to Europe had either been civic, or
federal, or essentially aristocratic, or a combination
of all three. Milton's ideal republic was an aristocracy, Cromwell's very practical Commonwealth a
mixture of aristocracy and dictatorship. The Swiss
cantons, the Dutch provinces, the ancient Republic of
Venice, were all governed upon aristocratic principles.
But the French Republic was very different from
all these. It was a great unitary democratic State,
founded in a sudden revolution and by a wonderful
manifestation of national energy. Compared with
the long process by which Venice had freed herself
from the Byzantine, and Switzerland from the Austrian
Empire ; compared with the protracted struggle which
had heralded the Dutch Act of Abjuration, and in
sharp contrast with the complete absence of formed
political doctrine which had accompanied all these
movements, the political conversion of France had
all the air of a catastrophe. Everything about it

was new and startling, from its comprehensive and
attractive philosophy to the phraseology of its politics
and the manners of its politicians. As early as
October 1790, Edmund Burke had proclaimed the
fact that the French Revolution, being entirely
unlike any previous revolution in history, being at
once more logical, more self-conscious, more comprehensive, more destructive, and, above all, more
contagious, was a danger to the whole fabric of
European civilization : and what Burke said in
1790 the conservatives of Europe have believed ever
since.

The doctrine of the perfectibility of men, which
was one of the central convictions of the new French
philosophy, was sharply opposed to the teaching
of the Roman Catholic Church. It is impossible
to reconcile the view that man is infinitely perfectible
through human agencies and institutions with the
dogma that man is born in original sin, and that
only through the practices of his religion can he
succeed in wiping away some part of the evil which
is inherent in human nature itself. It is an ancient,
perennial controversy. The dispute is always with
us, though it does not always use the same terminology.
There is the school of heredity and the school of
environment ; there are those men who incline to
the view that education can effect nothing, and those
who would fain believe that it can produce angels
out of ogres. We have learnt now that we cannot
expect too much from human nature ; that happiness
is only to a limited degree dependent upon the political
mechanism, and that, legislate as we may, vice and
crime, illness and want refuse to be legislated out of
existence. The politicians who carried out the

Revolution in France were subject to none of these misgivings. They believed that there was no case of vice or crime or want or misery which could not be attributed to defective institutions ; they believed that bad men were the product of bad laws, and, conversely, that if the laws were good, the men would be good also. They did not regard happiness as dependent on individual temperament ; they viewed it as a compound of social chemistry, which could be manufactured as easily as bread or sugar and distributed in equal amounts to every member of Society ; and, starting from this foundation of sanguine psychology, they regarded it as being within the compass of human achievement to bring, first their own country, and then, through a necessary process of emulation, every other country in Europe into a state of Society so natural and perfect that war, poverty and injustice would be unknown.

Proceeding on this fundamental hypothesis, the Constituent Assembly had created a body politic which was different in almost every important particular from the old monarchy of France. Whatever may have been the virtues of the *ancien régime* —and it was not all composed of baseness and folly— efficiency was not among them. It was impossible for a King of France, however vigorous and well-intentioned, to carry on his trade with competence under the conditions which existed in the *ancien régime*. The action of the central power was thwarted either by the organized body of the Church or by the great legal corporations, or by the provincial estates or by the tenacious opposition of the nobility. An edict issued by the King might be rendered inoperative in Normandy by the refusal of the Parliament of

Rouen to ratify it. A measure, acknowledged to be expedient by all his ministers, might be quite outside the range of practical politics owing to the anticipated opposition of one of the great vested interests of the realm. All these obstacles the Constituent Assembly brushed away. It abolished the legal and industrial corporations, obliterated every trace of the old provincial system of France, its names, its boundaries, its historic assemblies, stripped the nobility of their titles, their exemptions, their privileges, and deprived the Church of its position as a great landed corporation specially exempted from the visits of the tax collector. Under the old monarchy French Society was constituted in privileged groups, which placed impediments in the path of individual liberty and central power. The new philosophy viewed the corporation as an infringement of human liberty and privilege as inconsistent with the equality of man, and so, abolishing all those intermediate groups which had sheltered the individual from despotism though not from the irregular action of caprice, it left nothing standing but the individual on the one hand and the State on the other.

Among the qualities which distinguished the revolutionary State there was one which, as it aroused the greatest consternation among contemporaries, so has continued from that time onward to be an enduring element in the republican movements of the Continent. The French Republic was anti-clerical. In its opposition to the Church it was very different from the republican movements of which the world up till then had taken principal note, from the struggle for Dutch independence, from the Commonwealth of Oliver Cromwell, from the revolt of the American Colonies, in all of which instances a community struggling for its rights and liberties found a cordial and a solace in religion. There is no mystery about the chain of causes which led to this result. Roman Catholicism as a creed is essentially absolute and exclusive. It claims that God has given to the world a single depository of inflexible truth, and, finding this depository in the Catholic Church, argues that no other creed can be tolerated because no other creed can possibly be true. The Protestant and the Jew can hardly be saved, but they can be suppressed or converted, and it is the business of the Christian State to suppress or convert them. Nothing but error and confusion can result from the policy of tolerating the public worship of dissidents. No State tolerates crime ; no State should tolerate that which is more serious than crime, the error which destroys souls and defeats the beneficent purpose of God. From these premises it follows that every member of the Christian State must necessarily be considered as a member of the Catholic Church. He is baptized, married and buried with Catholic rites. His education is conducted under Catholic supervision. No one save a priest possessing the appointed orders of the Church may wed him ; no one may dissolve his marriage. At all the solemn moments of life the Church intervenes with her holy sacraments and her imperious injunctions, emphasizing the original sin and depravity of man, and exhibiting, in contrast to this imperfection and reluctancy of fallen nature, the splendour of a spiritual renewal following upon an easy acquiescence in her rites.

Long before the outbreak of the Revolution this conception of the unity and fixity of truth had lost its hold upon educated minds in France. Scepticism was at work, eating the heart out of the old doctrine and exhibiting it to the contempt and amusement of the world in its motley guises of obscurantism, cruelty and folly. The judicial murder of Calas; the protracted and degrading wrangle between the Jesuits and the Jansenists; the wealth and frivolity of the upper clergy, exhibiting itself in startling contrast against the misery of the village curé, whose life was one long battle with starvation—all these circumstances tended to produce an anti-clerical feeling in the minds of the intellectual laity. The day for despotism in Church and State was over, and the time had come for full and fair investigation. " It is an insult," wrote Voltaire, " to reason and the laws to pronounce the words, ' Civil and Ecclesiastical Government.' The phrase should be ' Civil Government and Ecclesiastical Regulations,' and no regulation should be made save by the civil power." [1] Toleration was in the air, and when once this was granted, even to the smallest and most insignificant sect, the keys of the Catholic fortress had been given away ; for the civil power, which has granted liberty of worship to different professions, stands above the churches and outside them. Now, in 1787, civil rights were granted to the Protestants in France.

Two years later, a tract, by a young lawyer named Camille Desmoulins, was selling, edition after edition, in Paris. *La France Libre* is not a great monument of literature, but it is an admirable example of the fiery kind of stuff which was being swallowed eagerly all over France in the first months of the Revolution.

" Instead of a gay religion, of a religion friendly to enjoyment, to women, to population, and to liberty ;

in place of a religion which makes dances, spectacles
and festivities a part of its ritual, as was the case with
the Greeks and the Romans, we have a sad, austere
religion ; a religion which wishes men to be poor,
poor in goods, poor in mind ; a religion which hates
wealth and the sweetest promptings of nature, which
will have one walk backwards, like the Carmelites,
or live like an owl, as the Anthonys, Pauls and
Hilarions, which promises no recompense save to
poverty and pain, which is only good, in a word, for
the hospitals. Can one tolerate its anti-national
maxim ? Obey tyrants : Subditi estote non tantum
bonis et modestis sed etiam dyscolis. Paganism had
every recommendation except reason ; but reason
is scarcely more content with our theology, and folly
for folly, I prefer Hercules killing the boar of
Erimanthus to Jesus of Nazareth drowning two
thousand swine.''

The Assembly which met at Versailles two years
later, in May 1789, contained a majority which was
hostile to the existing ecclesiastical order. Some
were Jansenists, others were Protestants, many had
derived their theology from Voltaire. It was no
part of their intention to disturb the doctrine or
the ceremonial of the Catholic Church, however slight
may have been the value which they placed upon
orthodox ministrations. Even the most advanced
free thinker knew that France was a Catholic country.
But it was intended that the Church should be reduced
in wealth and influence, that it should be shorn
of its endowments and made powerless to arrest
the progress of a democratic State. Holding the
doctrine that the property of the Church was the
treasure of the nation—a thesis stoutly opposed by

the defenders of the ecclesiastical establishment—the Assembly proceeded to strip it, first of its feudal dues, then of its tithes, and finally of its land.

For a great, endowed, independent corporation it substituted a humble and salaried dependent of the State. In the work of transformation the most sacred scruples and historic associations were rudely violated. The monastic orders were abolished; the monastic vows declared to be invalid, as contravening the principle of human liberty. Since the Church was subservient to the State, it was argued that a French citizen could not safely be permitted to acknowledge any jurisdiction or authority outside the limits of his diocese. A bishop on his appointment might write to Rome to signify his communion with the Catholic faith, but there the connexion must end. The Pope was a foreign priest who had no authority within the French dominions. Bishops and *curés* were to be elected by the people, the bishop by the electors of the department, the *curé* by the Assembly of the district. And the Apostolic Church was invoked to support an arrangement whereby an atheist might choose the successor of Bossuet, and a local council of radical politicians regulate the length of his holidays.

If the principle be conceded that religions are all of equal value in the eye of the civil governor, or that all citizens, whatever may be their religious belief, have an equal claim on his justice and benevolence, it would seem to follow that the State should confine itself to the secular sphere and leave the confessions to regulate their own concerns. The Constituent Assembly did not accept this conclusion. Its zeal for liberty did not run to " a Free Church in a Free State."

It did not recommend, or dream of recommending, a scheme of disestablishment. A disestablished Church must necessarily depend upon the endowments of the faithful, and in a Catholic and orthodox country such endowments would be generous and perennial. It would be a labour of Sisyphus to attempt to weaken a body which could draw from a bottomless reservoir of treasure : and it was the distinct aim of the Constituent Assembly to weaken the Catholic Church. No other organized body in the State was based upon principles so antagonistic to the Revolution, or had so large an interest in defending the established order against them. The Church claimed a monopoly of the truth, protested against the toleration which had been recently given to the Protestants, and sided with the cause of the vested interests. Such a body could not be allowed to enjoy liberty. The interests of the Revolution demanded that it should be the hireling of the State, that instead of being rich it should be poor, that instead of rioting on endowments it should starve on salaries, that its ancient chapters should be abolished, its wealthy monasteries dissolved, and that its ministers should exchange the dignified security of royal or territorial patronage for the votes of a popular constituency. The old religious monopoly was broken down and could never again be mended. The Constitution of 1791 stated that in the eye of the law marriage was simply a civil contract.

The eye of the law was no longer the eye of the Church. The civil and religious elements in marriage were declared, not for the first time to be theoretically distinct, but for the first time to be practically separable. To the Church belonged the sacrament ; to the State a contract which could be made without the intervention of a priest, and could be dissolved in express defiance of the canons. These two institutions, Civil Marriage and Divorce, were incorporated in the law of France in September 1792. They are characteristic of the new democracy, and mark a stage in the growth of the Secular State.[2]

Seldom has a political assembly embarked on a more momentous course than did the Constituent Assembly when it agreed to accept those rules as to payment, discipline, and regulation of the Church which are known as the Civil Constitution of the Clergy. There is always a democratic side to the Roman Catholic Church, and in the first ecstasies of revolutionary excitement the sympathies of the village *curés*, who were drawn for the most part from the peasantry, were influenced rather by the miseries of the class to which they belonged than by the traditions of the profession into which they had been promoted. The *curé* had his own grievances, and those no less bitter and substantial than the grudges of the artizan or the peasant. He worked at starveling wages while the honey went to the drones. Proposals to reduce the great ecclesiastical establishments, to bring down the pride of the bishop or abbot, to restore the tithe to its proper purpose, and even to mulct the general revenues of the Church, provided the surplus were more equitably distributed, would have commanded a large measure of assent among the lower clergy. But the Civil Constitution of the Clergy drove hard through some of the intimate convictions of the Church. No scrupulous Catholic could accept an arrangement devised to sever the connection of the Church with Rome, or assent to the view that a

7

Bishop could be lawfully elected save by the faithful of his diocese. A schism was the inevitable result. The scrupulous minds refused to swear the oath to the Constitution; the timid, the careless, the time-serving, the men who were Frenchmen first and priests afterwards accepted it. The refractory priests became outlaws and suffered all the glories and hardships of persecution. The constitutional priests became officials, not much to be distinguished from the mayors and *procureurs*, and suffering under the stigma which always attaches to those who under a sudden stress abandon a point of honour and the principle of their caste. When the war broke out the gulf between the Revolution and the Church became wider than ever. The priest was the national enemy, the friend of the Kings and the émigrés, and the prime source of the civil convulsions which spread over the west and south of France. The embarrassed Treasury ceased even to pay the salaries of those who had sacrificed so much to accept the Constitution, and the Church was severed from the State, not from any conscious change of principle, but from the force of events, which had rendered it unwilling and unable to subsidize an alien and a suspect power.

The new Republic was distinguished by a third characteristic of equal novelty. It was inherently, and by nature of the principles which it possessed, an organ of propaganda. The Declaration of the Rights of Man, copied from America, was regarded as applicable to man in general, apart from all circumstances of time and place. Condorcet, who expresses in logical and coherent form the floating thought of the early revolutionary idealism, expressly controverts the idea of Montesquieu, that it is th business of a legislator to find out what laws may suit certain latitudes, or to adjust them to the passions, interests, and prejudices of certain classes. His duty is in fact just the opposite. He is not called to adapt laws to situations but to change situations by laws. " Whatever be the constitution of a country, freedom of commerce and industry, a direct land-tax, simple civil laws, humane and just penal laws founded on the nature of man and society and deduced from these principles by reason ought to be the same everywhere." . . . " Political writers therefore should try to discover what these laws should be and how they can be made as simple and perfect as possible." [3] The student of modern comparative legislation will acknowledge the substantial truth which underlies these observations. With the progress of civilization the laws and institution of different countries are becoming more and more alike ; the palpable cruelties of medieval jurisprudence have disappeared from our codes, together with those grave and capricious inequalities in justice and finance which characterized the declining age of feudalism in all the countries of Europe.

There is all the difference in the world between the slow process of peaceful penetration and the effort to propagate ideas by force of arms. If the leading principles of the French Revolution have converted Europe, if religious toleration and social equality and popular government are diffused over a wider surface of the globe, this is not because of, but in spite of, the wars of propaganda. Violence never makes genuine converts. The public law of Europe may have been ridiculous, but then it should have been changed by the agreement of the contracting powers. To close a great and noble river to the commerce of the world, as the Scheldt was closed under an international agreement, was doubtless a deplorable expedient; but if no other means could be found of adjusting acute national jealousies, if it was a necessary condition of peace between England, Austria, and Holland, that Antwerp should remain sterile, then the price may have been worth paying. The young Republic did not stoop to such a posture of circumspection. It claimed to alter the public law of Europe in virtue of principles which were anterior to all treaties. It declared the navigation of the Scheldt to be opened : it professed itself ready to annex any territories the inhabitants of which should freely desire to be conjoined with France. The destiny of nations was no longer to be determined by diplomats, but by the voice of the people, by that unknown, unfathomed general will which now at last, after centuries of silence and deference to a servile convention, was invited to express itself. As for the tyrants who make war upon a people to arrest the progress of liberty and destroy the rights of man, were they not the outlaws of society ? " They should be attacked," said Robespierre, " not as ordinary enemies, but as assassins and rebellious brigands. Kings, aristocrats, tyrants whoever they may be, are slaves in revolt against the sovereign of the land, who is the human race, and against the legislator of the Universe, who is Nature." [4]

" Nature, the legislator of the Universe." But what if Englishmen, Germans, Italians would not accept her law ? In his speech against the War delivered in 1792 Robespierre had himself pointed out that the Belgians were unripe for liberty ; and when France found herself with England, Austria, and Prussia on her hands, there was a school of prudence which preferred the methods of diplomacy to the Quixotic enterprize of the indiscriminate crusade. Narbonne, Talleyrand, Danton wished to limit the warlike liabilities of the country. In pursuance of an immemorial national ambition, they argued that the interest of France lay in the acquisition of Belgium and the Rhine frontier, and not in a philanthropic endeavour to free the suffering peoples of Europe. It was therefore the object of their policy to pacify England and Prussia, and to concentrate their efforts on a war with Austria to recover the national and classical frontier of ancient Gaul. The propagandist strain in French foreign policy was blended with the engrained national ambition of a proud and warlike people, greedy of that very glory which Voltaire despised as a senseless folly, and filled with that very spirit of territorial conquest, which its philosophy had so often condemned as inconsistent with the oracles of reason and of nature.

These two distinct aspirations continued to form part of the French Republican creed until the great disaster of 1870. There was the humanitarian impulse on the one hand; the warlike, the Chauvin impulse on the other. The early propagandist illusions soon blew away, for it became obvious that the walls of the royalist Jerichos would not tumble at the first blast of the Marseillaise. In 1795 France made peace with the monarchy of Prussia, the same year with the King of Spain who had drawn his very ineffectual sword in favour of a family connection; and then, two years later, the coveted prize of centuries was in the clasp of the Republic. The Italian victories of Bonaparte brought Austria to her knees so that she ceded to France the Rhine frontier and the Netherlands. Republicans did not forget that these territories were won under the Republic, held under the Empire, and lost at the Restoration, and all through the age of Metternich and long afterwards when Bismarck was laying the foundation of a United Germany, the Rhine was a symbol and a watchword no less sacred than the Rights of Man.

Such then were the characteristics of the Republic which was founded in September 1792. It was apt for centralization ; it was anticlerical, it was military and propagandist, full at once of new humanitarian ideas and of inherited instincts of territorial acquisition.

The humanitarian principle which in the Christian Buddhistic and Tolstoian systems is accompanied with the ascetic doctrine of Renunciation was, in the philosophy of the French Revolution, associated with an affirmation of the Rights of Man. It was founded not on humility, but on pride, not upon conviction of sin, but on an assertion of dignity. The pure gospel of fraternity has sometimes been the rule of saints and sometimes the profession of sinners but it has never governed political societies ; least of all could it be expected to dominate a country boiling with a sense of social injustice and barbarized by centuries of misgovernment. It is therefore no matter for surprise if the ideal of peace, fraternity and goodwill should have failed to be realised in France, seeing that it has never been realised by any nation in the world's history. The cause for surprise is that the emotion should have been felt, that th idea should have been diffused, and that the principle should have been proclaimed by a great European community. Infinite are the ironies of history; and the ironic contrasts of the French revolution, the professions of peace, the realities of war, the Federations of Man, the Massacres of September, the prelude of liberty, the finale of despotism, have been often described as the bankruptcy of idealism. Yet a treasure-trove is not disgraced because the seeker has missed his way.

Of these humanitarian aspirations we can find no better incarnation than the Girondin philosopher, Condorcet, to whom was entrusted the principal share in the drafting of the first Republican Constitution. Condorcet, like John Stuart Mill, is one of the saints of Radicalism. He was a savant of austere virtue, the friend and disciple of Turgot, a man consumed with a passion for the public welfare and animated by the most sanguine expectations of the future of humanity. Defective on the side of observation, and knowing little of the real workings of human nature, Condorcet paid the penalty of his ignorance. The every day world cannot be governed by the geometrician's compass ; and those who would draft constitutions for states must know something of the vulgar forces out of which states are composed. Condorcet, like John Locke, framed plans which were incapable of execution, indulged in many insubstantial speculations, and drew a horoscope of a golden future which no man has yet seen. But he possessed the quality which belongs to the clear, powerful, and independent intelligence of divining some of the great lines of human progress. His plan of free, secular, gratuitous education was only realized in France under the Third Republic through the efforts of Jules Ferry and has still to be realized in England. He was the first eminent Frenchman to champion the rights of women and to propose a scheme of co-education ; and in his thorough grasp of the fact that a sound democratic polity must necessarily depend upon a good system of national education he exhibited a truth which did not become the common property of the country till it was preached from a hundred platforms by the organ voice of Gambetta.

Yet the Constitution which Condorcet devised for the French Republic contains every defect which an unflinching pursuit of the principle of popular sovereignty is calculated to produce. The supreme executive council of the state was to consist of seven ministers elected by the primary assemblies and changing its president every fortnight. A president chosen on the American plan would not only be too powerful ; he would be demoralizing. He would excite respect and deference for his person ; feeble imaginations would forget the office in the man ; and blind instincts of personal devotion would supersede the exclusive use of enlightened reason. " A man, the living image of the law " : such words were void of sense and devised on the assumption that man is to be governed not by reason but by seductive fiction. So Condorcet proposed that the President of the French Republic should hold office for a fortnight. As for the legislature it was to be chosen for one year by universal suffrage. A legislature, however, even in the course of a year, may cease to represent the general will. To meet the difficulty two expedients had been discussed. The constituents might recall their deputies and choose others in their place so that every undulation of popular feeling might be transmitted to the Parliament, or else the electorate might demand that certain measures should be submitted to its own immediate decision. It was the latter plan which Condorcet favoured. He proposed the Referendum, and this in a form so extreme that, if adopted, it must have produced a complete legislative deadlock. He actually recommended that, upon the requisition of two departments demanding an amendment or a law or a measure of general policy, the legislature should be forced to summon all the primary assemblies of the Republic, and that, if the majority of these assemblies agreed to the proposition, a general election should be held.[5]

Such was the last word of practical wisdom bequeathed by the Girondin philosopher. A few months later, after a bitter struggle, his party was proscribed by the Jacobins, and he died by his own hand to escape the guillotine. His constitutional scheme was taken up by a Jacobin committee and rapidly revised by the facile pen of Hérault de Séchelles. Universal suffrage was retained but the referendum made more difficult. The executive council was enlarged to twenty-four and was still chosen by a system of popular election, the Legislature naming the members from lists of candidates drawn up by the electoral assemblies of the departments. The assembly was still to consist of a single chamber ; but whereas Condorcet had spread out a programme of democratic propaganda abroad, the final draft proclaimed the principle of non-intervention. Such provisions were calculated to please the democracy ;

and their electoral value was enhanced by an express recognition of the " sacred right of insurrection," and of the duty of the State to find work or sustenance for all its members.

Submitted to a *plébiscite*, the Constitution of 1793 was accepted by 1,801,918 votes ; but as war was raging on the frontiers, as the great city of Lyons was in insurrection, as the Vendée was in flame, and the whole fabric of the State was in imminent peril of dissolution, there was no intention of carrying its provisions into effect. On October 10 a decree was issued to the effect that " the provisional government of France is revolutionary until the conclusion of peace." The Constitution of 1793 was never put into force. It remained an ideal and a war cry with the working classes ; and of all the constitutions which have been devised on the popular model, none has sought to give so literal an expression to the view that government should be directly controlled by every momentary determination of the General Will.

The real French Republic which stamped itself upon history and upon the imagination of men was a very different thing from this airy scheme of popular anarchy. Formed under the stress of foreign war and civil discord, and relying upon the support of a small minority of resolute men, it created armies, cleared the frontiers, and saved the unity of France ; but this achievement, one of the most memorable in history, was accompanied by an organized system of atrocities, few, if we compare them with the crimes of the Inquisition, but enough to make the Committee of Public Safety a synonym for all that is despotic and sinister in the use or abuse of public power. In outline the scheme of this revolutionary Government was a small executive committee of the Convention, exercising plenary administrative powers over the armies and in the provinces through its delegates or representatives *en mission*. The Committee of Public Safety, as it was called, was the brain centre of France ; from it proceeded the orders which provisioned the armies, directed their movements, raised the supplies and carried on the administration of the country. It was assisted in its task by a subordinate police committee, known as the Committee of General Security, and specially devised to counteract reactionary movements in the capital. The Jacobins, who in virtue of their greater audacity had overawed the moderate and timid members of the Convention, had hold of the helm and did not intend to lose it. Violent themselves, they had reason to fear the violence of others. A mania of murderous suspicion seized upon the capital of the most civilized country in Europe, and was repeated in many a country town and village, with hideous and original variations, *noyades* at Nantes and *mitraillades* at Lyons, matching if not exceeding the atrocities in Paris.[6]

In each one of the forty-eight sections of the capital a revolutionary committee of Jacobin politicians, hired at the rate of forty *sous* a day, carried on a trade of blackmail and delation. The helpless victims of their suspicions or animosities were brought before a revolutionary tribunal, condemned without a shadow of honest investigation, and sent to the guillotine. The city government, fallen into the hands of that insurrectionary Commune which had established itself on August 10, 1792, was one of the principal centres of profligate terrorism, though for a time,

under the influence of Chaumette, murder and the
public profession of atheism were mingled with
sentimental schemes for the relief of the poor. To
complete the picture, we must imagine a starving
population, a tyrannical interference with the prices
not only of bread but of many of the necessaries of
life, trade and commerce prostrate, credit annihilated,
the country flooded with depreciated paper, a band
of six thousand ruffians, styled "the revolutionary
army," patrolling the streets of Paris, and, in their
appointed and lucrative task of executing revolutionary
laws, respecting no consideration of common decency
or justice. In this grim and terrible period, dating
from August 10, 1792, though not reaching its highest
point of severity until May 1794, and extending to
the fall of Robespierre in the following July, freedom
was an empty word. The last honest and independent paper—the *Mercure de France* of Mallet du
Pan—came to an end with the fall of the monarchy;
the *Vieux Cordelier*, the first newspaper which ventured
to appeal for clemency and the only piece of real
literature in all the Revolution, brought its editor
to the block. The city which had fêted Voltaire
was condemned to tolerate the foul and vulgar
blasphemies of the *Père Duchesne* and to look on while
two thousand six hundred and twenty-five judicial
murders were perpetrated by the Revolutionary
tribunal. "Terror," as Barère phrased it, "was the
order of the day," but not the wish of the majority.
The young and the brave were with the armies; the
members of the administration absorbed in their
tremendous task; and the general mass of moderate
men too numbed and broken by the sudden and
anomalous calamity to concert resistance to this

campaign of purposeless and irrelevant crime. To the quiet bourgeois what did it matter if the Jacobin proscribed the Girondin or the Girondin the Jacobin? Jacobins, Hébertists, Dantonists, Girondins were all revolutionaries. They adopted the September massacres; they constructed the Revolutionary tribunal; they declared war; they sanctioned the Commune; they sent Louis XVI. to the block. Let the wolves rend one another!

The passive majority which washed its hands of politics did not care to follow the swift and thrilling vicissitudes of the deadly struggle in the Convention. It was neither moved by the destruction of the Girondins, nor enlisted in the triangular contest between Robespierre, Hébert, and Danton. And so it permitted the fair name of the Republic to be stained by the atrocities of a faction which in the estimate of a careful observer never exceeded six thousand men.[7]

In this provisional and haphazard government every principle of the early revolution seemed to be violated. The Constitution of 1791 had provided a plan of extreme decentralization; but under the terror the wheel had gone round full circle and all executive authority was gathered into the hands of the Committee of Public Safety. The division of powers had been one of the most cherished doctrines of the early revolution. The Committee of Public Safety was a committee of the Convention. The first Assembly had introduced the jury into France and attempted to accredit it; the men of 1793 made the jury a farce and so far compromised its reputation that it ran a risk of disappearing under the Consulate. The first Assembly believed in freedom of commerce. The government of the Terror enacted the law of the maximum. In every department of government a despotic extension of State interference had superseded the legislative recognition of individual right.

In the reaction which followed upon the death of Robespierre the continuance of the French Republic was promoted by a crime. Partly through neglect and partly through ill-treatment, the Dauphin of France died in the Temple prison. The child was sickly, and it may well be that he would never have crossed the threshold of manhood ; but he was the hope of the Bourbon cause, and that could be said of him which could be said of no living male of his house, that he was clear of the contagion of Coblentz, and that he had had no part or lot in the camps or the counsels of the enemy. His uncle the Count of Provence, who now assumed the title of Louis XVIII., was not so situated. He had committed the crime of emigration in June 1791, and gave no sign that he was prepared to accept those parts of the new *régime* which were irrevocably fixed in the acceptation of France. It is open to argument that concessions would not have helped him, that they would only have estranged his friends without conciliating his enemies, and that in view of the fate of Philippe Égalité, the chief of the royalist House was wise to avoid the faintest suspicion of apostacy. That had not been the view of the Béarnais who held that Paris was worth a mass ; but Louis XVIII. was not Henry IV. And yet it seems that the chances of a royalist restoration were never so bright as in the months which succeeded the fall of the Jacobin tyrant, when in the sudden revulsion against the horrors of the last two years the country would gladly

have seen a constitutional monarchy provided that
it were guaranteed against the restoration of the
ancien régime. Louis XVIII. failed to grasp the
opportunity. He would not promise an amnesty.
He would never treat with a regicide republic ; he
would have nothing short of unconditional surrender,
believing that the chief of the *émigrés* could recover
the allegiance of France by the old forlorn expedients
of armed incursions and foreign gold, and perhaps
in his indolent vein of Pyrrhonism not very seriously
wishing to risk a plunge into the central maelstrom.
However this may be, the cause of the monarchy
was conducted as badly as possible, and a fruitless
effort to rekindle the flames of the Vendée, coupled
with a mad descent on Quiberon, completed the
discomfiture of the royalist hopes, and established
the French Republic in a fresh term of existence.

What particular shape that Republic should assume
was by far the most important question which confronted France, when the murderous cloud of the
terror had been rolled away. A fierce revolt known as
the Insurrection of Prairial (May 20, 1795), and having
for its war-cry " Bread and the Constitution," only
deepened the conviction which was now the common
property of all sensible men that the scheme of 1793
was but an alias for anarchy. But if this scheme
were abandoned, and if monarchy were impossible,
how should the Republic be organized ? It is the
nemesis of civil war that it does not admit of an
immediate sequel in the free working of a democratic
constitution. In France, where passions had run
so high and careers had been so deeply engaged,
there was no swift and easy road to liberty. The
Convention which had voted the death of the King

could not afford to risk elections which very possibly might result in a royalist majority. Between the abstract principle of electoral liberty and the preservation of their own very concrete skins the members of this Assembly had no difficulty in making a choice. The earlier schemes of the Revolution had been the fruit of youth and idealism ; the Constitution of 1795 was the product of a tragic experience. " We have lived," said Boissy d'Anglas as he introduced the measure, " six centuries in six years. Let not this costly experience be lost on you. It is time to profit by the crimes of the monarchy, the errors of the Constituent Assembly, the vacillations and eccentricities of the Legislative Assembly, the misdeeds of the decemviral tyranny, the calamities of anarchy and the misfortunes of civil war."

The misfortune most keenly remembered and bitterly bewailed had been the tyranny of Robespierre. That such a calamity might never recur the executive power was vested in a Directory of five, who were to hold office for a term of five years and were expressly debarred from the control of the Treasury, the personal command of an army or a seat in the Legislature. American experience was before the minds of the Constitutional Committee who knew that the executive head of the United States is chosen by the votes of the people. But, though the American plan was discussed, two considerations were fatal to its adoption. An Executive Committee depending on the direct vote of the people might easily defy the Legislature, and would not improbably be a royalist body. It was determined then that the Directory should be chosen not by the primary assemblies but by the Legislature of France. This body, unlike all the legislatures which had preceded it, was to consist of two Councils, renewable by a third every year and protected by a series of excellent provisions from the intimidation and disturbance of the mob. A few months before, an orator proposing a bicameral constitution would have expiated his temerity on the scaffold. Now the two Councils passed through the Convention almost unopposed. A single Chamber had failed to express the true will or the sober sense of the people. It had been the slave of the Commune, of the Mountain, of Robespierre, and had made itself the accomplice of a thousand acts of temerity, cowardice, and crime. Even the critics admitted that there could be no stable constitution with a single legislative chamber. Against the mob rule which had been the special curse of recent times the Constitution of the year III. took rigorous precautions. Universal suffrage was abandoned for a scheme which was both limited and indirect ; the large towns were broken into manageable districts ; the clubs and armed assemblies and tumultuous petitions peremptorily forbidden. It was the general design that power should be transferred from the democracy and lodged in the hands of the enlightened middle class. So great was the force of the reaction that only three members of the Convention rose to defend universal suffrage.

This Constitution was frequently and persistently violated. Whatever potency of virtue may have been implicit in its provisions, that potency was never allowed to develop. The experiment of the bourgeois Republic was shorter and far less honourable than the subsequent essay of the bourgeois monarchy. A regicide Directory, backed by a regicide party in the Legislature, could not permit the reactionary

8

feeling in the country to flow freely and at its appointed intervals into the central cistern of government. Engaged throughout the whole of this period in foreign war, unwilling to make an honourable peace, but possessing in its powerful armies a defence against the royalist reaction, the Directory did not scruple to preserve the ascendency of its principles by a military *coup d'état*, and afterwards by official candidatures and systematic interference with elections.

The life of the Directory is divided into two halves by the *coup d'état* of 18 Fructidor (September 4, 1797). In the earlier period there was a struggle carried on within the walls of the Chambers and under the forms of the Constitution between the party which desired to relax and the party which was resolved to maintain the penal laws against the priests and the *émigrés*. Throughout the country the tide was running in favour of clemency, moderation, and peace, and the partial elections of 1797 gave to the Constitutionalists a working majority in both Chambers. Carnot, the most eminent of the Directors, though as a former member of the Committee of Public Safety he had been associated with the horrors of the Terror, favoured the cause of clemency, and the new Director Barthélemy, who had the honour of negotiating the peace with Prussia, was of the same opinion. The laws against the priests were relaxed ; the relations of *émigrés* were released from police supervision and restored to civil rights. Then the Revolutionary party struck their blow. Representing, what has never been established and is indeed contradicted by all the evidence, that their opponents were working for the restoration of the monarchy, the Jacobin directors appealed to Bonaparte to save the Republic.

The young general of the army of Italy found it convenient to believe the charge and sent Augereau to Paris to do the business. The Constitutionalists of the Chambers were seized, sent across France in open iron cages, and despatched with every circumstance of rigour and barbarity to expiate their virtues in the torrid and fever-stricken village of Sinamary. Carnot, the organizer of victory, fled to Switzerland; Barthélemy was deported to Cayenne; the elections in forty-nine departments were summarily quashed. In every district a military tribunal was established to identify and to shoot *émigrés*.

Then ensued a period unredeemed by any gleam of grandeur, and marked by every species of corruption and violence. The laws against the *émigrés* and the priests were sharpened and enforced with increasing rigour, and for the first time since the age of Diocletian the whole mechanism of a powerful government was employed to destroy Christianity.

In the fury of party feeling the instinct of good sense and public policy disappeared. The Fructidorians, playing for their own hand and aware that foreign war supported the armies of the Republic, rejected a fair occasion for a general and an honourable peace. After the victories of Bonaparte had driven Austria to conclude the peace of Campo-Formio and to recognize the acquisition by France of Belgium, of Ancona, and the Ionian Islands, England sent Lord Malmesbury to treat at Lille. The British Government was prepared to make astonishing concessions, to recognize the European conquests of France, and to restore the captured French colonies, save only the Cape of Good Hope taken from the Dutch, and Surinam taken from the Spaniards. The Directory broke off negotiations upon the point of the Cape. It declined to make a peace which would have left France the most powerful State in Europe, mistress of Belgium, and exercising through the medium of the Cisalpine Republic a predominant influence in Northern Italy. And so the duel between the Republic and Europe endured, and the Directory repudiated two-thirds of its debt, furnishing to Europe the first example of republican bankruptcy.

In many of the careers which were fashioned in the great tempest of the French Revolution there is a high and stern note of civic passion, an austere moral beauty sometimes a little injured to our Teuton taste by a certain stiff classic affectation verging on the ridiculous. Victor Hugo has painted the type in that grand picture of the dying Conventionnel which he has set into the framework of " Les Misérables " ; and there is an image, not out of fiction but out of history, from the life of ·Jean Bon St André, who controlled the Naval Department during the Terror, which may hang as a pendant to that picture. But of all this high and strenuous purpose there is little trace during the last two years of the French Republic. The large issues had disappeared from the vision of the party which had secured its tenure of power by a crime. The Fructidorians cared only for themselves, for their own pockets and their own lives. They were a faction, and they fought for the ascendancy of a faction, believing, or affecting to believe, that the welfare of France was bound up with their interest. Few Governments have been less pure, less equitable, less honest. The spirit of plunder permeated the whole administration. Diplomatists extorted bribes from foreign powers ; the generals squeezed money and plate and pictures from conquered territories ; and in his sumptuous rooms in the Luxembourg, Barras, the most profligate of the Directors, gave an example which was faithfully copied through all the descending circles of the official hierarchy.

In the history of revolutions certain broad phenomena constantly present themselves. They rise out of real and admitted grievances, and receive support from the generous emotions and sometimes from the most enlightened speculation of the age ; they begin in moderation, they steadily increase in violence, they end in the ostracism of their opponents. Then an inevitable revulsion sets in. Men begin to ask themselves why they have been carried so far, and whether the policy into which they have been driven really expresses their original meaning. In proportion as their initial ideal was high, their disappointment is great at the harsh and ugly close of so many pleasant sentiments and hopes. But meanwhile the Revolution has created a mass of vested interests, swelling in proportion to its duration and dangerous to disturb ; and in this fact lies a problem of infinite difficulty. Hateful as is the present, the past was still more odious : the interests menaced by reaction coalesce together to defend their new acquisitions, and a dangerous period of uncertainty and oscillation ensues, marked often by a recrudescence of severity as one or other party obtains the mastery, and continuing until out of weariness or statesmanship some working compromise can be found.

So it was with the French Revolution. It began in the idealism of 1789, rose to the Terror of 1793, and sank to the compromise of 1799, which only the authority of a despot could procure and enforce.

It was while the movement was on the declining curve that France was governed by the Directory, a body of men whose collective epitaph may thus be written : " They preserved the land-settlement of the Revolution and introduced conscription into Europe."

De Maistre, the philosopher of the Catholic reaction, argued that States were never the product of an articulate process of deliberation, but that, springing from some hidden root, they grew in virtue of a mysterious organizing principle of which no man could render an account. A country was made, not out of calculation but out of patriotism, and lived, not by the lamp of reasoned self-interest, but by the inner glow of a national tradition. Men did not obey written constitutions or philosophies ; they obeyed mysteries. Active obedience could only be due to the deep inarticulate call of instinct. The Jacobins put out declarations of the Rights of Man, and established a system of popular government which was, as popular government always must be, nothing but organized ostracism. In so doing they were, according to De Maistre, ignoring the character of the world in which they lived. They believed that Justice could be realized on earth, whereas God is unjust in time though just in eternity ; they thought that the world was rational, whereas it is a system of profound, solid, and vigorous absurdities ; they believed in the existence of Humanity, whereas we can know nothing but individual men. None the less, having the sentiment of the indivisibility of their country, the Jacobins were the blind instruments of God. They saw that France should be a nation and they made her a nation. The long obscure process of history, begun in the dim Middle Ages, sanctified

by St Louis and Joan of Arc, glorified by Philip
Augustus and Richelieu, aided by the force of Louis
VI., the patience of Charles VII., the circumspect
prudence of Louis XI., the genial power of Henry IV.,
was brought to a completion by a generation of
republicans who, while appearing to flout all the
traditions of their country, were unconsciously serving
the oldest and deepest instincts of the French race.

CHAPTER VI

THE SOWER AND THE SEED

I do not believe that monarchy and aristocracy will continue seven years longer in any of the enlightened countries of Europe. —PAINE, Feb. 9, 1792

THE voice of Immanuel Kant sounding across the sandy plains of Prussia proclaimed in the French Revolution the advent of everlasting peace and a federation of European republics. In Germany, where romantic enthusiasm ranged at large with no formed habit of exact political calculation to check it, such expectations were freely entertained. The poets, the philosophers, the critics welcomed in the Revolution the emancipation of the human race from the enthralment of paralysing social and political conventions. But the literary class did not constitute Germany. In that archaic and anomalous polity there were depths of unrealized Teutonic sentiment, of affinities and repugnances, of loyalty to the old dynasties and hierarchies, for which no place was found in the cosmopolitan philosophy of the lettered middle class. The long pedigrees of the Saxon Wettins, the Bavarian Wittelsbachs, the Prussian Hohenzollerns, the Hanoverian Guelphs, were regarded as national monuments, and prized like the Niebelungen Lied or the Luther Thürm. Weave their dreams as beautifully as they might,

the professors of republican and cosmopolitan democracy were impotent to disturb the settled and rooted
tradition of the princely dynasties.[1]

But, whatever may have been the prospect of stable
republican developments in Europe, it was fatally
injured by the course of affairs in France.   The
execution of the French King, the outbreak of the
War, the Terror, the Vendée, the excesses of the
revolutionary armies on the Rhine, in Switzerland,
and in Italy, and finally, after ten years of tempestuous
agitation, the enthusiastic acceptance of a despotism
by the very country which had claimed to be the
prophetess of human liberty—all these circumstances
tended to throw Europe back into reaction.

In the passions evoked by the great European
struggle, the character of the polity which was set up
in France by the genius of Bonaparte was imperfectly
understood.   The enemy saw the obvious things, and
was blind to the things which were less acceptable to
a biassed intelligence.   He saw the soldier of fortune,
the *coup d'état*, the despotism, the contrast between
the promise and performance of democracy, the
shameful eclipse of the Republican idea, heralded
with ten thousand trumpets, before it had established
itself in the political traditions of Europe.   These
things were obvious and important.   The Republic
in France disappeared on that November night in
1799 when the deputies of the last revolutionary
Assembly were chased through the windows of the
Château of St Cloud, and save for the legend on the
coins which persisted till 22nd October 1808, there was
little in the new government to recall its existence.
The Republic then vanished, and the Consulate was
ratified by an overwhelming majority of the French

people.   But if the new polity was not a real Republic,
still less was it the *ancien régime.*   Bonaparte was
a man not of the old but of the new world.   In all
its fundamental aspects he represented the course of
the French Revolution.   He secured the new land-
settlement, and provided a shelter for the careers
which had been forged in the service of the republic.
He stood for government founded on the *plébiscite*,
for social equality, for the *carrière ouverte aux talents*,
which he held to be the core and heart of democracy.
Against the tradition of the Customs and the Ordinances, he maintained public trial, the jury, the
juges de paix, and, in a slightly modified form, that
equal law of division which was the corner-stone of
the revolutionary civil law.   Against the Pope, the
Roman Church, and the Canons he maintained the
Civil Marriage and Divorce.

True that he made peace with the Pope, recalled
the Roman Church into its Erastian connexion with
the State, and opened wide the gates of France to
the exiled servants of the ancient monarchy.   For
the religious policy of the Concordat he did not obtain
the forgiveness of the intellectuals of his own day nor
of the republicans of succeeding generations.   But
his object was broader than the views of any school
or faction—to unite the old France and the new, to
control all the spiritual and intellectual impulses of
his people, and to incorporate the vigorous traditions
of the Revolution in a State which should combine
the advantages of democracy with a discipline such as
no subject or citizen of France had ever known.

In the conquests of the Revolution, the Consulate,
and the Empire, the political gospel of the new French

nation was spread abroad through Europe, creating here feelings of violent revulsion, and here educating unsuspected and fruitful affinities. The quarter in which this influence proved to be most permanent was the peninsula of Italy.

Of all the countries in Europe Italy alone possessed ancient republican traditions ; but these had become so empty of democratic content, and ever since the fifteenth century had been so much overshadowed by the principalities and monarchies of the peninsula, that, as Napoleon observed to the Directory, there was less material for the constitution of republics in Italy than there was in France. From the numerous records of foreign tourists, from the delightful Des Brosses to the sage Goethe, as also from the memoirs of Goldoni and the autobiography of Alfieri, we can gather an impression of what Italian life and society must have been like in the period which elapses between the Treaty of Utrecht and the first contact of Italy with the French Revolution. The heavy hand of the Spaniard had been removed from Lombardy, but not before the Spanish dominion, which dated from 1540, and was accompanied by the tremendous instrument of the Inquisition, had crushed all the creative energies of the country. Patriotism was long dead, and the hopes which Machiavelli had derived from the transient success of Cesare Borgia were no longer plausible enough to animate any portion of public life. The Austrians were in Lombardy ; in Naples and Sicily the Hapsburgs were removed in 1737, only to be superseded by Spanish Bourbons, by the rotten branch of the most rotten trunk in the forest of European monarchies. Piedmont alone, with its rude subalpine population, possessed a certain sap and vigour. Here at least there was a national monarchy and a national nobility, though little else that can weigh in the scales of civilization : no art, or music, or science, or literature, or in fact any contribution to the splendid sum of Italian culture ; a land of priestcraft and superstition, using French for the language of polite society, and a patois more akin to Provençal than Italian in the staple converse of the people ; a tame country, dull as rectangular Turin itself, but possessing the virtue that belongs to a simple, robust, and loyal community. Of the ancient republics, two alone, Venice and Genoa, retained the external signs of former greatness ; but their empire was broken, their commerce had dwindled, and the failure of their outward energies was associated with a loss of political animation. These States, preserving the republican forms, but in reality controlled by civic aristocracies, had stiffened into a pose of stationary and dignified content. Their citizens were happy, they loved festivals and processions, the gossip and pretty trivialities of life, the pleasant chat in the piazza, the voices of choristers in the church, the flirtations, the verse-making, the *villeggiatura*. Their days were like a comedy of Goldoni, for they asked nothing better of life than life was able to give them. Heroic dreams did not trouble this pleasant tranquillity. Labour and the risks of political enterprise they were content to leave to the barbarians. In Tuscany alone there was a more strenuous tradition and a standard of government as high as any in Europe ; but Tuscany was no republic but a grand duchy under the House of Hapsburg-Lorraine.

The Italians themselves speak of their national

movement of the nineteenth century as a " Risorgimento," a resurrection, and no phrase could be more appropriate. It was a resurrection of a people once the centre of power and illumination in Europe, but long since fallen into an elegant and sterile decrepitude. And this process of recovery dates from the shock of the French Revolution. It would not, of course, be true to say that the land of Vico, the parent of political philosophy, had been altogether barren of sound and fruitful speculation during the eighteenth century. The names of Beccaria and Filanghieri may remind us that this was not so. As there were reformers before the Reformation, so there were precursors before the Revolution, whose influence was felt in the practical administration of the more progressive Italian States. But the summoning of the States-General to Versailles on May 5, 1789, is the real birthday of the Italian Risorgimento. The French Revolution roused Italy from her torpor, broke down the barriers which had obstructed the tides of national life, dislodged the Austrians from Milan, the Bourbons from Naples, and for the first time since the age of Justinian brought the whole peninsula under what was in fact, if not in name, a single political system.

The republican ideal, which was one of the forces working in the Risorgimento—differentiating by its continuous presence and importance the Italian from the German national movement—was not so much the product of the old classical and medieval memories, though these must be given a certain weight, as of the new democracy of France. Girondin newspapers were more important than the histories of Rienzo; the doctrine of popular sovereignty than the tradition of chartered rights; the sowing of new republics on

the French model than the chronicled victories of the
medieval communes of Lombardy.   The ancient
classical, aristocratic tradition had its votaries, men
who hated Kings and scorned the people, like Alfieri,
the greatest writer of tragedies in the Italian language,
and one of the first prophets of a larger Italian
patriotism.   But the age was full of stir and novelty
and, being swept into the whirlpool of the French
wars, Italy received from the French those impulses
towards democratic and republican ideas which, com-
bining with aspirations of a different origin, and
quality, finally secured her national union.

The new era was inaugurated by one of the most
thrilling exploits in all military history—the first
Italian campaign of Bonaparte.   Here was an Italian
epic, not mythical like the " Æneid," but a sequence of
substantial exploits unrolling themselves in a series of
swift and surprising revelations.   And the hero of
the epic was an Italian.   He came from France leading an army the like of which had never been seen
before, for it had a creed, and a mission to propagate
democracy.   The general was an adventurer.   No one
had explored his pedigree ; few had heard of him ; he
ruled an army of wild, rugged, and joyous comrades
involving everything that was sacred and established
in the spray of their light and impetuous contumely.
Yet in the course of a campaign he beat the Sardinian
and Austrians to a standstill, and was master of such
parts of Italy as it was germane to his purpose to
control.   An unknown Italian from Corsica had
proved himself more than a match for the Holy
Roman Emperor.   He had beaten him again and
again, pursued him into the Styrian Alps, and forced
him to make an ignominious treaty of peace.   By one

of the terms of this instrument the Emperor acknowledged a new political entity, the Cisalpine Republic,
composed partly of that which had been Austrian
Lombardy, partly of the Papal Legations, and partly
of the western provinces of Venetia and the Swiss
territory of the Valtelline. It was the first democratic republic upon a large scale which Italy had
known.

The constitution of the Cisalpine Republic was
modelled upon that of the French Directory, yet
since.it was no part of Bonaparte's design that the
new commonwealth should be independent of French
influence, he named its first directors, representatives,
and officials. The young general was no idealist,
and in the cynical destruction of the Venetian Republic had demonstrated to the world how little he
cared for political liberties. But finding an enthusiastic welcome among the radical idealists of the larger
towns, and carrying the commission of a democratic
republic, he chose to represent himself as the herald
of the republican idea and the creator of republican
States. No one, however, was more conscious of the
fact that these polities were unsupported by the
general mass of the people, or that the Italians were
as yet unfit for self-government. . You cannot change
the pyschology of a people by a *coup d'état*, or by
some quick process of political chemistry convert
an idle nobleman into a serious worker, or a
medical student into a full-blown statesman. The
letters of Napoleon to the Directors of Paris are
powdered with cynical gibes at the degenerate fibre
of the Lombards and Venetians. He wished his
government to understand that stable polities are not
based upon the transient excitement of the Piazza,

and that a tree of liberty or a red cap have no necessary relation to the art or science of government.[2]

When a political settlement has become hardened by prescription, even the most transient disturbance of it is a fact of moment. It dislocates the traditional mode of thinking and breaks the hard crust of usage. Even if the old order be restored, the restoration is never quite exact. It cannot reproduce a state of feeling of which one of the essential conditions was the bare fact of unbroken continuity. The old furniture may be replaced, but it is viewed not as a fixture but, as a movable ; and questions arise as to whether it looks well in its former position.

So it was with the short-lived Italian republics founded under the Directory. Ephemeral as they were, and the creatures of military coercion and financial greed, they broke an old tradition and started a new one. Rome, Naples, Milan, Genoa were capitals of republics, organized on French designs, and depending, so far as local support was concerned, upon the sympathies of the lettered and professional middle class, for whom little space had previously been found in the public life of the country. It is true that, in 1798, Austrian and Russian victories swept the French out of Italy, and that the Cisalpine, Roman, and Parthenopean Republics were brushed away like cobwebs ; but it was not in vain that the tricolour had waved over Milan, Rome, and Naples, and the brief Roman Republic formed a precedent for that larger design which fifty years later, thanks to the valour of Garibaldi, was printed so deeply on the Italian heart.

One incident there was in the year 1799 which made an indelible impression upon Southern Italy and may be regarded as the source of a long history of bitterness in the Neapolitan Kingdom, resulting in successive waves of secret republican and patriotic conspiracy. Bonaparte was in Egypt, his fleet had been destroyed at the Battle of the Nile, and the Neapolitan Court saw an opportunity of taking a handsome revenge upon the French. The arrival of Nelson with the victorious English fleet threw the Neapolitan royalists into transports of delight and assurance. Encouraged by the presence of an English admiral and an Austrian general, and believing that a rapid blow struck at the French positions in Central Italy would bring Austria into the coalition and save the cause of monarchy in Europe, the government of Ferdinand IV and Marie Caroline mobilized the army of the kingdom and dispatched it into the Roman State. The inefficiency of a Neapolitan army has often been proved, and it was proved then. General Championnet, drawing in his scattered troops, allowed General Mack and his Neapolitans to occupy Rome and then crushed them in detail as they marched northwards. Their defeats were for the moment decisive. The regular Neapolitan troops fled before the French bayonets, surrendering position after position, and the King and Queen in a paroxysm of fear basely abandoned Naples to its fate and escaped to Sicily on an English man-of-war.

But the capitulation of the regular troops did not imply the surrender of the capital. The Neapolitan Government was founded on a union of the Crown, the Church, and the lower classes, and as the French army advanced the priests and friars who adhered to the falling government roused the superstitious loyalty of the rabble, reminding them of the Queen's words, "The people alone remain faithful, for all the educated classes of the Kingdom are Jacobins." Nowhere indeed in Italy were the social contrasts more clearly marked than in Naples. The aristocracy was more cultivated and ambitious, the professional classes more enlightened than in any other Italian city ; but this island of civility was set in the midst of a dark ocean of barbarism. The lazzaroni of Naples rose at the call of the priests, equally prepared to sack the houses of the wealthy Neapolitan liberals and to resist the attacks of the imperious Frenchman. For three days they fought desperately for a King who talked their dialect, relished their dishes, and had himself kept a cook-shop in a poor district of the town. At length, on January 23, 1799, a combination of disciplined valour and dexterous diplomacy gave Championnet control of the city. More than three thousand Neapolitans had fallen in the fighting ; but though Naples was still red with carnage it welcomed the French general with delirious joy. When Championnet took his seat at the opera all the spectators rose from their seats, thousands of white handkerchiefs fluttered in the air, and vivas and bravos sounded for a space of a quarter of an hour. On January 26 the Parthenopean Republic was proclaimed, and on the following day St Januarius condescended to perform the miracle which consecrated the new order of things in the eyes of a superstitious Mediterranean people. "We adore St Januarius," wrote General Bonnamy, the French Chief of the Staff, to the Minister of War ; "we live as well as possible with the lazzaroni ; we accomplish miracles with the aid of the respectable cardinal. . . . The Commander-in-Chief has prayed like the devil. He has believed

hat was necessary, and the blood of St Januarius
flowed.   At the same moment Vesuvius has
hed forth flames, and a *Te Deum* has been sung to
ak Heaven for the entry of the French into Naples."
h the mobility of the South, the population which
savagely resisted the French attacks a few days
re, now took the tricolour cockade, and paraded
streets with cries in honour of liberty, St Januarius,
Championnet.   The French Commander-in-Chief
so much flattered by these spontaneous outs-
sts that he wrote to the Directory that Naples
sented the appearance of Paris in 1789 and 1790.
n reality the conditions were very different.   In
nce the Revolution was national and came from
hin ; in Naples it was imposed upon a people by
sign bayonets.   In France the Republic was a
hbol of patriotism ; in Naples it was associated
h the triumph of an enemy.   The forces which
fronted the French Republic were the Church, the
stocracy, and the foreign powers ; in Naples the
atest danger to republicanism was the cruel and
erstitious temper of a fickle and degraded mob.
a revolutionary party in France was composed of
the rough homespun of the nation, its peasants,
artisans, its laborious and zealous middle class ;
in Naples it was far otherwise.   Here the repub-
an was a man of property and culture, and the
resentative of ideals not only far in advance of
intelligence of his country, but antagonistic to
general direction of national instinct and opinion.
the paroxysm of fear caused by the excesses of
lazzaroni many refined men and women belonging
the noblest families in the country rallied round
cause of the Parthenopean Republic.   A con-

passages of Tacitus, and show that the classical spirit of the Republic was still alive in Italy. But for the moment fury and superstition were in the ascendant. As the victims passed to the scaffold the lazzaroni could scarcely be prevented from tearing them to pieces; suspect Jacobins were burned alive, women were flogged, and excesses were committed in the name of God and King which match, if they do not surpass, the utmost horror of the French Revolution. So the Parthenopean Republic was drowned in blood. No European capital, as Colletta observes, has ever lost so large a proportion of its elect citizens. The flower of southern liberalism was cut down, and, by the proscription of all that was noblest and most generous in the country, the forces of progress were deprived of sane and wholesome direction and driven into the underground channels of a dark and desperate conspiracy.[8]

With the return of Bonaparte from Egypt the fortunes of the Italian dynasties began to tremble anew. The battle of Marengo shattered the Austrian ascendency and precluded the return of the Sardinian house to Turin. The Cisalpine Republic was restored, and by swift stages the dominion of France was extended throughout the peninsula. But while this process was being accomplished, and while the greater part of it was still in the future, the government of France had passed from a disguised Republic into an undisguised Empire. The mask once thrown away in France, Napoleon could refashion Italy in free disregard of democratic theorem. The Cisalpine Republic was in 1804 converted into the Italian Kingdom, and when two years later the King and Queen of Naples were again chased from the capital, the form

of government established by the French was not a
republic but a monarchy. Whatever may have been
the ultimate intentions of Napoleon, it did not enter
into his scheme to fortify that republican tradition
to which his earliest victories had given a new and
powerful impulse. The devices which were employed
to strengthen the Empire in France were applied to
support the monarchical principle in Italy, and if time
had been permitted, the French dynasty or dynasties
established in the peninsula would have been supported by a cluster of noble and dependent families,
whose princely estates, descending by the privileged
method of primogeniture, would tower over the
dwindling properties of the middle and lower class.

Fourteen years passed and the power of Napoleon
was broken. The French dominion in Italy which
was founded on force crumbled to pieces with the fall
of its creator: the Pope returned to Rome; Ferdinand and Caroline resumed their odious rule in
Naples; the Austrian flag flew in Milan and Venice,
and superstition returned to Turin in the wake of
the Sardinian exiles. Of the old Italian republics,
San Marino and Lucca alone remained. Venice was
Austrian; Genoa was Piedmontese; in outward
semblance the cause of free government in Italy
appeared to have been retarded rather than advanced
by the expansive force of the revolution and the
Empire. This, however, is the reverse of truth.
Napoleon sowed the idea of Italian unity, and a
republic was among the modes in which patriotic
Italian minds came to conceive that great result.
The dynastic tradition had been interrupted, the old
boundaries temporarily effaced, and with this revolution in affairs, ephemeral as it may appear to be, the

twin spirits of loyalty and locality lost something of their hold upon the instinct and intellect of the people. More important than all, the population of Italy had been compelled to take sides in a great and living issue.   Part had served the French ; part had offered to them an active or a passive resistance.   In every quarter of Italy, and behind all the varying conditions of Italian political life, this underlying dualism remained the groundwork of public affairs.   The old dynasties were pitted against the revolutionary faith ; the canons against the Civil Code, the index against the belief in liberty, the doctrine of obedience against the gospel of natural rights.   Hateful as were the oppressions of the Empire, there was not a town in which some family or group of families had not contributed to establish the new *régime* and to strip from the old fabric its traditional supports ; and this great connexion, when the lamp of the Empire was extinguished, continued to cherish the thoughts which arose from the understanding of that strong and finely-wrought machine.

The republican tradition in England, represented by the writings of Milton, Harrington, and Sidney, and illustrated by the triumphs of the Commonwealth, survived the Revolution of 1688 only as a literary memory.   The Whig settlement, by circumscribing the prerogative of the Crown and fixing the succession in the Protestant line, gave substantial satisfaction to the constitutional feeling in the country.   In the first half of the eighteenth century the Hanoverian throne was threatened, not by republicans but by Jacobites, and, when at the beginning of the reign of George III., a radical movement sprang up in the City

of London, and " Wilkes and Liberty " became the
war-cry of the city mob, the attack was directed not
upon the monarchy but upon the ministers of the
Crown and the constitution of Parliament. The
radicals of that period were not wanting in courage
or decision. They advocated universal suffrage,
annual parliaments, and electoral pledges : but all
this under the shelter of Whig principles and with
the claim that they were the true and lawful heirs
of the Bill of Rights. If the monarchy during the
eighteenth century had been an active principle of
evil, some party might have been formed for its
destruction ; but the growth of cabinet government
was slowly transferring the responsibility for the
conduct of affairs from the King to his ministers.
The process was indeed neither swift nor continuous,
and it suffered a dangerous interruption during the
twelve years of Lord North's administration, when
George III. was practically his own Prime Minister,
and directed the policy which resulted in the loss of
the American colonies. Had that intermission been
prolonged, had the King been able to break down
once and for all the system of government by party
cabinets which Burke in his " Thoughts on the Present
Discontents " defended as the essential condition of
wholesome public life, a considerable strain would
have been imposed on national loyalty. The famous
motion introduced into the Commons in 1780, that the
" influence of the Crown has increased, is increasing,
and ought to be diminished," indicates the presence of
discontent which might have ripened into mutiny ; but
there is a wide difference between a monarchy which
exercises its power through parliament and a monarchy
which exercises its power outside it. George III.

indeed ruled for twelve years as an absolute master, but he obtained his ascendency by procuring subservient majorities in the Commons and pliant instruments in the Cabinet. Stiffen the Cabinet, free the Commons, and the Crown would become what under the Bill of Rights it was intended to be, the dignified figurehead of the Commons. The measures by which this result could be obtained were inscribed upon the programme of that Whig party, whose brilliant talents in opposition illustrated the dark days of Lord North's administration,—they were the restoration of the Cabinet system, the reduction of the King's power of patronage, and the widening of the parliamentary franchise. Of these three objects the first two had been secured when the roar of the great French conflagration startled the ear of Europe.

With a temperament profoundly conservative and with no just grievance against their ancient constitution which a moderate enlargement of the parliamentary franchise might not remove, the English people were as impenetrable as granite to the extreme logic of leveller or republican. "We have real hearts of flesh and blood," wrote Burke, "beating in our bosoms. We fear God, we look up with awe to Kings; with affection to Parliaments; with duty to magistrates; with reverence to priests, and with respect to nobility." In the first moments of enthusiasm the French were eagerly congratulated upon the courage with which they had shaken off an odious tyranny and procured for themselves liberties which had long been familiar in England. Charles Fox enthusiastically exclaimed that the fall of the Bastille was the best and grandest event which had ever happened; and the generous sentiment found an

echo in every Whig or radical conventicle in the
country. But as the revolution developed itself, as
it was realized that the movement was in every
respect dissimilar from the fancied precedent of 1688,
that instead of being orderly it was anarchical, that
instead of being devised to assist the established
Church it was busy with the confiscation of its
property and the destruction of its influence, the first
glow of enthusiasm died down. Approval was succeeded by doubt, doubt by distrust, distrust by horror
and repugnance. In October 1790 Burke wrote that
famous piece of philosophical invective which expressed and at the same time determined the general
attitude of England towards the French Revolution.
The King said that it was a good book, a very good
book, and that every gentleman should read it.[4]

In the sermon at the Old Jewry which provoked this
grand explosion, Dr Price, a Unitarian preacher and
one of the most notable supporters of the French
Revolution in England, maintained that George III.
was almost the only lawful King in the world because
he alone owed his crown to the choice of the people.
The argument, as Burke proceeded to show, was not
very solid, but the exception at least is significant.
The French Revolution acted as a cordial to English
radicalism, and political societies sprang into being in
every town in the kingdom. Some of these societies
corresponded directly with the French Convention, and
we have it on the authority of John Binns, an Irish
radical who ended his life as Mayor of Philadelphia,
that in the weekly debates of the Corresponding
Societies the more violent members not infrequently
crossed the line which divides the radical politician
from the avowed enemy of monarchy. Economic

causes, aggravated by the war, tended to produce a
spirit of bitter disaffection among the poorest class in
the great towns. Bread was dear, taxes were high,
and as the King drove through London to open
Parliament in 1794 he was mobbed with cries of
" Down with George, down with Pitt, down with the
War." Stones were thrown at his carriage, one of the
leaders was killed, and the King himself was half
dragged out of his carriage by a ruffian who on that
same evening recounted his exploit to an admiring
circle of his fellow club-men. As the song went—

> How happy a thing
> Is having a King
> That tenderly feels all our woes.
> How well we are fed,
> How well we are led,
> Ah ! prettily led by the nose.
>
> The King, I am sure,
> Is all that is pure,
> But then sure the devil is in it.
> There's Pitt at the helm,
> A-sinking the realm,
> And sinking it all in a minute.
>
> But, say what you will,
> Pitt taxes us still—
> Our tea, our wine, and our drams;
> They have taxed our light
> By day and by night,
> Our lawyers, poor innocent lambs.

But although the operations of the political
societies gave ground for legitimate alarm, they were
for the most part confined within constitutional
limits. Of this fact there is a sufficient, if not a
decisive, test. In 1794 Hardy, a shoemaker who
founded the Corresponding Society, Horne Tooke, a

radical philologist, and others, were tried upon a charge of high treason. Their offence was that they had summoned a convention to meet at Manchester to discuss the question of Parliamentary Reform, but it was believed that investigation would disclose designs of a darker and more subversive complexion. The law officers of the Crown may be supposed to have chosen their ground with scrupulous care. If there did indeed exist, as was asseverated in a thousand pamphlets, a nefarious conspiracy to subvert the realm, these men would be at the bottom of it, and, being brought under examination, would enable the whole skein to be unravelled. Yet after eight days of dramatic tension the whole prosecution broke down. There was nothing in the speeches and writings of the incriminated men which could give the faintest colour to a charge of treason. The jury acquitted Hardy and Horne Tooke, and the less important prisoners were released without bail.[5]

There was then no republican party in England. Republican sentiment was not uncommon ; republican opinions may be traced, but not any overt or organized action for the overthrow of the monarchy. In one of his St Helena conversations Napoleon told O'Meara that had he succeeded in invading England he would have been well received by the *canaille*, and that after dethroning George he would have founded one republic in England and another in Ireland. If this plan was really entertained, it was founded upon a complete delusion as to the political complexion of the country. There was indeed a poor and starving proletariat ; and there were some educated republicans. There was Mrs Macaulay of whom Dr Johnson said that he did not mind her reddening her

face if she would give up blackening other people's
characters ; there was Hollis the publisher of the
classical literature of the cause ; and Tom Paine and
William Godwin, together with a wonderful constellation of young men fresh from school or college,
Wordsworth, Southey, Coleridge, Landor, Shelley.
But of this miscellaneous group one alone was a force
in politics and those not the politics of his native
country. It is difficult fully to share the admiration
which has been bestowed on Thomas Paine by Dr
Moncure Conway, his learned American biographer.
Paine's private morals were never of the best, and in
political prudence he had much to learn ; but he
undoubtedly possessed great courage, a robust independence of received convictions and a considerable
capacity for clothing his views in the form which was
most likely to appeal to a wide circle of readers.
Paine was a Lewes exciseman who escaped to America
with a grievance against the British Government just
when the clouds were gathering which broke out into
the War of Independence. A man of the people, he
found in the New World a scope for the character
and the energy which had received no adequate
recognition in his native land of rotten boroughs and
country squires. He plunged into American politics,
wrote pamphlets against the British cause, and published his philosophy of politics in a work entitled
" The Rights of Man," and his philosophy of religion
in a book, which has had much influence, called the
" Age of Reason." Paine, to put it bluntly, was a
republican and a deist, representing both in his political
and in his religious convictions the very opposite pole
of thought to that which is contained in Burke's
" Reflections on the French Revolution." Burke was

an English patriot ; Paine was a cosmopolitan who quitted England to become an American citizen, and then for a time abandoned America to become a citizen of France. Burke regarded society as bound together in an organic whole by the mysterious cumulative force of tradition ; Paine as an aggregate of separate units connected by an artificial contract. To Burke hereditary monarchy was sacred, to Paine it was the abomination of desolation and the one form of government which the sovereign people was not entitled to set up. The greatest crime of the French Revolution consisted in the eyes of Burke in the spoliation of Church property and the destruction of ecclesiastical corporations ; Paine on the contrary regarded these acts as constituting a superb victory in the secular campaign of light against darkness, of reason against the forces of priest-craft and superstition. Compared with Burke's resplendent and massive eloquence Paine's " Rights of Man " sounds thin and hollow. But if he had not the polish or culture of his adversary, if he was lacking in poetic vision and historical imagination, Paine at least grasped one side of the French Revolution which had entirely escaped Burke's attention. He saw—and this Burke never chose to see—that the French Revolution was a protest against intolerable wrong, and that the sufferings of the court weighed light in the balance against the misery of an oppressed and starving people. In the one phrase of the " Age of Reason " which is often quoted, he remarked that Burke had pitied the plumage but had forgotten the dying bird.

If Paine drew his political doctrine straight from America, William Godwin represents a more subtle and sophisticated compound. His intellectual genealogy may be traced partly to French and partly to English sources. He was the author of an excellent History of the English Commonwealth which the combined labours of Guizot and Gardiner have been required to displace, and he was also a student of the French philosophers. But in the abstract and generalizing cast of his mind he was, despite his historical acquisitions, more French than English. There was no feature of human society in which he did not desire to see a radical alteration. Starting from the principle that man possesses no innate tendency to evil, he concluded that all evil must be the result of government. Government then was bad, punishment was bad, property was bad, and marriage, as the most degrading form of property, was worst of all. These propositions being accepted, very little is left of the Ancient British Constitution; certainly not the Church, for religion obstructs the free operations of the human reason, nor yet the monarchy, for a king is the most irrational instrument of coercion which is in itself essentially injurious. On the other hand, if force is wrong, there can be no justification for a violent revolution, and Godwin is consistent enough to condemn the storming of the Bastille. He may, therefore, be regarded as an exponent of anarchy and nonresistance, anticipating as he does some of the doctrines which in our own day have been preached by Bakunin and Tolstoy. But the '' Political Justice '' was far too fantastic and loosely reasoned to disturb the judgment of the country, and had it not been for the singular influence which Godwin's teaching exerted over the mind of Shelley, he would have been a negligible factor in the organic development of English thought.[6]

And now we come to that constellation of plastic and imaginative young minds for whom the French Revolution seemed to open new and radiant horizons of happiness exhibiting—

> A people in the depth
> Of shameful imbecility uprisen
> Fresh as the morning star.

And again—

> A time
> In which apostasy from ancient faith
> Seemed but conversion to a higher creed.

In every case we meet a repetition of the same story. Enthusiasm passes into disenchantment, and disenchantment into repulsion by stages which vary in rapidity with the different temperaments and natures of the persons concerned. Southey, who was a free thinker and a republican when he went up to Oxford in 1792, experienced a first rude shock at the downfall of the Girondins, and lived to become a pillar of Church and Crown, and the mark for the angry defiance of Byron. The political orbit of Coleridge is very similar. He begins as a republican and a Gallophil, he ends by being, in the phrase of John Stuart Mill, one of " the seminal minds " of English conservatism. His conversion, which was marked by the apearance of a splendid ode entitled Recantation, was definitive in 1797 and had been prepared four years earlier when the domination of the Jacobins was established in France. In all this there is no need for surprise. Southey and Coleridge both in reality belonged to the conservative wing of human opinion, Southey because he was a plain Englishman set in conventional lines. Coleridge by reason of a deep mystical belief in the worth did not need to dig liberty and equality out of folios; he found them by the peat fire of the dalesman's cottage, and on the open air-washed spaces of the mountain side—

> Love had he found in huts where poor men lie,
> His daily teachers had been woods and rills,
> The silence that is in the starry sky,
> The sleep that is among the lonely hills.

Growing up then without any formed or explicit political theories, but deriving from the social and natural harmonies around him a strong bias towards the cause of freedom and social justice, Wordsworth was attuned to sympathize with the French Revolution. From the very first, however, his faith in liberty experienced shocks which would have proved fatal to a plant less securely rooted in the depths of a profound nature. Travelling through France in 1791, he fell in first with a merry swarm, chiefly of delegates returning from the Feast of Federation, and then with a band of armed rustics commissioned to expel the blameless inmates of the famous convent of Chartreuse. Sunshine was followed by shadow; the triumph of freedom was stained by the guilt of sacrilege. Wordsworth's compassion for the monks was, however, overpowered by his enthusiasm for " new-born liberty," and he returned from his travels with no serious misgivings. As yet he knew nothing of the inner workings of French politics. So he revisited France in 1792, and, after gathering a relic from the rubble of the Bastille, settled down for the summer in Touraine. Here he fell in with a certain Captain Beaufoys, a revolutionary, to whose gracious and enthusiastic character Wordsworth has dedicated a noble passage in the " Prelude." To-

gether they discussed politics and condemned the idle
and selfish courtier's life.

> Painting to ourselves the miseries
> Of royal courts and that voluptuous life,
> Unfeeling where the man who is of soul
> The meanest thrives the most ; where dignity,
> True personal dignity abideth not :
> A light, a cruel and vain world cut off
> From the natural inlets of just sentiment,
> From lowly sympathy and chastening truth.

The summer passed in pleasant colloquy among the
castles of the Loire, and then, in October, Wordsworth
was back in Paris. The Tuileries had been stormed,
the King and Queen were prisoners in the Temple,
and the horror of the September massacres hung like
a blood-red cloud over the city. The French State
having repulsed the hordes of Brunswick had

> Spared not the empty throne, and in proud haste
> Assumed the body and venerable name
> Of a Republic.

Despite the massacres, Wordsworth still remained a
staunch believer in the Republic. The horrors were
ephemeral, the Republic would be eternal. Returning
to England he found London excited by the agitation
for the abolition of the slave trade. Wordsworth con-
soled himself by thinking that the defeat of Wilber-
force's bill was only a temporary rebuff, since the
success of the French Republic would bring in its
train the abolition of slavery throughout the world.
These dreams were, however, almost instantly shattered by the outbreak of the war between England
and France. That England should fight the democracy
of France seemed to Wordsworth the height of impiety.

He defended the execution of Louis, argued that
a republic was the best of all constitutions, and
rejoiced at the miscarriage of English arms. Terrible
as was the tyranny of Robespierre, Wordsworth remained obstinate and inflexible. He still trusted in the
people of France. With grim desolating determination he quelled the patriotism which was gnawing at
his heart, and refused to retract a single thought.
But when the Directory fell, when the French submitted to the yoke of Bonaparte, when it became clear
that the wars waged by France were not for defence
but for aggression, when the extinction of the Venetian
Republic was followed by the subjugation of Switzerland, by the imprisonment of Toussaint l'Ouverture
and the threatened invasion of England, the wheel
turned round full circle. France, the apostle of liberty,
had become for the moment the instrument of despotism, and, in the series of sonnets dedicated
to National Independence and Liberty, Wordsworth, since Milton the greatest and staunchest of
English republicans, wrote that immortal palinode
in which true liberty is distinguished from its garish
counterfeits.

CHAPTER VII

AUTOCRACY AND ITS CRITICS

Then night fell ; and as from night
Reassuming fiery flight,
From the West swift freedom came,
Against the course of Heaven and down,
A second sun arrayed in flame,
To burn, to kindle, to illume.
From far Atlantis its young beams
Chased the shadows and the dreams,
France with all her sanguine streams
Hid, but quenched it not ; again
Through clouds its shafts of glory rain
From utmost Germany to Spain.
—SHELLEY " Hellas "

FORCE is the antithesis of liberty. The wars of the Revolution and the Empire involved changes which were too violent to be durable, and in its essential features the Europe of 1815 does not differ from the Europe of 1789. But the reaction was not limited to the sphere which a Congress of Vienna may control ; it spread over the whole surface of human interests, and was no less comprehensive than the creed which had been shamed on the Place de la Bastille and beaten on the field of Waterloo. As the Revolution was anti-clerical and dogmatic, so the counter-revolution re-discovered the sentiments and beliefs which clustered round the central column of historic Christianity. Savigny attacked the French Codes, and championed the principle of historical development against the claims of ideal construction. De Maistre built up a compact edifice of shining paradox in honour of Absolutism in Church and State ; the beautiful eloquence of Chateaubriand was poured out in copious floods to commend the claims of the Christian religion to the admiration of a cultured and æsthetic intelligence. In every quarter of intellectual activity brains were working to re-establish and decorate the principle of authority. Alexander of Russia, who began life as a theoretical republican and ended it as the accomplice of Metternich, may serve as a type of that European generation who watched the shattering of their youthful ideals and passed out of the warmth into the cold.

Though in some degree or other it had affected every people in Europe, the storm of the French Revolution beat most directly upon the Latin races. The Bourbon monarchy was torn up by the roots in France, Spain, and Naples, and its place was filled up by governments which in all the great affairs of life proceeded upon an opposite principle. From these facts it was natural to deduce the conclusion that the cause of monarchy would be less secure in the Latin than in the Teutonic and Slavonic races of Europe. Spain had lived for six years, Naples for nine years, France for twenty-five years, without the legitimate monarchy whose necessity was proclaimed by the Congress of Vienna ; and it was reasonable to suppose that the strength of the restored dynasty would vary inversely with the term of its exile, —that the monarchy would be less secure in France than in Spain, less secure in Spain than in Naples, and that, if Europe were ever to become that federation of republics which Brissot had preached and which Kant had predicted, the first mutter of the storm would be heard within the Latin zone, and the decisive explosion within the capital of France.

It was recognized from the first that Fra
the point of danger. In the five-and-tw
crowded history during which she had re
life and filled Europe with the noise of
how could France remember the Bourbo
no part or lot in the national achieveme
dropped out of the national memory, a
enter into the framework of national
(New habits were formed, new interests w
new generation had grown up to whom
of an exiled dynasty was alien and unfa
so, when the Bourbon dynasty was restoi
arms, it suffered under every disadvanta
dynasty could be subject.   Its latest cred
as France could recollect them, were a
connected in the public mind with those
old social system which the Revolution h
and which the people of France were re
never be restored. It was imposed upon t
foreign foes and as the result of victori
tracted the greatness of the nation an
pride. To the French mind persons co
and on this computation what chance had
against the fallen Napoleon ? At best
was an anti-climax ; at the worst it m
disaster.)
(Between the extremes of the ancie
the Republic there was a, middle way
constitutional monarchy. ·It was a pat
France had not yet trodden—for the v
cannot be counted—and no other route
to lead into safe places. Acting on the
allies and recognizing the pressure of
Louis XVIII. consented to be a constituti

He granted a Charter based upon the English model with an hereditary Chamber of Peers and an elected Chamber of Deputies, and appended a list of specific assurances with respect to the freedom of the press, religious toleration, the liberty of the subject, and the land-titles of the Revolution. All the main institutions of the Empire were preserved, the Codes, the University, the Church, the Legion of Honour, the Bank of France, the prefects, the imperial nobility. The social structure of the country remained and was destined to remain as it had been fashioned under the Revolution and the Empire : but the mechanism of the central government was new and its success was problematical.)

In the minds of Englishmen the rule of Parliament is associated with democratic control. The affairs of the country are governed by the Cabinet, the Cabinet is responsible to the House of Commons, and the House of Commons is responsible to the nation at large. The government of France under the Restoration did not conform to these conditions. The Chamber did not represent the nation, and the Ministers did not necessarily represent the majority of the Chamber. The King regarded himself as the source of the Constitution, and the guiding wheel of the political machine. Whatever might be the balance of parliamentary parties it was for him to choose the Ministers ; the Cabinet was responsible not to the Chamber but to the Crown. To the logical mind of the French such a system was a standing anomaly. The Civil Code proclaimed the equality of all French citizens ; the electoral laws confined political rights to a select oligarchy ranging under the restoration from 89 to 110,000 persons. The fundamental creed of the Revolution was that the people was sovereign, the

source of all law, the will behind a
The monarchy of the Restoration based
not upon the general will, but upon its e
the principle of legitimacy.   A cons
has grown with a growth of a nation has
If change is wanted, it is made within t
Constitution, and in accordance with p
the Constitution is believed to emb
constitutional monarchy of France was
but an expedient ; and while there was
pledged to support it, there were two
nation who challenged its validity and e
circumstance which seemed to impair
The ultra-Royalists wished to abolish th
and the party of the tricolour wished
King.

The Republican movement during t
period suffered from a complaint which
all political parties which find themselve
minority.   Misfortune makes strange be
minorities in opposition enter into
combinations which involve some sacrif
and obscuration of aim.   The French
been overturned by Bonaparte with
stance of ignominy.   He had silenced
muzzled the press, reintroduced the h
ciple, and stamped out, so far as a powerf
can suppress a vital thing, every re
pensity in the nation.   Yet, in the com
which followed the defeat of Waterlo
and Bonapartists drew together.   Th
principles which divided them and ren
those upon which they were agreed.
represented the tricolour which Loui

unwisely discarded; equally they were the children
of the Revolution, cherishing a common hatred for
Kings and Jesuits; and resolved that never again
should the peasant pay feudal dues or tithes, or the
noble escape his due share of taxation.) In the minds
of the statesmen who made the American nation the
Republic stood for peace, concord, and non-intervention. The French republicans cherished no such ideals.
It was their aim to reverse the European settlement of
1815, and to help the cause of liberty wherever it was
struggling against oppression. They sympathized
with the Spanish Americans revolting against Spain,
with the Poles conspiring against the Russians, with
the Greeks fighting against the Turks, and with the
subtle meshes of secret conspiracy which were spreading over the whole Italian peninsula. They wanted
war and plenty of it. They were clamorous for the
Rhine frontier. They regarded it as an obligation of
honour to unlock the unnatural union between Belgium
and Holland, and to recover for France its lost
ascendency in Europe. They viewed a monarchy
which had come packed up in the enemy's baggage as a
standing disgrace to their country, and in every phase
and incident of its foreign policy were quick to read a
servile compliance with an enemy's command. In
the Chamber the party was led by Manuel and
Lafayette; in the streets and cafés of Paris the war-
songs of Béranger were a programme in themselves.

A movement containing so many subversive and
revolutionary elements was naturally suspect to those
who moved within the narrow channels of the Constitution. After the first paroxysm of reaction had spent
itself, the Liberals—a name recently imported from
Spain—began to be successful at the polls. They

gained twenty-five seats in 1817, forty-five in 1818
ninety in 1819. Conservative Europe was seriously
alarmed. The Republic was raising its ugly head, and
if nothing were done, the old troubles and confusion
would begin again, and Europe would be involved in :
fresh cataclysm. Louis XVIII. was urged to tak
strong measures. He was not himself an ultra, lik
his brother the Comte d'Artois, having a shrew
suspicion that a middle course was always safest, an
that if the monarchy were ever to become national i
must acquire confidence by respecting constitution
forms. But in 1820 the Duc de Berry was murdere
in the streets of Paris, and the Royalists raised a
outcry which the compliant temper of the King wa
unable to resist. A ministry was chosen from the Right
the electoral laws were revised ; and for the next seve
years the Government was carried on by the ultra
In this violent and furious reaction the Liberals we
practically driven out of parliamentary life. Th
movement which had begun with an attempt to captur
the parliamentary system ended with a conspiracy t
undermine it. The Charbonnerie, modelled on th
Italian Carbonari, divided into sections of twent
members, and, directed by a central committee, aime
at overthrowing the Bourbons by a military insurre
tion and with the help of revolutionaries in oth
countries. Revolutions which are brewed in barrac
rarely obtain a commanding or durable success. Th
movements of 1820 in Spain, Naples, and Piedmont we
easily crushed, and the French insurrections of 182
at Belfort, Colmar, Toulon, and Saumur were equal
ineffectual. When in 1823 a French army was se
into Spain to assist the cause of Absolutism it wa
confronted on the banks of the Bidassoa by a sma

body of Imperialists carrying the tricolour flag ; but the seductions which Bonaparte had once employed with success depended on Bonaparte and lost all their magic without him. Not a man was suborned from his allegiance to the white flag, and Chateaubriand could boast that, whatever elements of trouble might be found in the kingdom, the army at least was true to the Bourbon cause.

The wisest heads of the Restoration period, men like de Serre, Decazes, and Martignac, knowing that France was set against the *ancien régime,* held it to be a part of common prudence to send the revolutionary passions to sleep by abstaining from any course which might be construed as a menace to the revolutionary settlement. Charles X. was of a different opinion. In temper and intellect he belonged to the older order, to the narrow world of ultramontane theology and autocratic politics. As heir apparent he was deeply suspect, as King he rapidly converted suspicion into mutiny and mutiny into revolt. A bishop was appointed Grand-Master of the University of France, a premonitory symptom of the approaching victory of orthodox theology over free speculation. A thousand million francs were voted to compensate the *émigrés* for the loss of their lands in the Revolution, and a law passed against sacrilege was taken as an indication that offences against religion were henceforward to be treated as crimes against the State. By 1827 the Government had excited against it a coalition of Liberals, Jansenists, and manufacturers. The country was deeply stirred. The electoral currents ran against the ministry, and Villèle, in whom the ultras had found a bold and astute leader, resigned his portfolio. There were then two alternatives open to the King. He might take a ministry, if not from the Left at least from the liberal Right Centre, and attempt to acquire the confidence of the Chamber and the country, or he might send for the ultras, provoke a quarrel with parliament, and build up an absolute monarchy out of the ruins of the Constitution. He tried the first expedient for a year, and then, in a mood of levity and impatience, had recourse to the second. Summoning Polignac, an *émigré* and a mystic, to his counsels, he resolved to crush the opposition by a *coup d'état*. Ordinances were issued muzzling the press, restricting the franchise, and dissolving the new Chamber before it had met. Counting on the fidelity of the army, and rich in assurances of divine aid, the frivolous old King and his hair-brained minister were confident that they could rivet reaction upon France.

In the republican movement in France there were two psychologies, one exuberant, sanguine, reckless, abounding in joyous energies, the other Spartan, austere, and self-controlled. Of the latter type, which was not uncommon in the great Convention, Godefroy Cavaignac was an example. He believed in the Republic with that fixity, narrowness, and concentration with which John Knox believed in Holy Writ or Charles I. in the Divine Right of Kings. He was suckled in the creed and never dreamt of contesting its credentials. The Republic was to him the symbol of reason in politics ; the ideal for which the heroes of the Revolution had striven and suffered, but to which by a series of uncontrollable calamities they had never been able to attain. The logic of the fanatic is never applicable to the perplexed conditions of political life. Cavaignac argued that the troubles of France were due to the suspension of the Constitution of 1793, and that they would be cured by the adoption of that fanta. and impracticable design. In Paris there were alwa^{amy} two elements of disorder, the students of the Lati^{se} quarter and the workmen of the faubourgs, and Cavaignac, who was a man of deeds, knew where to find an army of the tricolour. The reply to the Ordinances of the mystical Prince were the barricades of the practical republican, and to the surprise of those who confided in military discipline the reply was sufficient.

Three days' street fighting were enough to decide the fate of King Charles. The men of the barricades pushed Marmont out of Paris, and the Revolution was left master on the stricken field. The number of men engaged on the barricades was probably not more than eight or ten thousand, and, had the royalist troops been handled with decision and properly reinforced, a course of autocratic government might have received an appropriate baptism in blood. But, having thus surprised a victory, the republicans were in turn the victims of a surprise. The politicians of the Palais Bourbon were not prepared for a republic, and they knew that France was as little inclined to that prospect as they. -The Revolution had not spread outside the capital, and it was still open to the King to appeal to the loyalty of the provinces against a wicked and impious faction. There was a party in the Chamber and there were organs in the press who favoured the claims of the Duke of Orleans. His father had embraced the cause of the Revolution; he himself had been admitted as a boy to the Jacobin Club, had fought for the armies of the tricolour, and had then experienced the hard and laborious vicissitudes of exile. Thiers drew up a proclamation commending the Duke. "He

mirs at Jemmapes.   He is a citizen King.   He has
Rörne the tricolour standard in the midst of battle, he
alone can bear it again.   He awaits our call.   Let us
issue this call and he will accept the Charter as we wish
it to be."   The Duke was brought to Paris, rode across
the armed city to the Hotel de Ville, and there annihilated the chances of a republic.   Appearing on the
balcony with Lafayette, he embraced in the presence
of the mob the man who stood out as the ornamental
figurehead of the republican movement.   And so in
July 1830 a new monarchy was etablished in France
by means of a republican revolution.[1]

About this time a little old man, quaintly dressed in
a Quaker-like brown coat, brown cassimere breeches,
and white worsted stockings, was punctually scribbling
twelve to fifteen folio pages daily of a Constitutional
Code.   Now and again he would put a straw hat
upon his head and trot out into his garden to look at
his flowers, for he loved flowers and cats and music,
and lived all by himself on a handsome income in a
grand country-house in Somersetshire.   His name was
Jeremy Bentham, and it was a famous name, for though
he was a recluse from society and full of whimsical
habits and curious opinions, he had been writing on
jurisprudence, politics, and morals for fifty-six years,
and was an established oracle on the art and science of
codification, not in England alone but in Russia and
Greece, and among the constitutional reformers of
Spain and Portugal.   Of the leaders in the march of
European intellect one alone could vie with him in
length of years, the stately poet of Weimar who
happened at this very time to be composing, in the
second part of Faust, his final message to the world.

But of Goethe and his mysterious sublimities Jeremy
Bentham knew and cared less than nothing. " Prose
is when all the lines except the last go to the margin,
poetry is when some of them fall short of it." This was
his final verdict on the language of the higher emotions.[2]

To Bentham's very practical English mind the logic
which had inspired the men of 1789 was as unpalatable
as their sentiment. The doctrine of the rights of man
was an " anarchical sophism," which could not stand
serious investigation, and which it was his pride to have
demolished in a slashing treatise. But while avoiding
the faulty high *a priori* road Bentham was drawn into
practical conclusions hardly differing from those of the
French Jacobin. He began by attacking specific legal
abuses, found them to be an inseparable part of the
Constitution and government of England, and was thus
led to challenge the whole structure of the English
state. If the greatest happiness of the greatest number
was not realized in English institutions, that was because the English government had no interest in promoting it. How could a small governing class have
any interest in furthering the happiness of human
beings outside its own social pale ? Only in a pure
democracy, a government of all by all, could legislation
be framed in the true interests of general felicity. A
monarchy therefore was necessarily evil, and the situation of a monarch, even of a limited monarch, " at all
times that of an enemy of the people," acting by force,
fear, corruption, and delusion through his three human
instruments, the soldier, the lawyer and the priest, to
produce in all times and at all places " the greatest
infelicity of the greatest number." It followed that
the only good act which a monarch was capable of
accomplishing was to abolish his own office, but this he

11

was most unlikely to do since the " natural tendency
not to say the constant effect of a monarch's situation
is to place him not at the top but at the bottom of the
scale of moral worth." The Holy Alliance and the
madness of George III. no doubt suggested other un-
flattering features in an institution which Bentham had
come to regard with slaveholding as one of the plagues
of human society. " While to one another," he writes
" all monarchs are objects of sympathy, to all monarchs
all subjects are objects of antipathy ; of a sort of com
pound sentiment made up of fear, hatred, and con
tempt ; something like that which women and children
are made to feel for a toad." Moreover, though th
madness of a monarch can hardly ever add to the evil
which he inflicts, monarchs are most probably mad
" In every monarchical state the great probability
always is that in proportion of several to one, at an
given period, the fate of all its members will be in th
hands of a madman." It might be asked how Europ
had come to accept in tranquillity and with apparen
acquiescence so absurd and iniquitous an institutior
Bentham's answer is—By force of custom. " Almos
all men are born under it, all men are used to it, fe
men are used to anything else ; till of late years nobod
ever dispraised it, . . . men were reconciled to mixe
monarchy in England by the same causes by whic
they were reconciled to pure monarchy in Morocc
Turkey, and Hindustan." [3]

In these cheerful and robust observations Bentha
was expressing an opinion, then very prevalent
Europe and firmly held by philosophical radicals
England, that the ultimate and perfect form of gover
ment was necessarily republican. It was still t
fashion to idealize America and to find in her institutio

the type of pure and successful democracy. "Fortunate Americans ! " exclaims the tiny sage, " fortunate on so many accounts, if to possess happiness it were sufficient to possess everything by which it is constituted, this advantage is still yours ! Preserve it for ever ; bestow rewards, erect statues, confer even titles so that they be personal alone ; but never bind the crown of merit on the brow of sloth." [4] At least Bentham could feel confident that whatever chaplets might be reserved for trans-Atlantic brows, the great Republic would never summon a lunatic to the White House. To the generation of Europeans who lived through the autocratic reaction and felt the thrill of the Greek War of Independence, America, a land of philosophers living, it was assumed, blameless and beautiful lives, was the last human fortress of Freedom.

> Darkness has dawned in the East
>   On the noon of time :
> The death-birds descend to their feast
>   From the hungry clime.
>
> Let Freedom and Peace flee far
>   To a sunnier strand,
> And follow Love's folding star
>   To the Evening land !

Before Bentham's Constitutional Code was given to the world, the merits and demerits of monarchy as an institution were submitted to a formal debate in Brussels with a result diametrically opposed to the true calculus of happiness. In 1830 when the storm of revolution was searching all the weak places in the political fabric of Europe, when the monarchy of Charles X. fell with a crash in France, and there were risings in Poland and Saxony, in Hanover, Brunswick,

and Hesse Cassel, the kingdom of the United Netherlands, which it had been one of the principal achievements of Lord Castlereagh to create, was seized by a
violent convulsion. The southern provinces split off
from Holland, declared their independence, and were
confronted with the task of framing the design for a
new polity. Some of the revolutionary movements of
this year were mere protests against unintelligent
tyranny ; in Belgium the outcry against specific
grievances grew into a demand for national liberation.
The Belgians had never asked to be united with the
Dutch from whom they were divided by more than
two hundred years of antagonistic history. The Dutch
were Calvinists, the Belgians for the most part
Catholics and Ultramontane Catholics. The Dutch
spoke a Teutonic language ; the educated population
of Belgium, whether Flemish or Walloon, used French
as the medium of education and social intercourse
The Dutch were saddled with a big debt, part of the
interest of which was now charged on the Belgian
taxpayer. The Dutch, being a seafaring people, were
advantaged by freedom of trade, the Belgians, a race
of manufacturers and farmers, insisted on protection
The civilization of Belgium was in the main derived
from France, the civilization of the Dutch provinces
from Germany or England. It had been the pride
of the Dutch that they had secured their liberty by a
tremendous struggle against the overwhelming power
of Spain, in the agony of which the inhabitants of the
southern provinces had basely deserted them, and that
through all the changes which had ensued, they had
maintained their independence until they were forcibly
assimilated to the French Republic. In contrast to this
record of heroic and sturdy liberty the Belgians had

been distinguished by uniform subservience to alien rule. They had allowed themselves to be ruled first by the Spaniards, then by the Austrians, and finally by the French ; and it was no doubt for this reason the more readily believed that they would not recoil from being governed by the Dutch.

Had the first King of the United Netherlands been a man of more pliant temper, this expectation might not have been disappointed. The Belgians had not a little to gain from a situation which secured them from foreign invasion, freed the river Scheldt for navigation, and opened out rich and sunny colonies to their trade ; but men are not exclusively governed by considerations of material self-interest, and the Belgians were human beings with susceptibilities which it was the duty of statesmanship to take into account. Unfortunately William I. was both a stout Dutchman and a strong Calvinist, and the Belgians were very far from being either the one thing or the other. In the two particulars in which the susceptibilities of a nation are most delicate, religion and language, a government controlled by Dutchmen went out of its way to outrage the feelings of the Belgian population. It made the Dutch language obligatory for admission to public office and employment, and interfered with the sacerdotal practices of a most sacerdotal nation. There were other grievances such as heavy taxes on corn and meat falling with special weight upon the poor of the southern provinces, but none were so keenly felt as these two main grievances of language and religion. Opposing them the Belgian population, which had been sharply divided into radical and clerical factions, discovered for the first time a common ground of action and a national unity.

The game of politics is full of surprises. The
Belgian, hated the Dutch language, the Dutch taxes
the Dutch press laws, the Dutch debt, the Dutch
religion, but in a long course of political agitation did
not directly contemplate a disruption of the Union
A full measure of administrative autonomy would have
stanched their wounds and silenced their cries.   They
had grown wealthy under the rule of King William
and were not blind to the material advantages which
flowed from their connexion with a prosperous colonia
power.   There were socialists and republicans in
Belgium as there were socialists and republicans in al
the great artisan populations of Western Europe, but
as yet their influence was inconsiderable.   Nobody
seriously proposed to overturn the monarchy o
argued that the hereditary principle was necessaril
inconsistent with the welfare or freedom of a progres
sive people.   The King, indeed, was far fallen in publi
esteem, but the heir to the throne was popular and i
the opinion of capable observers a few moderate con
cessions would even at the eleventh hour have save
the Belgian provinces for the House of Orange.   Thes
concessions were not made.   The news of the Pari
Revolution gave the signal for an outbreak in th
Belgian capital.   The Government piled blunder upo
blunder.   A street tumult grew into a revolution
The moderate men fell into the background, th
extreme men came to the front, and in less than si
weeks after the first token of disorder (October 4
1830), a provisional government in Brussels declare
the Belgian provinces to be an independent State
and summoned a National Congress to give it
constitution.[5]

In the memorable debate which ensued, th

question was raised, and for three days discussed, whether the new nation should be a monarchy or a republic. To those statesmen who were schooled in the French democratic tradition there was no reply to Condorcet's remark that the inheritance of political functions was not only a clear violation of natural liberty but an absurd institution, since it assumed the inheritance of appropriate qualities. But the abstract arguments, which had seemed so conclusive with earlier generations, played a subordinate part in this debate. Seron, one of the republican leaders, dilated on the expensiveness of thrones, cited the breakdown of the monarchy in France, and asked his hearers whether they could name a country more exactly calculated than Belgium to prosper under republican rule, a country where the nobles were liberal, the priests patriotic, the merchants prosperous, and the artisans enlightened. Another speaker related the crimes of the Holy Alliance and asserted that so long as the conspiracy of Kings should continue, he would never be a party to sending them a recruit. A third orator asserted that there was a general tendency in Europe towards the republican state, and that Belgium should march with the spirit of the age, but the argument which had most weight with an assembly of practical men was the supposed expensiveness of monarchical establishments.

European politics are, in the main, very conservative, and though the Belgian National Congress was elected in the midst of a successful revolution by a system of universal suffrage, it decided by 174 votes to 13 to recur to the familiar forms of monarchy rather than to affront the unknown perils of a republic. The Belgian people had always lived under Kings, limited, it is true,

the principal concerns of diplomacy to bridle the insurgent democracy of the West. The proclamation of a Belgian Republic would be viewed as a challenge to the existing order, and as a menace to all the crowned heads in Europe. Nor could any course be more prejudicial to the young and ill-established monarchy of Louis Philippe in France. In that country there was a strong republican party anxious alike to overturn the throne and to resume the broken epic of the revolutionary wars. Proclaim the Republic in Brussels, and the " party of movement " in Paris would receive a call to action to which it would instantly and powerfully respond. The new Belgian nation relied upon the moral and political support of the French King who owed his throne to that popular triumph at the barricades which had given the signal for their own revolution. If Belgium declared for a monarchy it would strengthen the hands of Louis Philippe. If it proclaimed a republic it would forfeit the friendship, if not compass the downfall, of its only ally in Europe.

The terrible drama of the Polish insurrection supplied an additional weapon to the logical armoury of the monarchists. The calamities of that unfortunate nation might be traced to the partitions of the eighteenth century, and these in some measure to the fact that the Polish Kingship was elective and not hereditary. The evils which followed from this unwise arrangement—the diplomatic intrigues, the civil broils, the pretexts for foreign intervention and the like—belonged to the most threadbare commonplaces of European knowledge, but on every fresh advertisement of the Polish tragedy the old lesson received a new and lurid illustration. Could there be a more awful example of the consequences of an

elective Headship ? Was Belgium to enter on th
path which had brought Poland to the abyss ? An
the warning voices did not come from the East alon
There were " the bloody and retrograde fluctuatioi
in the republican states of Southern America," exhibi
ing a violence of party-spirit, peculiar, it was though
to polities which permit the highest prize of politic
ambition to be scrambled for, and confirming tl
general belief that republican government is necessari
unstable. Such was the tenor of much of the argumer
Others laboured to exhibit the truth, which had be
obscured by the doctrinaires of the French Revoluti<
that heredity was " a neutral institution " equal
consistent with tyranny or freedom. The form of t
executive was not in itself a matter of primary ii
portance. Taxes could be reduced under a monarc!
as they could be increased under a republic. T
citizen could go and come as freely under the one d
pensation as under the other. Heredity, said t
democrat, would lead to despotism ; but the real pi
tection against despotism was not an elective Preside!
but an elective legislature, a responsible cabinet,
independent judiciary, together with guarantees :
freedom of worship and speech and education. Th<
were the really important principles which, once fiy
and established in the constitution, would carry w
them every liberal consequence which the most i
compromising apostle of human freedom could desi
And such was the spirit which gave shape to the c<
stitutional monarchy of Belgium.[6]

CHAPTER VIII

THE SECOND REPUBLIC IN FRANCE

L'Univers n'est qu'un laboratoire de magie où il faut s'attendre à tout.—PROUDHON

Rien de médiocre sous la République.
La grandeur est sa nature.—MICHELET

Au premier mot de république le premier cri des gens de campagne a été; "Plus d'impôt, à bas les impôts."—GEORGES SAND

ONE of the principal supports of the Restoration Monarchy in France had been the acute and painful recollection of the governments which immediately preceded it. However ill the mass of Frenchmen thought of Louis XVIII., they thought far worse of the Terror, the taxes, and the tyranny from which they were so recently delivered. But as time went on memory began to work its accustomed marvels. The Revolution appeared to be a humanitarian, the Empire a liberal movement. The ugly or doubtful features of either dispensation were seen either through a softening mirage or else they were not seen at all. After 1825 a habit grew up of viewing the Revolution, not as it really was, a succession of different though connected phases of a complex movement, some cruel or unwise, others noble, others unripe and ridiculous, but as a single thing, agreeing with itself, and with a distinct will and quality of its own which only the language of hagiology could adequately characterize. The historical revival which was so remarkable a feature of that age contributed to foster this respectful and even devotional attitude towards the French Revolution. Thiers treated it as a rational and progressive movement, every part of which was linked to every other by a chain of causation, so that transactions which had been wont to excite horror, surprise, and shame, appeared as the inevitable stages in the disclosure of a great and beneficent design. With Lamartine the Revolution was a beautiful idyll; with Louis Blanc a prelude to the complete emancipation of man. And very much the same process of transfiguration affected the retrospect of the Empire. As the St Helena Conversations became published abroad, the world learnt that it had entirely mistaken Napoleon. It had regarded him as the incarnation of military tyranny, whereas in reality he was preparing a peaceful federation of Europe upon liberal lines. It had read an ultimate design into transitional institutions, and harshly misjudged the greatest of mortals because it had refused to wait for the full divulgation of his plan. His purpose, which had been partially disclosed in his Italian and Polish policy and in the constitutional concessions of the Hundred Days, would assuredly serve as the liberating impulse in the future policy of Europe. He would have united Italy, freed -Poland, endowed France with constitutional liberties, and balanced the peaceful federation of the New World with a policy no less peaceful in the Old. The Napoleonic legend grew apace, and, when the bones of the great Emperor were brought to Paris in 1840, there were some who said that the Second Empire was already made.

The French Revolution was founded, not upon a

criticism of property, but upon a criticism of privilege. It effected sweeping social changes without any conscious purpose, which in modern economic terminology would be called socialistic. Tithes were taken from the pockets of the priests and put into the pockets of the landlords; peasant properties were created and extended; and the ground was cleared for the untrammelled play of free competition. These changes went very far, but had no tendency to promote communism or to weaken the principle of private property in the country. On the contrary, inasmuch as the Revolution increased the number of landowners, it fortified the economic interests which were connected with the defence of private property in land. It did not scruple to attack monopoly, than which Socialism has no firmer ally, or to establish a peasant proprietary, than which Socialism has no more deadly enemy. So far as economic legislation went, its ideal was freedom. Men could take what trade they like, sell in the dearest and buy in the cheapest market, and follow their interest to the top of their bent. Factory life was in its infancy, and there were no factory laws. Trade unions and strikes were forbidden, for the idea of an economic combination was suspect as savouring of those guild monopolies which, in pursuance of the most enlightened doctrine of the time, had been condemned as inconsistent with the stainless canon of human liberty. The problem of poverty still remained unsolved. With the growth of machinery and the concentration of capital, it developed features of which the men of the Revolution had not dreamt, and for which the Codes of the Revolution had made no provision. It was all very well to secure freedom of contract, but in what sense was a contract free, when the parties to it

were Lazarus and Dives ?   The rule of the physiocrats
laissez faire, laissez passer, was a valuable protest
against the meddlesome interference of an archaic
government and the stifling restrictions of feudal
caste, but was it the last word of economic science ?
Did it guarantee society against waste ? Did it
shelter the weak from the strong ?   Had it cured unemployment or raised wages or improved physique ?
Was not the anarchy of competition as distinct and
palpable an evil as the sheltered and privileged torpor
of the guilds and monopolies ?   These and similar
questionings began to claim in an increasing measure
the attention of serious minds in France during the
reign of Louis Philippe.   In 1838 a Frenchman, by
name Pierre Leroux, coined a term which has since
become a battle-cry all over the world.   The term was
Socialism : its meaning, social control as opposed to
individual liberty in the sphere of economic production
and exchange.

One of the earliest and far the most brilliant of the
French writers who attempted a radical criticism of the
economic basis of society was Claude Henri, Comte de
St Simon.   Few Frenchmen have printed so deep a
mark upon the thought of their age.   Men of the calibre
of Auguste Comte and Augustin Thierry submitted
to the fascination of this aristocrat, who made it his
maxim to lead the most original and active life possible
to explore every class in society, and to become acquainted with the whole range of human theory and
practice.   St Simon's doctrine is in extreme outline as
follows : The French Revolution had intended to
abolish privileges of birth, but had only half-completed
its task.   It had abolished birth privileges in matters
relating to public functions, but not in matters relating

to economic functions. It had done away with hereditary legislators and hereditary judges, but it had left
hereditary wealth and hereditary poverty. It had
been an epoch of criticism, not an epoch of construction,
and the law of human progress was that epochs of
construction should succeed to epochs of criticism.
Of this new age St Simon proposed to be prophet and
founder. He would complete the abolition of birth
privileges by transforming private property into a
kind of life interest or trust held under the State.
This need not involve a violent revolution. By the
abolition of collateral inheritance and by progressive
death duties the State would gradually and without
disturbance convert private into public property ;
and so, owning all the land and all the means of production, would be able to organize industry upon the
principle of distribution for all, " to each according to
his capacity, and to each capacity according to his
works." The anarchy of trade would be cured by the
organisation of industrial communities, whose output
would be regulated by statistics, whose gains would be
distributed according to the services of the individual
producers, and whose activities would be stimulated
by promotion according to merit, and by pensions for
old age.

In the system of St Simon, as in that of his contemporary Fourier, there is enough of the fantastic
and absurd to blast any ordinary reputation for sound
sense. But, viewed in the context of their own age,
these two pioneers of Socialism exercised a just and
intelligible influence. They saw with great distinctness terrible disparities of happiness, and urged that
the State had the duty and power to remove them.
Their writings mark a wholesome reaction from the

military spirit of the Napoleonic age. St Simon, in this respect anticipating Herbert Spencer, but unfortunately not the true course of history, proclaimed that the world was passing from a military into an industrial stage. He announced that the problem of curing poverty was more important by vast and immeasurable degrees than the conquest of territories ; and in his works, as in those of Fourier, this problem is handled in the broadest way. These men did not weigh out palliatives in a grocer's scale ; they offered to reorganize society from roof to basement. Their horizon was not limited by the frontiers of political economy ; their economics were affiliated to laws of progress, to cosmologies, to comprehensive, original, and mostly very absurd speculations as to the nature of man and the past and future of the Universe. Nothing arrests attention more successfully than a mixture of sound sense and paradoxical nonsense, especially if it be subtly compounded and addressed to the remedy of admitted evils. St Simon startled France into serious sociology ; and the impulse, communicated from his writings, spread in widening circles through the whole framework of French society. There were Socialist songs, Socialist novelettes, Socialist pamphlets, besides solid criticism of the old political economy in such an organ as the *Globe*, and from such pens as those of Buchez, Carnot, and Duvernier. The most attractive programmes were put out based upon the thinnest gauzes of visionary psychology. Cabet's " Voyage en Icarie " depicted a Utopia governed by the pure ethics of the gospel, in which the rich made a voluntary renunciation of their wealth and the State distributed commodities, not according to the aristocratic principle of desert, but according to the charitable principle of need. The doctrine disseminated by Fourier that nature, under proper direction, could be taught to produce a superior race of men and animals, was widely, if not explicitly, held by those who had everything to gain by a social revolution and nothing to lose by a comfortable dream.

In the general intellectual ferment watchwords were coined which have done service in the currency of Socialism for many generations : property is theft ; to each according to his needs; rehabilitation ; emancipation ; solidarity ; scientific and industrial organization. The literature of the movement was neither learned nor profound, but it was full of large and seductive ideas. The title of Louis Blanc's famous treatise " L'Organisation du Travail," was in itself a programme for humanity. Reading it at a distance of some seventy years we are struck with its slightness and brevity. National workshops aided by state capital, electing their own officers, paying equal wages to their operatives, are gradually to eliminate the individual producer. Competition is to disappear, capitalism is to retreat before the superior type of these democratic, co-operative, and State-aided groups. That is all. There is no attempt to meet difficulties, to push the argument home, or to support it on a basis of economic knowledge. It is as flimsy a raft of dialectic as any upon which a great mass of social appetite has voyaged on the sea of politics. But in comparison with most of the proposals of the day Blanc's programme was precise and substantial, and, when the Revolution of 1848 broke out, the idea of the National Workshop was firmly lodged in the brains of the Paris artisans.

A Socialist State might be governed by an hereditary

12

monarchy. There is nothing inconceivable, though there would be something anomalous, in such a policy. Anton Menger, a modern German Socialist writer of an advanced type, thinks that the government of his ideal State may be entrusted to a weak hereditary monarch rather than to a republican president.[1] This, however, was not the view of the French Socialists under the government of Louis Philippe. They tended to be republican because they were aware that no pressure could wring a scheme of socialism out of a selfish bourgeois government. Thus the idea of the Republic began to acquire a new content and significance. Individualists of the old school, who believed in the Republic, either because their fathers had fought for the Revolution, or because the Republic was associated in their minds with military glory and expansion, no longer held the monopoly of that political faith. A new generation had arisen, who worked for the Republic, not on the ground of what it had done in the past, but in the expectation of what it might do in the future. They did not want the old Republic; they wanted La République sociale, with established economic security for every workman in the State.

The two charges which John Stuart Mill brought against the government of Louis Philippe have never been disproved or shaken. First, it was "a government wholly without the spirit of improvement," and second, "it wrought almost exclusively through the meaner and more selfish impulses of mankind." It was stationary and it was corrupt. In a nation of thirty-four millions it was content that the Chamber of Deputies should rest upon an electorate of a quarter of a million votes, and that electors and deputies alike should be subject to every form of official pressure and corrupt inducement. All proposals to widen the franchise were met with an unqualified negative, and it was stated that three circulars upon pauperism addressed by the Minister of the Interior to the prefects constituted the total sum of energy expended by the government upon social amelioration during a period of eighteen years.[2] No government can long subsist upon a policy of negatives. Louis Philippe came to the throne in difficult times. The men of the barricades were consumed with the " maladie de 1815," and it was part of their ideal that the Revolution should triumph abroad as well as at home. To meet the special emergencies of the time a great minister, Casimir Périer, devised what was called the policy of resistance. He made it the principal object of his government to crush revolution at home and to reassure the foreign powers as to the pacific intentions of France. It was a strong, prudent, and necessary course, but it was not a sufficient policy for a dynasty which wished to establish itself in the esteem of a progressive and high-mettled nation. The country demanded more of its government than that it should be able to master the conspiracies of the factory and the riots of the street. It was deeply dissatisfied with a foreign policy which, until the rift over the Spanish marriages, bore the appearance of truckling to England and was afterwards plainly enlisted in the system of reactionary alliances. The one military achievement of the dynasty, the conquest of Algeria, brought no compensation for the tranquil acquiescence in the loss of the Rhine frontier, and for the abandonment of the Italians, the Poles, and the Protestant democrats of Switzerland. Dissatisfaction spread apace. While the general public was shocked by the steady increase of parliamentary placemen, by the revelation of some flagrant cases of political corruption, and by a terrible murder in the highest class of society, the politicians were irritated by the long ascendancy of Guizot. In 1847 the agitation for political reform spread from the Chambers to the country. Reform banquets were organized, speeches were made, and though the movement was professedly constitutional, it was carried out in an atmosphere charged with republican sentiment. The hero of this oratorical campaign was Lamartine,the lyric poet of France, and the author of that sentimental history of the Girondins which had recently been acclaimed by men and women of republican sentiments throughout France.[3]

The foundation of the Second Republic was not contemplated by the organisers of the reform banquets. They wished to break down the dictatorship of " Lord Guizot," to enlarge the franchise, to cure the body politic of corruption, and to open the door to social reforms. They desired a foreign policy neither Ghibelline at Rome and Milan, nor sacerdotal at Berne, nor Austrian in Piedmont, nor Russian in Cracow, but framed upon the very antithesis of this reactionary spirit, and adjusted to the old republican tradition of France. Some of the agitators who spoke at these banquets, notably Ledru-Rollin, were known to cherish republican traditions ; others, like Louis Blanc, were avowed Socialists ; others, like Lamartine, had put out at one time or other in their career large programmes, including universal suffrage, free education, the extinction of an hereditary aristocracy, the separation of Church and State—programmes which were unlikely to be realized under the constitutional monarchy. But if any of these men had been asked at the beginning of February 1848 whether they expected to see a republic within the year, they would certainly have replied in the negative ; and most of the reformers would have added that they would not have it if they could, and that France was neither fit nor willing to receive it. Odilon Barrot depicted the dominant frame of mind when he spoke of his ideal as "a monarchy supported by republican institutions." [4]

A battle in the streets, arising indirectly out of the prohibition of a reform banquet, brought about the resignation of Louis Philippe. He was unmade, as he was made, by the barricades. It was a popular revolt, a revolt of artisans and students, neither led nor supported by the bourgeois, but despite this, conquering Paris with astonishing ease, and owing its victory rather to the lukewarmness of the defence than to the weight and fury of the attack. The three days of February have been described by many eye-witnesses, by De Tocqueville, by Flaubert in his "Éducation sentimentale," and best of all by Maxime du Camp, who went out with Flaubert to watch the fighting in the streets. To him as to many other contemporaries the whole affair was a disgusting surprise. They knew that the government was not very glorious ; but they conceived that it was well enough, and that given a change of ministry and a dose of parliamentary reform, it would be made acceptable to the general sense of the country. On February 23, there were some disturbances in Paris, some processions of students and workmen, an attempted barricade in the Rue St Honoré, and in the night a bonfire of the chairs in the Champs Elysées. Such scenes had not been uncommon in Paris, and the government of Louis Philippe had triumphed over many a more formidable demonstration ; but there was one ominous sign.   The National Guard was on the side of Parliamentary Reform.   When the *rappel* was beaten on the afternoon of the 23rd, only six hundred of the eight thousand men of the second legion came to the Mairie, and on the following day the news was more disquieting still, for the guard turned out in the morning with cries of *Vive la Réforme*.   Upon this Louis Philippe took the step which he should have taken before, he dismissed Guizot and sent for Molé. When the news spread through the capital there was a general sense of relief.   Houses were illuminated. People went mad with joy.   Groups of men rushed through the streets carrying paper lanterns and crying, *Vive la Réforme ! A bas Guizot !* The crisis seemed to be surmounted.   The great obstruction to the impatient flood of reform had been removed.   Suddenly, towards ten in the evening, the sharp crackle of musketry rang out into the air.   A detachment of the 14th regiment of the line, posted before the Ministry of Foreign Affairs in the Rue des Capucines, had fired a volley into the crowd.   A Corsican sergeant, by name Giacomoni, fired the first shot. " What followed," writes De la Normandie, an eye-witness, " is indescribable.   In an instant the road emptied.   Some twenty dead and thirty wounded lay on the ground.   The first movement of stupor over-past, the crowd returned, howling, exasperated, in a paroxysm of fury.   It took up the corpses, escorted them through the streets by torchlight, crying, ' Vengeance ! Treason ! To arms ! ' " [5] The grisly procession did its work.   Gun-shops were rifled ; pavements taken up ; the church bells sounded, and before daybreak sixteen hundred barricades were up in Paris.

Had Louis Philippe been a strong man, he would have levelled every paving stone of the barricades before making a concession to rebellion. But he was old, stricken by the recent death of the Princess Adelaide, his sister and principal support, and honourably averse from shedding the blood of his subjects. He appointed Marshal Bugeaud to command the troops, and then obstructed the only plan of action which would have led to certain success. Almost to the end he believed that an excited mob could be pacified by soft words and promises of reform and dissolution. Then, as the storm of the insurrection beat up against the Tuileries, he signed a deed of resignation in favour of his grandson, and appointed the Duchess of Orleans Regent of the kingdom. "Eh bien! Puisqu'on le veut, j'abdique." It was not heroism; but at least it was fatigue and common-sense.

The Republic was announced a few hours later. Immediately upon the conquest of the Tuileries a band of advanced Republicans swooped down on the Hôtel de Ville and proceeded to appoint a Mayor for Paris and a Committee of Public Safety for France. On the same day and almost at the same hour two distinct governments were constructed in different buildings in Paris. The Hôtel de Ville government was Socialist, devised in the office of *La Réforme*; the Palais Bourbon government individualist, and drawn up by the more conservative politicians who wrote for the *Nationale*. Had the issue then and there been decided by force, the extremists would probably have prevailed; but Lamartine, whose eloquence and renown had given him the leadership in the Palais Bourbon on that critical afternoon, was determined to avoid a struggle. With a capacity for action rare, if not unique, among poëts, he marched to the Hôtel de Ville, disarmed the authority of the Socialist commune by accepting three of its members, Blanc, Marrast, and Albert, as secretaries to the provisional government, and took the decisive step of proclaiming the Republic.

As the royal family drove off along the quays, the Duchess, leading her little boy by the hand, walked to the Palais Bourbon and appealed to the chivalry of the Legislature of France. But the Revolution was master of the city, and though the Chamber would probably have voted the Regency had it been a free agent, an armed mob bursting in at the doors and windows compelled it to name the members of a provisional government.

Such was the birth of the Second Republic. It was launched on the world by the pressure of the Paris mob, and without any knowledge on the part of its principal promoters whether it would be acceptable to the general body of the nation. So surprising and thorough was the success of the Revolution that the Republic was greeted with lyrical enthusiasm as heralding the dawn of a new age, not only for France but for humanity in general. In a few days Louis Philippe was so thoroughly expunged from memory that he might, as De Tocqueville remarks, have belonged to the Merovingian dynasty. Every ingenious wit about town was busy constructing his Utopia—one in newspapers, another in placards, a third in posters, a fourth in open-air harangues. " A proposed to destroy the inequality of fortunes, B the inequality of intelligence, C the most ancient inequality of all, the inequality of men and women. Specifics against poverty and remedies against work, the evil which has tormented humanity since its beginning, were proposed." [6]

The Provisional Government, of which Dupont de l'Eure was the nominal head, but Lamartine the soul and spirit, was faced with a crisis of extraordinary peril and perplexity. In a city seething with the ferment of successful revolution, it was debarred by its own antecedents and credentials from the employment of armed force. Three of its members, with what measure of support behind them no man could calculate, were hotly impelling their colleagues down the paths of Socialism. Another body of opinion, enthusiastically held and more strictly belonging to the republican tradition of the country, urged the instant undertaking of a crusade to relieve the suffering peoples of Europe from the tyrants who oppressed them. Again and again the government was besieged by organized mobs and compelled to make promises which it was no part of wisdom to perform. Yet, despite many difficulties and not a few mistakes, these men who, without any preparatory experience, suddenly found themselves called to conduct the government of a great country, exhibited a truer apprehension of the highest states-manship than all the experienced parliamentarians of the Guizot *régime*. They did away with slavery in the French colonies, abolished the death penalty for political offences, made an end of imprisonment for debt, legalized trades unions, and decreed that the future Chamber should be elected on a system of uni-versal suffrage. To the finer parts of the republican tradition they were true ; the dangerous or deplorable elements they were emphatic to reject. They adumbrated a scheme of free primary education ; they declined to be drawn into a war of propaganda or to admit that the guillotine is the lawful arbiter of political difference. While thus attempting to clear the name of the Republic from the legacy of suspicion which it had inherited from the past, they were anxious not to be drawn into the madcap raid upon the principles of property. Lamartine rejected the red flag of Socialism as the emblem of the new Republic. " The tricolour," he said finely, " has made the round of the world, the red flag has only made the round of the Champ de Mars ! " At the same time concessions were made under pressure to Louis Blanc and his following. The State guaranteed work to all citizens, and proceeded to establish national workshops to carry out this tremendous undertaking.[7]

A people which, ever since the sixteenth century, has possessed State workhouses, cannot complain of the French for accepting the principle of the *droit au travail*. It is, however, a principle which, unless it be accompanied by a number of most essential safeguards, is liable to obvious abuse. The experiment of the *ateliers nationaux*, as it was tried in Paris, could not but lead to disaster. The work provided was easy, unproductive, and overpaid, accompanied by no restrictions on liberty, and presenting every form of seduction most calculated to destroy the industry and independence of the working classes. In a few weeks more than a hundred thousand artisans were engaged in doing work which nobody wanted for salaries which the State could ill afford to pay, and to the serious dislocation of private industrial enterprise. To secure discipline the men were organized on a military plan in battalions and companies, and the Provisional Government seems to have cherished the idea that if it came to a conflict with the Red Socialists, the national workshops would be on the side of property. How great was this delusion was soon made apparent.

On returning to his estate in Normandy, De Tocqueville asked his steward what was thought of the Revolution. The man, who was himself half a peasant, replied that when the peasantry learnt that Louis Philippe had been given his discharge they said that it was well and that he deserved it ; but afterwards, learning of the disorders in Paris, of the new taxes, of the possibility of a general war, seeing that commerce was at a standstill, that money was hiding itself, and especially when they heard that the principle of property was attacked, they experienced a revulsion of feeling. In this report of De Tocqueville's steward we have the chief explanation of the downfall of the Second Republic. The country was not prepared for the Republic and was thoroughly alarmed at the prospect of Socialism. No nation fortunate enough to possess a large landed proprietary will readily accept a government which spreads a feeling of insecurity about land. Accordingly, when the Constituent Assembly met in Paris on May 4, and it was the first Assembly in Europe to be elected upon a system of direct universal suffrage, it was found to be a body of a thoroughly conservative complexion. De Tocqueville remarks that no French legislature had ever contained so many nobles, clergy, or large proprietors. Some four hundred out of a total of eight hundred and forty members were monarchists, and no fact was of greater significance than that Louis Blanc and Ledru-Rollin, who were regarded as the chieftains of the Socialist and Radical doctrine, were returned at the bottom of the Parisian list.

The Assembly, having no other option, was prepared to accept the Republic, but it was very clearly determined that it would have nothing to do with Socialism.

The struggle which ensued was one of the most terrible of which a civilized capital has ever been witness. Ever since the February Revolution, the workmen of Paris had been excited by the golden prospect of a complete reversal of social conditions : the poor were going to be rich, the rich were going to be poor ; the scullery maid would go in her mistress's silks, and the page boy would live upon the wings of the chicken. There was to be no more unemployment, no more exploitation, no more misery. The rich should be taxed to support the poor, and the Republic of equals should march off to help the Poles, and destroy all the tyrannies in Europe. In every political meeting—and the men who were employed in the national workshops were able to devote half their time to political discussions—these ideas formed part of the common stock of oratory. On May 15, a great mob, excited by the news of the sufferings of Poland, invaded the Chamber, decreed its dissolution, and declared war against the kings of Europe. Fortunately, the National Guard arrived in time to rescue the deputies and to restore order. The unpleasant experience revealed the necessity of taking strong measures. The leading conspirators were imprisoned, and on June 21, the government took the strong but necessary step of dissolving the national workshops. Then an insurrection began which lasted for three days and is known in history as the days of June. The insurgents fought without a war-cry, without chiefs, without flags, but with an organization little short of marvellous, and with a fierceness and courage which could not be surpassed. On the night of June 23, half Paris was in their hands, and before Cavaignac's army had reconquered it, ten thousand men had been killed or wounded in the struggle, and more French officers had lost their lives than in any of the most glorious victories of the First Empire.

On the day on which the Tuileries was captured a crowd collected round a statue of Spartacus in the Tuileries garden and crowned it with a red cap of liberty made out of the cloth which had been torn from the throne of Louis Philippe. The Spartacus who led the great servile war of June, if indeed there was any single leader of that desperate enterprise of organized poverty, is unknown to us. The Revolution was as anonymous as a convulsion of nature : it sprang up, like the sudden spurt of a volcano, spread desolation, and was then extinguished. For this very reason it left a deeper mark upon the public mind than if it had been the work of an organized and palpable political organization. Were the elemental fires so incalculable, so fierce, so close beneath the crust of convention ? A panic spread through the country which was not the least among the psychological conditions which brought about the Second Empire.

In the midst of these terrible anxieties a committee of the Assembly sat down to draft a constitution. Its most distinguished member, Alexis de Tocqueville, informs us that the discussion was poor and perfunctory, the main object being to construct some sort of government, the stronger the better, with as little delay as possible. A month of intermittent work, a report which many of the Committee had not read, and then a full dress debate in the Assembly, in the course of which the most important question of all was decided by an irrelevant flight of rhetoric, and the Second Republic was duly constituted. The first question which had to be determined was whether the Legislature should consist of one or of two Chambers.

The Directory had two Chambers, the monarchy had two Chambers, the American Republic had two Chambers. De Tocqueville advanced the arguments for the bicameral system which are familiar to every student of constitutional questions ; but he was beaten in the Committee and in the Chamber. " Two Chambers with a President," exclaimed Garnier-Pagès, " is the image of royalty. I want a single Chamber because I want a strong Chamber, a Chamber capable of resisting the executive power. By craft or force that power had always mastered us. The Committee of Public Safety devoured the Convention as Bonaparte devoured the Councils." These arguments prevailed. That the monarchy had two Chambers was felt to be a very particular reason why the Republic, which must be different, should have one; and to this intelligible but irrational prejudice was added the suspicion that were two Chambers established, the executive would be able to establish a tyranny by playing one off against the other.

As to the Executive power itself it was generally agreed to vest it in a single person. There was to be a President of the French, as there was already a President of the American Republic. The troubled experience of France during recent months had not improved the reputation of plural executives. It was a plural executive which had sanctioned the right to labour, formed the national workshops, and permitted a formidable insurrection to break out in Paris. It was a single executive, a military dictator, who had rescued France in the days of June. On all hands then the Presidential system was admitted, and no one can doubt that, in deciding to have a President, the Chamber was taking a prudent step. The success of the experi-

ment would, however, entirely depend upon the nature
of the safeguards provided against the conversion of
the Presidency into a despotism.   France was a
country with monarchical traditions and a centralized
administration.   " In France," writes De Tocqueville,
" there is only one thing which cannot be created, and
that is a free government, only one thing which cannot
be destroyed, and that is centralization."   A President
of the French Republic, controlling the administration,
directing the thousands of functionaries who spread
the name and influence of the central power through
every household in the country, could not fail to be
a very powerful person and might easily be a very
dangerous person.   Especially would this be the case if
the President was elected by the direct suffrages of the
people upon a plan adopted from America.   He would
then exercise a power co-ordinate with that of the
Legislature, and, as himself the direct representative
of the people, might defy with impunity a body whose
title to represent the sovereign will was necessarily less
distinct than his own.   Either then the presidential
power should have been expressly limited, or an
attempt should have been made to decentralize the
administration, or the election of the President should
have been entrusted to the Chamber.   No one of these
courses was pursued.   The Constituent Assembly
desired a strong executive and was averse to interference with that " modest action of the *sous-préfet*,"
which, according to one orator, was the barrier against
the recrudescence of feudalism, and according to
another, had prevented Alsace and Lorraine from becoming German.   But the fatal step was taken when
Lamartine threw in his lot with those who advocated
that the Head of the State should be directly elected

by universal suffrage. That vote gave the Presidency to Louis Bonaparte and prepared the way for the Second Empire.[8]

It is easy to scoff at the Second Republic, its origin, its illusions and errors, its swift and complete catastrophe ; and those who follow through the newspapers and pamphlets of the time the story of the first few weeks, when a generous wave of emotion was passing over Paris and everything seemed possible which the imagination of humanitarian fancy could suggest, when the clergy were blessing trees of liberty, and Georges Sand from her sordid attic in the Rue de Condé was pouring out her fevered dreams for universal regeneration, and good-humoured jests were flying about concerning Louis File-vite, and politics were governed by the phrases of a lyric poet, will not be the last to feel the full force of the ironic contrast. But the experiment of the Second Republic was not without a permanent effect on the political tradition of the country. It brought with it universal suffrage ; it introduced the presidential system, and it exhibited the fact that within the circle of republicans there were two distinct currents, one bourgeois, the other socialist ; one desiring to defend the bureaucracy, the land laws, the capitalistic system, the other desiring to overthrow them. To thoughtful minds it suggested the conclusion long ago anticipated by Condorcet that a republic would never be firmly established unless it were supported by a system of free secular education. But the effects of the Revolution of February were not limited to France itself ; they extended with the gravest developments to every animated polity of the Continent.

CHAPTER IX

ITALY

Hither, O stranger, that cry for her
Holding your lives in your hands,
Hither, for here is your light,
Where Italy is, and her might;
Strength shall be given you to fight,
Grace shall be given you to die for her,
For the flower, for the lady of lands.
SWINBURNE, " The Halt before Rome "

THERE is no more remarkable example in history of the contagious quality of ideas than the sudden spread of revolutionary excitement through Europe in 1848. In the course of a few weeks the established order seemed everywhere to be crumbling to pieces. The Revolution began in Palermo, crossed the Straits of Messina, and passed in successive waves of convulsion through Central Italy to Paris, Vienna, Milan, and Berlin. It has often been remarked that the Latin races are of all the peoples of Europe most prone to revolution ; but this proposition did not hold good in 1848. The Czechs in Bohemia, the Magyars in Hungary, the Germans in Austria rose against the paralysing encumbrance of the Hapsburg autocracy. The Southern Slavs dreamed of an Illyrian kingdom ; the Germans of a united Germany ; the Bohemians of a union of all the Slavonic peoples of Europe. The authority of the Austrian Empire, the pivot of the European autocracy, had never been so rudely

13

challenged, and if the Crown succeeded in recovering its shattered authority it was due to the dumb and unintelligent loyalty of its Slavonic troops.

In all these movements, which were complex as all movements must be which spread over several countries, there was a republican element. At different times during the course of two tumultuous years republics were proclaimed in France and Hungary, in Baden, Venice, and Rome. The chances for republicanism in Europe were never so good ; the spirit of the Republic was never so widely diffused ; the prestige of monarchy was never so low. To account for these circumstances there is no need to look much beyond the character, policy, and influence of Prince Metternich. Born in the Rhine provinces and having experienced in early manhood the evils of the French Revolution, Metternich had made it the guiding principle of his life to uphold the forces of order against the powers which make for political and social upheaval. He had seen Austria vanquished, humiliated, stripped of her fairest provinces by the great captain of revolutionary France, and the lesson sank deep into his soul. When Bonaparte was beaten and the Austrian Empire recovered its position, it was Metternich's aim so to direct the governments of central Europe that all free political thinking should be forthwith impossible. He provided Germany with a slow unworkable Federal Constitution exactly calculated to check the tide of national aspirations and to secure the ascendency of Austria. He resisted the grant of constitutions to the several States. At the first symptom of popular effervescence he worked upon the German governments to muzzle the Press and the universities.

And this repressive influence, which was exerted effectually enough in the German federation, was worked with a yet greater degree of minute particularity in the hereditary States of Austria. Here no book, paper, or pamphlet of a liberal tendency was admitted. Here there was neither parliament nor any minor organ for the expression of local grievances. The Government was a pure bureaucracy and was intended to exhibit to the world the model of a stationary and orderly State. Such a policy could not endure. The world was moving on and Austria stood still. It is impossible to draw a spiritual cordon round a great people. The Teutonic races felt, doubtless in a less degree than the French and Italians, but still in a notable measure, the liberal impulses of the world. They followed the liberation of South America; they marked the triumph of Greece and the success of Belgium; they were immediately affected by the fall of Charles X. of France. The cause of monarchy incarnate in such men as Louis Philippe and Frederick William IV. of Prussia and Ferdinand of Austria, so far from appearing sacred, was not even dignified. It was a not uncommon opinion that the monarchies of Europe were anomalous obstacles which it was the duty of a vigorous and enlightened civilization to clear away from its path.

It is needless to say that there had never been an Italian republic. The republican tradition of the country, such as it was, was civic and separatist, not national or making for consolidation, but as the spirit of the French Revolution sped through the country with its disintegrating doctrine of the Rights of Man, these ancient maxims of collective and honourable egotism became unfashionable with that class which is affected by literary movements. The Italian republican of the new school was the citizen of an ideal democracy, the geographical frontiers of which it was irrelevant to determine. In his library you would find French books and French pamphlets, and the careful analyst might trace the stream of his political reflection to its fountain head in some old file of Girondin newspapers full of that radiant cosmopolitan eloquence which captured the young heart of Giuseppe Mazzini. The downfall of the Napoleonic Empire could not interrupt the progress of a type of thinking which was fixed in the political consciousness of Europe. The Revolution continued, but it was driven underground and made to take many undesirable and obscurantist forms. The Italian republican of the Restoration period joined the society of the Carbonari—a body which had developed out of Freemasonry in the kingdom of Naples during the French period, and which not only spread its network over the whole Italian peninsula but possessed affiliated branches in other countries as well. It is the nemesis of despotism that it degrades those who oppose as well as those who serve it. The Carbonaro was bound to implicit obedience and served an organization which combined with the new and wholesome spirit of liberalism not a little of the ancient venom of the Italian vendetta. By degrees, as the society became more cosmopolitan, as its ritual became more elaborate and esoteric, it lost whatever educational value it may once have possessed ; and the cause of Italian liberalism, discredited by the failures of 1820 and 1831, was far fallen when it was raised on to a higher plane by the moral genius of Mazzini. Among all patriotic and enlightened Italians it was

common ground that the Austrians must be driven beyond the Alps. It was bad enough that they should
occupy the two splendid provinces of Lombardy
and Venetia, but even worse that behind every
corrupt and backward government of Italy there was
this overwhelming support of unintelligent and alien
power. So long as the Whitecoat garrisons were
quartered in the valley of the Po, no attempt to obtain
reformation in the States of the Church or in the
Kingdom of Naples could be carried out. Of this fact
there had already been two flagrant and painful
demonstrations. In 1820 the Austrians had crushed
the constitutional movements in Naples and Piedmont ; and eleven years later, when the Romagna
burst out into insurrection against the intolerable
government of the Papal legates, the same sinister
interposition baffled the cause of enlightenment and
reform. Judged indeed by her government of
Lombardy and Venetia, Austria should not be described
either as a barbarous or as a cruel power ; but her
mission was to be stationary, and her removal was
therefore an essential preliminary to the vital and
wholesome progress of the Italian people.

So far the patriots were agreed. Beyond there was
room for every variety of hypothetical construction and political ideal. Some desired an Italian
federation under the Pope ; others an Italian
monarchy ; others a federation of republics ; others
a unitary State on republican lines. Of those who
professed this last opinion no one was so eminent
or influential as Mazzini. The son of a Genoese doctor,
Mazzini was born in 1808 while Italy was still under
the French dominion. As a member of an ancient
city republic, he was suckled in the historic tradition

of civic freedom and in that peculiar distrust of the neighbouring monarchy of Piedmont which was the heirloom of centuries of bitter contest.   He grew up in an atmosphere of patriotic resolves and shrouded counsels.   The sight of the fugitives of the foiled insurrection of 1821 begging their bread in the streets of Genoa fired his austere and generous imagination. From that day to the end of his life he went clothed in black, wearing perpetual mourning for Italy.   He became a Carbonaro, suffered imprisonment and exile, and lived a life of constant conspiracy and patriotic propaganda.   In the eyes of Europe his name was a symbol of revolution : to his fellow-countrymen he stood out as the prophet of the Italian Republic.

It is a fallacy, nowhere more completely exposed than in the case of Mazzini, to imagine that the great human influences in the sphere of politics must necessarily be exerted by statesmen.   Few men constantly occupying themselves with politics have been so devoid of statesmanship as Mazzini.   His estimate of the political forces of his time was almost always wrong ; his particular plans almost always miscarried ; his horoscope of the future was signally falsified in the event.   The spirit of accommodation and compromise, the recognition that life presents but a choice of evils, qualities essential to successful statesmanship, were alien to his proud and lofty temperament.   At an early period of his life he convinced himself that the Republic, being the only form of government in which the popular will was faithfully expressed, was the only pure and perfect polity ; and then with a mystic belief in the destinies own land, nourished not only by the study of the classics but by a profound and exalted passion for Dante, he concluded that this perfect form must be designed for Italy. To those who held out for a monarchy he would reply, firstly that the old Italian tradition was republican, and secondly that there was no means of adjusting the rival claims of the Piedmontese and Neapolitan crowns. That the Piedmontese monarchy would ever be worthy to unite Italy was a supposition entertained at one fitful moment and then rejected and combated with blind and unflinching ardour. What indeed was Piedmont ? An autocratic priest-ridden State, without culture or light, which had absorbed the Republic of Genoa and persecuted the Carbonari.

Having once fixed this impression of Piedmont in his mind, Mazzini never changed it. He would not appreciate the series of great and fruitful measures by which, under the guidance of Cavour, Piedmont became the most progressive State in Italy ; and when in 1870 the Sardinian King entered Rome and the scattered members were at last gathered together in a single body, the triumph of a union so accomplished was to Mazzini the tragic inversion of his sacred and most cherished hope.

The real clue to Mazzini's power lies not in any faculty of adjusting means to ends, but in the much rarer quality of sustained moral elevation. He was great, not because he could show people how to circumvent difficulties, but because he could persuade people to confront them. The ordinary rules of political arithmetic had little meaning for a man who consistently weighed practical possibilities in the scale of his moral convictions. Some men win confidence by steady and substantial gifts of judgment, others by the force of a coherent philosophy, others again by some charm or glitter of eloquence ; but Mazzini belonged to no one of these classes. The source of his influence was the same as that which has furnished the saints and martyrs of the Church, the unfaltering conviction of a devoted and beautiful nature. Although his sphere of activity was political, the type of his genius was not political, but religious or prophetic. Hobbes thought that religion was part of law, Mazzini held that politics was part of religion. He did not therefore agree with Quinet, who traced the failure of the French Revolution to its refusal to cut itself adrift from the Catholic Church. Rather he viewed the Revolution as the last stage in the evolution of Christianity, a religion, as he conceived it, of sublimated egotism destined to give way before a higher type. The failure of the French Revolution, for he could not but acknowledge that the failure was disastrous, was due to the fact that it insisted upon rights, not upon duties ; upon individuality, not upon association. The Republic of the French was a temple of all the egoisms. The new Republic would be established upon a nobler foundation and a more positive faith. In a letter which shows a strange inability to penetrate into the life of alien institutions, Mazzini invites the Pope to abandon Roman Catholicism and to inaugurate the religion of the future, a creed of which the citizens of the Republic would be the only priests, and the practice of the Republic the only ritual. It was part of Mazzini's patriotic optimism to maintain that Rome would be the centre of that new stream of political illumination which would spread through Europe, and that Italy, under the guiding hand of Providence, being destined to provide the first type of the ideal Republic would reconquer her old position as the schoolmistress of European civilization. The new Republic would not teach Socialism which was material, but association which was spiritual. It would not cry up wages, but exalt character; it would not achieve economic equality, but establish moral unity. States may be prosperous and self-centred; living upon a low plane of duty and disinterestedness they may show a fine surplus and a long array of peaceful and unruffled generations; but such was not to be the ignoble destiny of the Italian Republic. That visionary polity was to be a fashioning tool for the moral improvement of the races of Europe. So far from wrapping itself in the selfish doctrine of non-intervention, it would throw the whole force of its vivid and spirited sympathy into all the great human causes of the world. It would help the Poles and Hungarians to be free. The electric shock of its moral conviction and military ardour would bring the monarchies of Continental Europe quivering to the ground. From Italy would spread the religion of the Republic, a doctrine founded on Theism and on a belief in the invisible but benign hand of Providence effecting its large and splendid purpose through the dark and perplexed tissues of human history.

Such in outline was the creed of the new Republic, a creed deriving some of its elements from the Ghibelline vision of Dante, others from the radical Catholicism of Lamennais, and, as Mazzini preached it, so in essentials was its spirit absorbed by thousands of young Italians who, without the transforming power of that high idealism, would have been delivered up to a soulless rage against priestcraft and tyranny.

Mazzini did not work miracles. He neither m
the Republic nor came within measurable dista
of making it. He could not liberate Italian pol
from mean ambitions or violent appetites or f
its inveterate malady of jealous suspicion.
intervention in affairs was often fatally injured l
disastrous intolerance, leading him to disbel
that history or morals could be patient of any c
solution but his own. But if he suffered from
limitations of the fanatic, he had also the un
power which belongs to a life strung upon a si
idea. He made Italy a moral unity, before
Piedmontese monarchy made it a political u:
A young obscure exile, he launched a propag:
which inflamed every Italian heart not alr
close sealed against the generous appeal of patriot
The Association of Young Italy was founded
garret in Marseilles, and designed to replace the
symbols of the Carbonari by a reasoned and instru
faith in the past and the future of Italy. Comme
by Mazzini's eloquent pen, the *Giovane Italia* raj
conquered adherents, and the republican movem
of the '48 with their youthful ecstasies of lyric
thusiasm are in no small measure the products c
missionary enterprise.[1]

The Italian Revolution of 1848 is the result n
a single stream but of many converging curr
Monarchists and republicans combined with lib
of every type and shade of opinion in a simultar
protest against the Austrian rule with all its
wholesome corollaries. Unfortunately the con
aversion from the Hapsburgs was not suffici
strong to efface the internal animosities and divi
of Italy. Instead of beating the enemy first and

settling upon the political organization of the country
the Italians confounded the two operations with
fatal results. While the struggle was still undecided
in the North, the Piedmontese government invited
the provinces of Lombardy and Venetia to declare
by means of a *plébiscite* whether or no they would
consent to be fused in the Piedmontese monarchy.
At a time when the attention of all Italy should have
been concentrated on the war, it was diverted to the
consideration of a grave political issue. The spine
of Italian resistance to Austria was the royal army of
Piedmont, and the monarchists not unreasonably
claimed the two Austrian provinces as the legitimate
prize of a royal victory. To the republicans on the
other hand such an attempt to prejudge the destinies
of Italy was, of all omens, the most sinister. They were
in no mood to sacrifice person and purse only that
Piedmont might be enabled to devour another leaf of
the Milanese artichoke. They were full of distrust of
Charles Albert. His record was dubious, dark, and
vacillating ; his hands were embrued with the blood
of patriots ; he was not clean of the taint of priest-
craft ; a paroxysm of dark superstition might throw
him back into the ranks of the clerical coalition and
leave his republican allies exposed to the furies of
Austria. Such suspicions and forebodings were not
uncommon and received some encouragement from
the radical papers in Milan. At the crisis of
her fate, when unanimity was of all things most
precious, the national movement was marred by bitter
suspicion and active recrimination.

The idea of a united Italy, whether organized upon a
monarchical or a republican plan, was not yet within
the compass of practical politics. It was hardly

likely that the Catholic world would tolerate the
disappearance of the Papal State, or that the Cabinets
of Europe would calmly acquiesce in the formation
of a united Italian polity.   Charles Albert himself
never dreamed of anything more ambitious than a
territory extending from the Alps to the Adriatic,
and a Piedmontese monarchy thus extended in the
north might co-exist with a variety of minor States
in the centre and south of the Peninsula.

In August 1848 the Piedmontese army was severely
defeated at Custozza, and the King compelled to sign
an armistice at Salasco. The Austrians were again
masters of Milan, and, with reaction triumphing in
Naples and France, the prospects of the Italian Revolution were indeed slender.   But in the midst of a
prospect, generally black and stormy, there were two
points of bright light.   The city of Venice, under the
inspiring direction of Daniele Manin, a Jewish lawyer,
had already thrown off the Austrian yoke, and had
signified its readiness to accept the dominion of
Piedmont when the armistice of Salasco suddenly
interrupted its purpose. Finding itself abandoned
by the Piedmontese, the Venetian government had a
fair and honourable excuse for making terms with the
Austrians.   But while they were resigned to fight
under the colours of Sardinia, the Venetians were yet
more eager to show that fifty years of servitude had
not extinguished the memory of ancient liberty, and
the lieges of St Mark determined to prolong a life of
gallant and desperate independence as a republic.
For a year the city of lagoons bade defiance to a great
and well-appointed army, which found to its cost
that one of the most languid and luxurious communities in Europe could be steeled to endure priva-

tions in the cause of freedom.   Eight thousand white-
coats perished in a siege which redeemed the name of
the Republic of St Mark and enlisted the admiration
of liberal Europe.[2]

And a not dissimilar scene was enacted in another
quarter of Italy.   The city of Rome had been a prey
to violent political excitement ever since the accession
of Pio Nono in 1846 had aroused expectations of
radical reform.   Clubs were formed ; crowds were
addressed by itinerant orators and schooled under the
shadow of St Peter's in the ways and words of revolution.   The outbreak of the war with Austria increased
the confusion in a city which had long been divorced
from the steady practice of politics.   The Pope, who
in quiet times would have been well disposed to liberal
courses, was not inclined to burn his fingers in a
struggle with the greatest Catholic power in Europe.
To the patriots who clamoured wildly for war, he
replied with an allocution which committed the
Papal State to an inglorious policy of peace.   From
that moment a revolutionary situation arose.   The
Roman democrats could find nothing good in a policy
of moderate constitutional reform accompanied by a
betrayal of the larger interests of Italy ; and, in the
fury of party passions, Rossi, the minister who represented the unpopular policies of peace and moderation,
was foully murdered on the steps of the Chamber.   A
few weeks afterwards (November 24) the Pope fled from
the Quirinal and sought refuge from the tumults of
Rome in the Neapolitan fortress of Gaeta.   It was only
then, after it had been abandoned by the Pope and
was thrown upon its own resources, that the city of
Rome showed that its politics were not all compounded
of sordid and violent elements.   With the failure of

the campaign in the north a wave of republican patriotism spread downwards through Italy. There was a revolution in Genoa, a second in Leghorn, a third in Florence where the progress of patriotic democracy was so triumphant as to oblige the Grand Duke of Tuscany to flee from his dominions. In these circumstances it is not wonderful that the City of Rome should have formally repudiated the sovereignty of the Pope. It was heartily sick of the mixture of incompetence, cruelty, and superstition which had so long been offered it in lieu of a government. It saw, or rather the guiding spirits of the movement saw, that there was a radical incompatibility between Italian patriotism and Papal rule. But it was one thing to escape from Papal bondage and another to construct a substantial polity in its place. A Parliament elected by universal suffrage met on February 5, 1849. Mamiani argued that the future of the Roman State should be determined by a Constituent Assembly summoned to decide upon the fate of all Italy; but this view, since it involved delay, was overborne by the impatient clamour of the democrats, and amidst a scene of wild excitement it was decided that a Roman Republic should be forthwith proclaimed.

A few weeks went by, and then began the most memorable struggle in the annals of modern Italy. The republican movement in Tuscany, never widely popular, had been crushed, before it had time to establish itself, by the combined opposition of the priests and the peasantry. Piedmont had stamped out the revolution in Genoa, and was herself utterly beaten on the field of Novara; and there remained only Venice and Rome to stem the rising tide of reaction. At this juncture the Roman Republic was assisted by the two most remarkable Italians of that time, Garibaldi and Mazzini. They were both convinced Republicans, both ardent patriots, but in all other respects as different from one another as two men can be. Mazzini had been brought up in the glories of Italian literature, and was himself one of the finest masters of a pure and elastic Italian prose. Garibaldi was a child not of books but of nature. His youth had been spent upon the waters of the Levant, his early manhood had passed amid the exciting struggles of South America, where he had served the cause of liberty both on sea and land. He had now returned to his beloved Italy, the hero of a thousand adventures and an accomplished master of irregular warfare. Of politics as a science of government he knew nothing, for his mind was constituted in a few simple propositions based upon a corresponding number of profound and passionate instincts. He hated priests, he worshipped liberty ; he was determined, if he could, to make Italy a free republic. With his following of brawny redshirts, their heads covered with conical-shaped hats decked wih black waving plumes, their long unkempt hair flowing over their shoulders, their shaggy beards and bare necks, he seemed to have brought the wild air of the Pampas into the marble capital of the ancient world.

The enemy was France. To conciliate the Catholic vote, Louis Bonaparte, the new President of the French Republic, determined that the Pope must be restored to Rome by French arms. A force under General Oudinot was dispatched to Civita Vecchia, and the Roman Republic was faced with the alternative of a politic surrender or a forlorn resistance. Mazzini had

no hesitation. " It was essential," he wrote aft
wards, " to redeem Rome ; to place her once ag
at the summit, so that the Italians might again le
to regard her as the temple of their common countr
The battalions of the National Guard defiled in fr
of the Palace of the Assembly with shouts of " Guer
Guerra ! " drowning the timid scruples of their leac
in a great insurgent wave of warlike exciteme
The French were told that the Roman Republic wo
fight, and learned on April 30 that it could fight w
success.   Then an interval ensued during which
French general obtained substantial -reinforceme:
while the Roman triumvirs were amused by an
hibition of insincere diplomacy.   The attack '
renewed on June 4, and for twenty-six days "
degenerate remnant of the Roman people," as
was styled by the *Times* newspaper, held out agai
the schooled battalions of France.   It was no m
artillery duel.   " I saw Garibaldi," wrote En:
Dandolo, describing the last battle of the siege, " spi
forward with his drawn sword shouting a popi
hymn."   But at last weight of numbers and wei
of guns prevailed over the careless enthusiasm of
Roman   volunteers.   On   June   30,   S.   Pietro
Montorio was in the hands of the French, and G
baldi announced to the Roman Assembly that i
few hours the French guns could reduce the city
ashes.   There was then no choice but to yield.

The chronicle of republican failure ends wit
brilliant and romantic epilogue.   Garibaldi was
cided never to surrender his sword to a foreigner u:
Italian soil.   Riding into the Piazza of St Peter's
invited all who wished to follow him.   " I offer,"
said, " neither pay nor quarters nor provisions.

offer hunger, thirst, forced marches, battle, and death." Four thousand men elected to follow him on the desperate chance that they might rally Central Italy to their cause and relieve the blockade of Venice. The army of the retreat struck across the Apennines with French and Austrians, Neapolitans, Spaniards, and Tuscans thrown into the scale against it. Its numbers rapidly dwindled, and as town after town declared its opposition or neutrality the chances of making an effective stroke for Venice or Italy melted away. Upon the immediate political situation the forced marches and hairbreadth escapes of Garibaldi had no perceptible effect. The last survivors were hunted down like wild beasts, and the restored government of the Papacy was no whit the weaker or less intolerant for this splendid demonstration of republican courage. Yet in the long series of conflicts which marked the regeneration of Italy there is no incident which has made a deeper impression upon the Italian heart than the retreat of Garibaldi's four thousand men, with its romantic incidents, its thrilling vicissitudes, and its tragic close.[3]

The republican experiments of these two years were not without their permanent effects. Though the papal government was restored in Rome, the Pope had been exhibited as the enemy of Italy and as the friend of foreign powers, and the moral foundations of the Temporal Power were proportionally impaired. To obtain Rome as the capital of a free Italy became henceforth a leading principle of the Republican creed. At the same time it had become clear to all who were possessed of sound political judgment that the liberation of Italy could not be effected on the Mazzinian plan. Spirited as the Republican parties had proved

14

themselves to be, they could never be a match for the leagued powers of theocracy. Mazzini had despised foreign alliances, and contended that guerilla warfare among the mountains would, if conducted with persistence, be sufficient to secure the freedom of his country. That idea was now exploded. Manin, who possessed a real instinct for statesmanship, learned from his experience as Dictator of Venice, that Italy could not be helped out of bondage without the army of Piedmont and the support of France. Accordingly, in the succeeding decade the Republican party loses the allegiance of the best Italian minds. The National Society organized by La Farina succeeds to the place once occupied by Mazzini's " Young Italy "; and as the constitutional government of Piedmont embarks on a course of active improvement, the intractable democracy of the older generation gives place to a spirit of patriotic opportunism, willing to take as the war-cry of the future, " Italy and Victor Emmanuel."

CHAPTER X

THE GERMAN REVOLUTION

O Namen, Namen festlich wie Siegesgesang !
Tell ! Hermann ! Klopstock ! Brutus ! Timoleon !
O ihr, wem freie Seele Gott gab,
Flammend ins cherne Herz gegraben
—STOLBERG, " Die Freiheit," 1775

Quand les hommes s'attroupent, les oreilles s'allongent.—
VOLTAIRE

IF we look back to Germany as it stood on the brink of this Revolution, we see a country which, despite flourishing schools and universities, was paralysed by the most irrational constitution in Europe. In Russia, in France, in Spain, in Piedmont, in the Kingdom of Naples, there was a national government which could levy money, raise armies, and make treaties. In Germany the sovereign power was divided among thirty-six States, some great, others small, but all tenacious of their respective rights, and solicitous to preserve them unimpaired. Nowhere in Europe was there so sharp a contrast between the strength of the national consciousness and the weakness of the political organ designed to give it effect. The Federal Diet was a mere shadow, a congress of diplomatists acting under the instructions of the several States without sovereign power or moral influence. Nobody read its debates. The smallest government was bold enough to defy its conclusions, unless they were supported by the two predominant powers in the Confederation, Austria and Prussia. There was no capital as in France. There were no great cities like Paris or Lyons, teeming with an intelligent and independent artisan population. Such as they were, the German towns were for the most part inhabited by small shopkeepers and unorganized craftsmen ; and a labouring population in any sense independent of the custom of prince, lord, or burgess had as yet no existence. The tillers of the soil still lived under the shadow of the castle, and, save in those parts of Germany which had come under the direct influence of the French, were either feudal tenants of the medieval type or leaseholders. There was a great deal of quiet happiness in the life of those times ; but there was a feeling abroad that other countries were becoming great and rich, while Germany remained weak and poor. German emigrants from America would write home of the free community beyond the seas where life was easy and wages high ; and many a society was founded in the United States for the purpose of spreading revolutionary principles through the Fatherland. Tracts advocating the expulsion of kings, princes, and dukes, the abolition of the nobility, the banishment of the Jews, the assassination of government officials, were carried over the Atlantic Ocean and found readers in the poor quarters of the larger towns.

But this influence from America was only one among many elements in the revolutionary education of the German proletariate. The annihilation of the Polish nationality has probably done more to endanger the monarchies of Europe than any one political act accomplished since the monarchies of Europe were

first founded.   To trace its effects in all their various
ramifications would lead us a long way.   It is sufficient here to notice that the destruction of Poland, like
the destruction of Jerusalem, produced a Polish dispersion, and that as the Jews of the dispersion have
discharged a peculiar office in the economy of the
world as usurers and financiers, so too have the Poles
of the dispersion, as agents and vectors of revolution.
In all the republican movements of the Continent the
Poles have played a leading part.   They are to be
found in the Saxon riots of '48 ; in the Berlin barricades ; in the struggle for the Republic in Baden ; in
the Italian and Hungarian wars of liberation ; in the
Chartist movement, and in the French Commune.
Homeless and fearless, schooled in war and made reckless by calamity, they have been the nerve of revolution wherever they have been scattered by the winds
of misfortune.   Their influence was in the ascendant
in the generation which succeeded the violent suppression of the national rising in 1830, and perhaps
reached its climax seventeen years later, when Austria
suppressed the Republic of Cracow.   Then every
Chancellery in Europe was familiar with their woes ;
and the exiles of Poland, being scattered far and wide
over the Continent, formed a cosmopolitan network
of conspiracy, and were the means of bringing into
a loose communion the disaffected portions of the
European proletariate.   In the Leipzig of Robert
Blum, as in the Paris of Louis Blanc, the restoration
of the Polish nationality to be obtained through the
defeat and downfall of the Russian, Prussian, and
Austrian monarchies was a cardinal point in the
Republican creed.[1]

The story of the Republican education of Germany

would not be complete if to the instigations of American emigrants and Polish exiles we did not add the examples of Switzerland and France. The Swiss enjoyed a Republican Constitution long before they became a democracy. Their Constitution was very complicated and their society very aristocratic when the flame of the first French Revolution spread up into their mountain valleys and gabled towns. By the light of that furious conflagration all the inner discords of Swiss life were suddenly revealed—the industrious democracies in the Protestant towns, the feudal society of the Catholic cantons—and a contest began between the old and new order which lasted far into the nineteenth century. The democratic school, taking its lessons from France and receiving the support of French bayonets, established a Helvetian Republic with a central executive, a common parliament, a uniform Swiss citizenship, and all the guarantees for liberty and equality which formed part of the revolutionary creed. Their action was premature; their cause was stained by violence and pillage, and by the odium which attaches to any party which cannot achieve its objects without foreign help. They offended the religious feelings of the Catholic cantons; they outraged the deep-set loyalties of the forest and the mountain, and in their zeal for national unity miscalculated the force of Swiss separatism. Bonaparte, who understood the life of secluded mountain valleys better than the Jacobin orators of Berne, framed a scheme which united the social equality of the new school with the cantonal independence of the old. But though his Act of Mediation was partially undone in the reaction, though the Federal Pact of 1815 weakened the guarantees of individual liberty and diluted the power of the central executive, the old variance of religious creed and political conviction still remained the fundamental factor in Swiss life. On the one hand there was the party of State rights, on the other the party of the Union, the first aristocratic and Catholic, the second representing the Protestant democracy of the larger towns and the tradition of the Helvetian Republic. The quarrel broke out violently in 1830, and continued in an ascending scale of vehemence until November 1847, when the league of the seven Catholic cantons, the *Sonderbund* as it was called, was crushed in a brief and brilliant campaign. The lesson of this agitation, providing as it did a kind of working model of the way in which the democratic and unitary principle may be made to prevail in a federal State, was not lost upon Germany, and the example and literature of radical Switzerland was one of the principal factors in shaping the political convictions of the workmen in the southwestern corner of the Germanic Federation.

But after all the first, last, and most dominant influence was France. However great may have been the revulsion from the Napoleonic despotism—and the anti-Gallican spirit ran high in the War of Liberation—Paris still remained the tribune of European democracy, and to those Germans who were restless under the yoke, a source of political illumination. In the darkest days of the Metternich ascendancy voices from the French Chamber, the oratory of a Foy or a Manuel, kept alive the flame of German liberalism, and the French Revolution of 1830 was repeated on a smaller, but less vigorous, scale in Brunswick and Hesse-Cassel, in Saxony and in Hanover. These movements were not indeed republican. The idea of founding a unitary German Republic was too bold a conception for the political leaders in the thirties. But as the Republican propaganda advanced under Louis Philippe in Paris, it began to spread across the Rhine. Turn for an example to Arnold Rüge's " Deutsche-Französische Jahrbücher," published in 1834. " Every attempt," we read, " to make science service-able to the world, every union of science and state-craft implies immediate union with France. To be against France is to be against statecraft, to be against statecraft is to be against freedom. France stands for the political principle, for the pure principle of human freedom in Europe, and France is alive." German workmen in Paris caught the infection and joined the Marianne, a revolutionary club with the Republic as its goal ; and the teaching of the French Socialists was already widely diffused among the artisan class in Germany, when the news of the fall of Louis Philippe produced a spontaneous rising through the country.[2]

Karl Marx, the father of modern Socialism, has left an account of the German revolution of 1848, which is remarkable as coming from the pen of a prominent Socialist and revolutionary of the period. He first exhibits those features in the social state of Germany which he conceives to have been adverse to the effective spread of revolutionary principles, the strength of the feudal aristocracy, the absence of political concentration, the numbers of petty trades-men and artisans, the imperfect development of the factory, and the effect of the economic structure of the country in encouraging deferential habits among the poor. He then lacerates the National Parliament at Frankfort for the pitiable imbecility with which it squandered all the treasure house of revolutionary hopes. Instead of using the first moments of enthusiasm to claim the exclusive sovereignty of the nation, to form an army, to defy the State governments, and if necessary to draw Germany into a patriotic war against Russia and Denmark, the Frankfort Parliament did none of these things. There was never a body so deficient in the wholesome spirit of iconoclasm. It would neither disperse the old Confederate Diet, nor assert its supremacy over the State governments, nor take any means to secure that its decisions should be carried into effect. It placed an Austrian Archduke at the head of a provisional executive, and offered the imperial crown of Germany to the King of Prussia. Reckless alike of time and enthusiasm it spun out elaborate discussions on fundamental rights, accepted a humiliating truce with Denmark, and sank by swift degrees into universal contempt. This, however, is only part of the story. The real destiny of Germany was not decided by the debates in the Pauluskirche in Frankfort, but in the streets of Berlin and Vienna. If the Revolution triumphed in the Prussian and Austrian capitals it would win all along the line, whatever might be the hesitations of middle-class doctrinaires. There was a time in the early spring when the hopes of revolution were unusually bright. The March days in Berlin had persuaded the King of Prussia to summon a Constituent Assembly, to promise a Constitution, and to wear the black, red, and gold of the German Revolution. " Preussen geht in Deutschland auf "—" Prussia is merged in Germany " —this promise, given in a royal proclamation, would undoubtedly be exactly coeval with the spell of royal timidity, and whether this spell would be indefinitely

prolonged depended upon the fortunes of the Haps
monarchy.   In the opinion of Karl Marx the fa
the German Revolution was decided in Vienna.   In
month of October the Emperor of Austria,
Slavonic troops and backed by the Slavonic men
of the Diet, crushed the Revolution in his capital.
famous band of students was broken, that bod
young Germans, four thousand strong, who for a
months dictated a policy to an Empire.   Vi
was allowed to stand a siege and to fall unaided,
the cause of the Revolution from the Carpathia
the Rhine were not involved in its defence.   An
the reaction triumphing through Austria, Fred
William IV. of Prussia recovered from his co
sions and timidity, and expelled his Prussian P:
ment at the point of the bayonet.   Autocracy,
the brute forces of the Slavonic world, had bl
the promise of Teutonic liberty.

The real truth is that republican principles
little hold on the general mass of the German pe
Professors and students dreaming of Harmodius
Aristogeiton, or deriving their political philos
from the French Revolution, scattered knot
artisans, nowhere very numerous save in Baden
the Bavarian Palatinate, did not constitute the
body of the German nation.   Political tradition
not outgrown in a night, and the political tradit
of Germany, being rooted not only in the Holy R
Empire but also in the numerous hereditary dyn
which had flourished under its shadow, was
against the abstract teachings of democracy.   T
was indeed a painful lack of unity and distinctn
the political ideals of the reformers.   Some wish
include German Austria in the new State, other

exclude it ; some dreamed of a revival of the old Empire in a modern vesture of constitutional rights and liberties, others of a central directory ; some thought of the Germany of the future as a Federation upon the American model, others as a strong and united republic ; but the great central body of the nation, holding that no project could succeed without the support of the princely governments, did not advance beyond the conception of a federation of constitutional monarchies. It is interesting to notice that Bismarck, who first rose to prominence in 1848 as a leader of the high Tory party in Prussia, comes to the conclusion that had the Prussian King then taken full advantages of his opportunities he might have formed a stricter and stronger union of Germany than was possible in 1870. Frightened by the Revolution, the rulers of Bavaria and the smaller German States would have made concessions which Prussia was in no position to demand from her allies in the Franco-Prussian War. Thus, while Marx thinks that the situation in '48, if properly handled, would have led to a democratic republic, Bismarck, with a saner estimate of moral forces, detects in it the squandered hope of a powerful Empire.

The story of the Republican party during the German Revolution is that of a hopeless minority driven into desperate courses and eventually shattered by the overwhelming force of the monarchical feeling in the nation. The men who led the party in the first instance, Friedrich Hecker and Von Struve, were already prominent in the public life of Baden, the first as a deputy, the second as a journalist. They were the Apostles of the radical South-west, the hope and pride of the young men. In appearance, temperament and intellectual preparation it would be hard to imagine a greater contrast. Hecker was a type of the careless poetical student who took his politics from Schiller and plunged into the Revolution for the love of stir and movement and generous ideas. Struve was a doctrinaire of the library. The one was tall, healthy, massive, his voice a full rich baritone, "very beautiful," writes an admiring lady, "with a Christlike head and long fair hair and a face of rapt enthusiasm." The other was small and bloodless ("lives only on vegetables," said his friends) with a cheek of parchment and dim, abstracted eyes. The charm and high courage of the one was supplemented by the considered revolutionary doctrine of the other.[3] The original programme sketched at a meeting of the Radical party at Offenburg on September 12, 1847, did not specifically demand a republic, though it aimed at undermining the power of the monarchies by requiring that the standing armies of the German States should be replaced by a militia of the whole people sworn to respect the Constitution ; but, in revolution, seed ripens fast, and in the frenzy caused by the news from Paris the seed of German radicalism ripened into the full grain. Fifty-one influential men met at Heidelberg on 5th March to consider what measures were to be taken towards the attainment of national unity. Hecker and Struve urged the immediate proclamation of a German Republic, and were met by the reply that the goal of liberal effort should be, not a republic but an empire. Feeling mounted fast and high ; on March 13 the Revolution was master of Vienna ; on March 21 it was master of Berlin ; and when ten days later a preliminary parliament met at Frankfort to concert measures for a national representation of Germany, the republicans believed that their goal was near.

It was an early spring; the first delicious shimmer of green was on the trees, and to the sentimental soul it seemed as if the palace of liberty were to rise like an exhalation from a Garden of Eden. Groups of artisans pressed against the shop-windows, staring at the pictures of the French provisional government—the famous poet, the simple workman, "a heavenly dream and yet all true." When the Baden men showed in the streets, the air rang with plaudits, for it was known that they went far and that the South had a commanding majority in the Vor-Parliament. At the theatre the piece was naturally Schiller's "Don Carlos," and as Posa came on to plead for the liberty of the Netherlands the house rocked with applause. Men and women were transported with enthusiasm. A new era had begun. A German Parliament had met. "I wished," writes Malvida von Meysenburg, "that the enemy were at the door and that we could all go out singing Luther's Chorale to fight for freedom or to die." Careless of Northern opinion, and disregarding the purpose for which the Vor-Parliament was summoned, Struve rose to urge the immediate proclamation of an indivisible German Republic. But at the very threshold of parliamentary debate, and in the first glow of the Revolution, he and his followers suffered an overthrow the significance of which they refused to acknowledge. Defeated in the parliament, the Republican leaders turned to the people. The South was covered with a network of Radical societies; and in April Hecker, with a hare-brained temerity which fatally discredited his cause, raised the standard of revolt in Baden. His hasty levies fared as ill as an auxiliary force sped from Paris by Hervegh, one of the least competent among German poets. A rising in Poland was equally unfortunate, and in the revulsion caused by these events three-fourths of Germany voted monarchists of some shade or other into the parliament which was to shape the new Constitution.

Thus the cause was already more than half-lost when the great debate opened in the Pauluskirche in Frankfort. The two hundred Republican deputies were hopelessly outmatched in numbers, and, with a political instinct which from their own standpoint was not unsound, attempted to sustain the passions of the country by a foreign war. All over Germany good patriots believed that Schleswig and Holstein were inseparable, and that, Holstein belonging by general consent to the German Federation, the Danes had no right to incorporate Schleswig. A war had broken out ; the Germans in the Duchies had been supported by a Prussian army, and then foreign powers intervened and Prussia was compelled to make a truce at Malmö. The parliament at Frankfort was violently convulsed by news which was generally read as a national humiliation. It first voted that it would not, and then that it would, confirm the action of the Prussian monarchy. Never did feeling run so high ; never were the debates more violent, for it was the Republican calculation, that, were the German nation to say " We will have war " while the Prussian monarchy said " We will have peace," a fatal blow would be dealt to the cause of monarchy all over Germany. When the second vote was taken on September 16, and the war party was defeated in a narrow division, rioting began in the streets of Frankfort. The deputies of the majority were branded as traitors to German liberty and German honour; barricades sprang up, and two members of the Assembly who had voted against the war were foully murdered on the outskirts of the town. Again the Revolution had miscalculated its strength: regular troops poured into Frankfort and had little difficulty in restoring order, and the only result of the incident was to associate the cause of the Republic with anarchy in the minds of the great mass of German citizens.

There was still one convulsive spasm, and it was not devoid of pathos or heroism, before the cause of Republican unity was finally effaced. After long and wearisome debate the Frankfort Parliament patched together a Federal Constitution and offered the Imperial Crown of a reconstructed Germany to the King of Prussia. Had Frederick William IV. been a man of imagination or resolve he would have accepted a gift which, whether or not it involved him in a war with Austria, would have implied the foundation of a great national State framed on liberal lines in Central Europe. But he first declined the Crown and then repudiated the Constitution. The South-west, still true to the cause of liberty, fled to arms; the regular troops of Baden joined the insurgents, and the fire spread right down the Rhine to Cologne and Düsseldorf and across the Thuringian Forest to Leipzig. Some of the noblest and most generous spirits in Germany were to be found in this last and most desperate venture to maintain the cause of liberal unity against the sinister opposition of the German crowns. It was all in vain. Democratic idealism fell, not for the first or last time, before the trained battalions of Prussia;

and the doom of the German Republic was de
mined at Rastadt, the little frontier town which
1798, had witnessed the first preliminary stages in
demolition of the fabric of the medieval Empire.
19th May 1849, Freiligrath, the bard of the Revolut
wrote his last poem in the final number (defia
printed in red ink) of Karl Marx's *Neue Rhein*
Zeitung :—

> Wenn die letzte Krone wie Glas zerbricht
> In des Kampfes Wetten und Flammen ;
> Wenn das Volk sein letztes Schuldig spricht,
> Dann stehn wir wieder zusammen
> Mit dem Wort, mit dem Schwert an der Donau, am Rl
> Eine allzeit treue Gesellin
> Wird dem Throne zerschmettenden Volke sein
> Die Geächtete, die Rebellin.

But the Republican party in Germany has n
recovered the blow which it received in Baden in 1
and the unity of Germany was destined to be achie
by men to whom the tradition of Revolutionary Fr
represented everything that was hateful and dange
to society.

The republican ideal most prevalent in the so
west of Germany, while always deriving much o
inspiration from the poetry of Schiller, was spec
circumscribed, both by the example of the S
cantons and by the humble economic conditions w
prevailed in that quarter of Germany.   "
Southerner," says a modern writer, " wished fo
republic, conceiving it, however, as a soft Arca
a small state of peasants and burghers, neither
rich nor very poor, and devoid of the great contras
historical and political life.   He wanted to ab
princes and the Civil List, and the nobility and

standing army, and, if possible, would have dispensed with taxes : on the other hand, he had no ambition to play an active part in history, and cared nothing for foreign politics, a great industrial development, or a world commerce. If it had been possible for Germany to fall into a number of such tiny republics, it would have vanished from the ranks of the great nations more completely than before." [4]

Numerically inferior to these southern idealists was a group of men fashioned of harder metal, who, desiring a united and republican Germany, scanned the whole political horizon and preached the duty of a general war. The writers in the *Neue Rheinische Zeitung* had no sympathy with little Republicans or Federalists, and with those who believed in Slavonic union. Their programme was a popular war against Russia and Denmark prefaced by the liberation of Poland. In autocratic Russia they saw the great obstacle to a European revolution; in Denmark the ally of three counter-revolutionary powers, and moreover " a brutal, dirty, piratical, old Northern nationality, rough to women, permanently drunk, its Berseker rage alternating with tearful sentimentality ! " Nobody has ever accused Karl Marx of " tearful sentimentality." And a policy of union through blood and iron was neither the invention nor the monopoly of a Prussian monarchist.

One day, late in February 1848, a certain German student at the University of Bonn was sitting in his attic at work upon a tragedy. The youth proposed to himself one of those quiet and dignified academic careers which are the reward of successful industry at a German University. Suddenly a friend burst in upon him with the intelligence that Louis Philippe

15

was overthrown and the Republic proclaimed in
France.   Carl Schurz threw down his pen, rushed into
the street, and never touched the manuscript again.
To him and to his fellow-students it seemed as if the
hour had struck for founding a powerful national
government upon a broad, democratic basis.   School
memories of ancient republics mingled in his brain
with a sentimental affection for the medieval Empire,
and an enthusiasm for the ideas of the French Revolution.   He was for the convocation of a national
parliament, for freedom of speech, freedom of the
press, freedom of public meeting, responsibility of
ministers, communal self-government, the right of the
people to carry arms, the formation of a civic guard.
He shared all the enthusiasms and all the illusions
of his time, and, being as fearless as he was generous
and enthusiastic, was ready to stake his life for his
political convictions.   When therefore the Frankfort
Parliament did at last issue a Constitution, and when
the monarchy of Prussia refused to accept it, Carl
Schurz, himself a Prussian subject, took up arms to
defend the work of the Revolution.   He fought in the
campaign of Baden, and then, when all was over,
contrived to escape into Switzerland.   Not long
afterwards a brilliant act of devotion made this obscure
student one of the heroes of the beaten cause.   His
professor and friend Gottfried Kinkel, a man of
singular fascination and no little reputation as a poet,
had been among the Baden insurgents.   At the
capitulation of Rastadt, the last town which stood out
for liberty, Kinkel was taken, condemned to imprisonment for life, and thrown into a common gaol.
His wife appealed to the young student, and thoug
it was to the peril of his life that he set foot in Germa

Carl Schurz did not fail her. He never rested till
Kinkel was freed, and, among exciting records of
adventure, the liberation of Kinkel as told in Schurz's
" Memoirs " deserves to rank with the famous episode
of the *Château d'If* in *Monte Cristo*.   In the eyes of
the Prussian Government the youth was now doubly
damned.   His own country in its present mood was
closed to him, and yet so long as hope was possible he
continued to cherish it.   London was full of the broken
men of the '48.   There was Kossuth, whose splendid
oratory had taken England by storm, and Mazzini,
the soul of the moral movement for Italian unity.
Every straw of hope was clutched at by these exiles
in their anxious and attentive survey of continental
politics ; but then came the news of the *coup d'état*.
France, the mother of the Revolution, had turned apos-
tate.   The last Republican rally had been shot down
in the Boulevards of Paris by the nephew of Napoleon.
Schurz made up his mind that the cause of liberty
was lost in Europe and that its broken fortunes could
never be mended.   Wandering out into Hyde Park on
a foggy December morning, when the intelligence of
the *coup d'état* was freshly received in London, he
sank upon a bench and resolved to emigrate to America.
He had sat musing for about half-an-hour when he
noticed at the other end of the seat a little man with
his gaze fixed on the ground.   The man lifted his
head and turned a pair of weary eyes upon his neighbour.   It was Louis Blanc.   " Ah, c'est vous, mon
eune ami !   C'est fini, n'est ce pas, c'est fini."   And
the French Socialist clasped the German's hand.
Thenceforward the biography of Schurz, like the story
of Hecker and of many another republican of that
time, belongs to the history of the United States.[5]

CHAPTER XI

THE THIRD REPUBLIC

She, killed with noisome air,
Even she ! and still so fair,
Who said, " Let there be freedom," and there was
Freedom ; and as a lance
The fiery eyes of France
Touched the world's sleep, and as a sleep made pass
Forth of men's heavier ears and eyes,
Smitten with fire and thunder from new skies.
SWINBURNE—"To Victor Hugo"

À coup sûr je ne crois pas être suspect quand je parle de mon
horreur pour les chimères, pour tout ce qui ressemble aux utopies,
aux systèmes par lesquelles on s'imagine qu'il est possible de
refaire violemment la société.—GAMBETTA

NO government founded on a crime can ever be
really stable. However showy its exploits,
however substantial its services, the indelible stain
remains and the invisible Furies pursue. The Second
Empire conferred some services on France, but it
was founded upon proscriptions and a *coup d'État*.
At first the Emperor was popular enough. His name
worked miracles with the peasantry ; his court, if not
pure, was at least showy and brilliant. By fusillades
and cannonades, by summary trials and wholesale
deportations he had scared away the Red Spectre of
Socialism, and informed men of property that forthwith they might sleep quietly in their beds. The
Roman Catholics exulted in this bland husband of a
devout Spaniard, who restored the Pope to the Vatican,

encouraged the clerical control of education, and championed the rights of the Latin Church in Palestine. To such as thirsted for military glory the Crimean War was a sufficient apology for the new *régime*. The soldiers of the Empire had stormed the Malakoff, the pride of Russia was abated, and the treaty of peace was negotiated in Paris.

But this communion of applause was not of long duration. The Emperor, who, in his youth, had belonged, if not formally, at least in sympathy, to the society of Carbonari, was drawn into the war of Italian liberation. A French army marched into Italy to assist Piedmont against Austria, and by 1861 all Italy save Venice and Rome was united in a single polity under the Sardinian crown. From that moment the French Empire lost the confidence of the Roman Catholics. It had helped the Piedmontese, who persecuted the faithful, and had promoted an impious revolution against Austria, Naples, the Papal State, the established bulwarks of the Roman Church. The withdrawal of clerical support would not in itself have been sufficient to undermine the Empire. Great as was the power of the Catholic Church in France, the tradition of the Revolution was stronger still. Napoleon III. alienated the Catholics and failed to conciliate the Liberals. He supported the Temporal Power of the Pope against the Italian Revolution, experienced diplomatic rebuffs in Denmark and Poland, and went out of his way to court the endless humiliations of the Mexican campaign. It was part of the liberal tradition in France to preach the doctrine of natural frontiers, and to maintain that it should be the prime concern of any government, solicitous for the good name of the country, to extract from the Powers of Europe, either by peaceful acts or by the power of the sword, a radical revision of the treaties of 1815. Louis Bonaparte shared these aspirations. As the price of his assistance in the affairs of Italy he wrung Savoy and Nice from Piedmont and then addressed his diplomacy to securing an extension of frontier towards the Rhine. In this project, however, he met with a grave reverse. War broke out in 1866 between Austria and Prussia ; and the Emperor, believing, as most people then did believe, that the struggle would be long and costly, was confident that he would be in a position to impose his mediation upon two exhausted combatants and to arrange a settlement of Europe of which France would be the principal beneficiary. But these calculations were disconcerted by the speed and completeness of the Prussian victory. In six weeks the war was over and victor and vanquished had come to terms. Prussia had gained all Germany to the Main, France had gained nothing at all, not a yard of Belgium, of Luxemburg, of the Palatinate, not a single German hamlet or a single German cottage. She had not been quick enough to intervene in the war ; she had not been invited to intervene in the peace. The balance of power in Europe had been changed adversely to her interests and she had not stirred a finger to prevent it. She woke up as it were from a fool's paradise to find that Prussia was the first military power in Europe, and at this unwelcome revelation a quick current of rage, apprehension, and wounded vanity ran through the whole body politic.

There is something to be said for a frank autocracy, for a despotism which is what it seems to be and does not pretend to be any better than it really is. The Second Empire was not frank. It was founded upon a sham and it lived upon an artifice. It created a parliament, but so circumscribed its functions, that it would neither propose a bill nor question ministers, nor debate large aspects of public policy nor appropriate supplies. It retained universal suffrage, but by a close and vigilant system of electoral pressure ensured the return of none but official candidates. From 1852 to 1860 political life was entirely extinguished in France. The press was muzzled, an insolent hierarchy of officials served by an army of inquisitive police dominated the country. Innocent men were deported at the whisper of an informer.

Eight years passed and then the Emperor resolved to relax the rigour of his system. Having lost the favour of the Catholics, he was desirous of conciliating the parliamentary Liberals. The Press restrictions were abated, the *Moniteur* was permitted to publish full reports of the debates in the Chamber, and the popular Assembly was empowered to draw up an address in response to the speech from the throne, a concession which enabled it to review the whole surface of public policy. These concessions did not go very far, but they were sufficient to revive public activity. The parliamentary opposition which had risen from nothing to five in 1857 leapt up to thirty-five in 1863, and reached one hundred in 1869, and as the faults of the Government were many and grave, so was the parliamentary opposition searching in its criticism and fierce in its attack.

In this opposition there were two parties, one believing in the possibility of a Liberal Empire, and the other resolved to overthrow the tyrant and establish a Republic. The leader of the first party was a man who is still alive and is widely known as the author of an apology, still unconcluded, in fourteen brilliant and seductive volumes. Émile Ollivier began his parliamentary career as a strong republican, as one of the famous five who during seven years of darkness and silence offered an unflinching resistance to the Empire. But then in 1864, when some few draughts of air had already been let into the engine-room of despotism, he was drawn into personal relations with the Emperor and became convinced of the possibility of founding a permanent and wholesome alliance between the Empire and the democracy of France. Such an union had already been foreshadowed in the constitutional concessions of the Hundred days, in the talk of the great Emperor at St Helena, and in the *idées Napoléoniennes*, composed by his nephew fifteen years before the *coup d'état*. Ollivier at least honestly believed that a Liberal Empire, an Empire with a ministry responsible to a free legislature, would appease the political hunger of France ; and such an Empire he claims substantially to have procured.[1]

Between 1867 and 1870 concession after concession was wrung from the enfeebled grasp of a dying sovereign. The Chamber acquired the right of initiating legislation, of cross-questioning ministers, of amending the budget clause by clause. Ollivier himself became the President of the Council. It was not in the strict sense of the term a parliamentary government, for the Emperor reserved the right to compose his ministries independently · of the majority in the popular House, and he could always alter the constitution by the votes of the Senate, a body named by himself ; but the liberal Imperialists of the Chamber were satisfied with the compromise, and believed that in this series of organic changes, which were ratified by a *plébiscite*, they had found the political formula for which France had been vainly searching ever since Louis XVI. summoned the States General to Versailles.

Less numerous in the Chamber, but far more formidable in the country, were the republicans. The *coup d'état* following upon the days of June had been more damaging to them than to either of the royalist parties. Their leaders had been shot down or proscribed, their organization was shattered, their programme was involved in that vague but deadly form of discredit which attaches to imputed schemes of crime, anarchy, and communism. But in Paris, Lyons, and in the other great industrial centres of France the idea of the Republic had taken a firm root, and as there were Orleanist families and legitimist families scattered up and down in country houses, so in the huge and hideous cities of toil there were families attached to the revolutionary tradition, and numbering martyrs and exiles for the republican faith. No liberal Empire, however plausible its professions, could content this great republican connexion. They argued that the Empire was a crime, that the concessions were illusory, that the experiment of the Republic had never been honestly tried, and there could be no peace or happiness for France until the usurper was deposed. The corruption, the extravagance, the inefficiency of the Government were held up to the derision and contempt of the Boulevards by the wittiest and least responsible of French publicists, Henri de Rochefort. The story of the *coup d'état* was dug out, recounted in grave, elaborate, and remorseless details by the serious historian, and flung at the face of the Government on every occasion and by every device which malignant and watchful hostility could discover.

Translated into the popular imagination of Paris, the actions and adventures of the Empire became in process of time a tissue of wanton and profligate cruelty, and it is characteristic of the changed atmosphere of Paris that a young southern advocate, Léon Gambetta, rose to instant fame by a splendid but irrelevant denunciation of the "crime of December," which sixteen years before had made Napoleon master of France.[2]

It will be remembered that the republican movement of 1848 came to an untimely end because of its connexion with socialism, because the river of revolution broke into two diverging streams, each adverse to monarchy, but one of them red while the other was tricolour. These two currents continued to flow on, however much they might be masked or obstructed by the Empire. The red republican, who was generally though not invariably, a working man, nourished a hatred and envy of the middle class analogous in intensity to the hatred which the middle class had entertained for the nobles of the *ancien régime*. He had been taught that the Revolution of 1789, which had humbled the nobility, must be succeeded by a new revolution of which the middle class were to be the victims. He believed that capital was evil and that the scene of waste and misery into which he was born could be converted into a smiling prospect by a wholesale revolution in the relation. of employer and employed. The annual meetings of the Internationale, an association of workers founded in 1864 and drawn from all the leading countries in Europe, helped to spread a familiarity, if not with the writings, at least with the principal conclusions of Karl Marx and Ferdinand Lassalle. By an inexorable economic process, given existing competitive conditions, the rich were getting richer and the poor poorer. All values were created by labour, and yet, however great the value of the product, labour was always ground down to the bare necessaries of subsistence. No palliatives would avail against a condition of affairs which was not confined to any one nation, but essential to the economic constitution of European society itself. Cosmopolitan labour must attack cosmopolitan capital without truce or remission until such time as the land and the instruments of production should be finally and completely transferred from the individual to the State.[3]

Such was the programme of the Red Republic. The doctrinaires of the older republican type did not trouble their heads with these large and questionable economic prospects ; they looked to the political machine. They believed that an untrammelled use of universal suffrage would, by a direct and logical process, lead to a republic, and that it was of the essence of a republic that offices should be elective, and that the State should provide free, secular, and gratuitous education to all its members. Of this school of thought Léon Gambetta, son of a grocer at Cahors, was in the declining days of Empire the best, because he was the most widely influential, representative. Gambetta's political philosophy was strung upon a few simple convictions held with great distinctness and tenacity and recommended to his fellow countrymen with all the authority which a fine voice, a rich and flexible vocabulary, and an energetic character are able to confer. The cardinal point in his code was a passionate belief in the beatific virtues of universal suffrage. Monarchies might profess to countenance universal suffrage, but it would be found on examination that no monarchy could look universal suffrage face to face. The Empire, for instance, had violated universal suffrage in five ways, by establishing heredity as a dogma, by establishing the immutability of the Constitution, by creating two Chambers, by making the chief of the Executive irresponsible, and by depriving the nation of Constituent Power. But once allow the fountain of the popular will to play freely over the Constitution, and taxes will fall, armies will dwindle, education will be compulsory, secular, and gratuitous, and as no official, however exalted, will be unaccountable to the people, so will no department of public policy be withdrawn from their control. " Universal suffrage cannot abdicate. The popular will of to-day cannot bind the will of to-morrow."

In Gambetta's election programme of 1869 all officials are to be elected, the standing army is to be suppressed, the Church is to be separated from the State, and the Government is to provide primary secular education for all at its own charges. Social changes would doubtless follow, but there was the less reason for tabulating economic prescriptions since in a true political democracy the maladies of society would cure themselves.

The Empire fell not before the radical propaganda of the students' quarter and the law-courts, but before the Prussian guns. When the news of the capitulation of Sedan was received in Paris on September 4, 1870, the Assembly was invaded and dissolved by an armed mob, and the deputies of the Left, headed by Jules Favre and Gambetta, proceeded to the Hôtel de Ville, pronounced the abolition of the Empire, proclaimed the Republic, and established a provisional government of national defence. There may well be two opinions both as to the policy and as to the morality of promoting an internal revolution in a country reeling under defeat and exposed to the calamity of foreign invasion. Favre and Gambetta, representing a section of Paris, took upon themselves to overthrow the Government of France. Their action was no more constitutional than was the attack upon the Tuileries on August 10, 1792. They had received no mandate from the country ; they had no means of gauging the sentiment of the army or its chiefs, and however much they may have been convinced that the Empire was fatally injured in popular esteem, they had certainly no reason to suppose that France was prepared for a republic. It is not, however, difficult to account for the sudden and impetuous city revolution which reversed the *plébiscite* of the whole country solemnly recorded four months before. There was a precedent, not older than seventy-eight years, and regarded as one of the most splendid memories of French energy and French valour. It would fall within the recollection of a very old man how, when France had been invaded by Austria and Prussia, when the enemy had advanced far across the frontier, had captured important strongholds and was within five marches of the capital, the democracy of Paris had stormed the Tuileries, deposed the King, and so communicated its victorious impulse through every fibre of the national being, that the enemy was driven across the frontier and the Republic founded in a blaze of victory. What had been done by the grandsires might be done again by the grandsons. On September 6 the Provisional Government declared in a circular to Europe that France would not yield either an inch of her territory or a stone of her fortresses. But Moltke was not a Brunswick nor Bazaine a Dumouriez. Within six months of this proud act of defiance Alsace and Lorraine were ceded to Germany.

Four and a half years elapsed before the Republic, hastily proclaimed at the Hôtel de Ville by the strong and impetuous son of an Italian grocer, was formally accepted by the legislature of France. It was then carried as the lame but ineluctable conclusion of a disappointing history without a ray of enthusiasm, and by the narrowest of all possible majorities. The Constitution of the Third Republic was the work of the left centre and bears the hall-mark of its manufacture. The minds out of which it was slowly and nervously extracted were as untouched by the geometrical rigour of the earlier republican theory as they were alien to its large and humane illusions. They did not believe that they were giving the law to Europe or that they were framing a perfect Constitution, or that their craftsmanship conformed to any classical and pre-ordained model of pure democracy. They spoke without rapture, without allusions to Solon or Lycurgus, as business men engaged in one of the complicated and difficult operations of practical life. Their main concern was to preclude a repetition of those errors and misfortunes which had been found to flow from a too literal interpretation of the doctrine of popular sovereignty, and so they decreed that the Chamber of Deputies should be checked by a Senate and that the President should be the creature not of the *plébiscite* but of a congress of the two Houses sitting together.

The series of events which led up to this meticulous and durable equipose is a curious page in the history of political conversions. "Passion," in the fine and

egnant phrase of John Bunyan, " will have all things
w," and the Republic was proclaimed in a fit of
.ssionate impatience by a handful of men to whom
·ance owed no sort of necessary intellectual allegiance.
hether " the revolution of disgust " would be rati-
:d by the maturer judgment of the country was a
iestion to which, while the armies of Germany were
[vancing on the capital, an answer could neither be
ught nor found.   The burden of the Provisional
overnment was already as heavy as any which human
.oulders can bear, and it was no time to institute
tose ancient and difficult logomachies which cling
>out the origins of a constitution.   Paris was invested
y the enemy, and from September 16, 1870, to January
3, 1871, the conduct of the defence devolved upon
ie men who had taken on themselves to proclaim
ie downfall of the Empire.   It is no part of our theme
> describe how Gambetta escaped in a balloon, how
e founded a delegation of the Provisional Govern-
ient at Tours, and how ruling over part of France,
ith powers which were practically dictatorial, he
:eated new armies, prolonged the national resistance,
nd shed a parting ray of glory upon a desperate and
eaten cause.   Whether the republican cause gained
r lost by his endeavours is a matter upon which
pinion may be legitimately divided.   Some praised
im for showing fight ; others ascribed to the culpable
anity of a self-appointed despot months of bloody
nd unavailing combat and a needless extension of the
ation's agony.   Be this as it may, when Paris was at
ist shamed into submission and when an armistice
/as granted in order that a National Assembly might
e gathered, competent to conclude a binding peace, a
rave of monarchical feeling passed over the country.

When the Assembly met at Bordeaux it was f
contain no less than four hundred monarcl
against two hundred republicans and thirty sup
of the fallen Empire. The most surprising feat
surprising result was the resurrection of the le
party, who after a political eclipse of forty yea
quered no less than two hundred seats. Their
denoted the activity of the priests and a re\
religious sentiment which among the Latin race
natural and inevitable sequel of national ca
Gambetta, who had preached the war à l'outra
fled into Spain to escape the rising tide of unpop
and his radical supporters were for the mo
beaten at the polls. At the bottom of the
mind was the sovereign need for peace, ord
reconstruction.

At this crisis of national affairs France disco
leader who, for the mass and brilliance of his
ments, stands out as one of the most eminent
in the nineteenth century. In the elections
Bordeaux Parliament, Thiers had been retur
twenty-six departments and had received nea
million votes. He was now seventy-three y
age, and ever since early manhood his name ha
a household word in French politics and h
spectacles and elfish body a fortune to the caric
Thirty years had passed since he had served
Prime Minister of Louis Philippe, forty-one yea
he had taken a principal share in procuring th
throw of Charles X. Babies had grown int
and grey-haired citizens while this exuberar
man from Marseilles was exhibiting the gl
facets of his various, irrepressible and inca
activities. Now he was known as the most for

journalist of the radicals, now as the author of the first cool and connected history of the French Revolution. He helps to establish Louis Philippe, helps to create the Napoleonic Legend, helps to found the Second Empire, and paves the way for the Third Republic. Every school of political thought into which France was divided might claim a fraction of M. Thiers, except the school of the dunces, the madmen, and the poltroons. Valour he possessed to the point of temerity, vanity to the point of ridicule, but the governing quality of his eager and domineering mind was a great lucidity and industry in affairs. Being a man who understood the niceties of Government, who had gone deep into the science of finance and had drawn from his studies of the First Empire a sense of the fascination of ordered power, he had not a particle of sympathy with revolution. He would shoot down red socialists with as little concern as a gamekeeper knocks over a jay or a magpie. When the roar of the barricades was surging up towards the Tuileries and the Court of Louis Philippe was twittering with timorous and divided counsels, Thiers advised the King to retire into the country, to allow the insurrection to gather head, and then to stamp it out with the armed forces of the monarchy. He prescribed the same drastic treatment in the days of June and followed his own prescription when Paris was caught by the fever of the Commune.

Such a man had nothing in common either with the Jacobin or with the Girondin tradition, save the horror common to all intelligent and progressive minds for the sacred unreason of the *ancien régime*. He was known as a constitutional monarchist of a somewhat advanced liberal type, as a friend of the Catholic Church,

16

and as an enemy of socialism.   But the circumstance
which at this juncture specially commended him to the
admiration of France was the recollection of his dash-
ing, free, and incisive criticism of the Second Empire.
When Thiers was elected to the Chamber in 1863, some-
one said that henceforth French history would resolve
itself into a dialogue between Thiers and the Emperor.
In truth a cloudy, ambitious and unsound policy could
not have encountered a more formidable antagonist
than this facile and fiery orator who knew the weights
and measures of Europe better than the Imperial
Foreign Office, and exposed with a desolating command
of technique the seamy finance and wavering diplomacy of a bad Government.   Again and again he
pressed his indictments in the audience of a people fast
moving down the planes of doubt and disaffection.
He exposed the wild folly of the Mexican expedition
with its ugly dash of financial speculation. He
denounced the apathy which accepted the bitter
political fruit of Sadowa. He predicted the military
ascendency of Germany, and, unless precautions were
promptly taken, the loss of Alsace-Lorraine. Almost
alone among French politicians he withstood the
passionate gust of frenzy which swept his country
into the Prussian War. He was not afraid to speak
unwelcome truths. He told France that while she
was unprepared, Prussia was ready ; he pleaded for
delay ; he protested against the idea that two great
nations should engage in a disastrous collision upon a
point of diplomatic susceptibility, and for the moment
he was the most unpopular man in Paris. A few
weeks passed and against the grim darkness of Sedan
he shone as the one oracle of wisdom. The Empress
appealed to him to save her, and the Paris mob which

had threatened to sack his house came about him and cried, " M. Thiers, tirez-nous de là." To Prosper Mérimée, the dying envoy of the dead Empire, he replied briefly, " Il n'y a rien à faire après Sédan " ; but if he could do nothing to raise the Empire from its grave, there was no service which in the pride and energy of his patriotism he was unwilling to render to France. As a last expedient he travelled round the Courts of Europe in search of mediation, followed at every step of his unavailing pilgrimage by the grateful eyes of his anxious countrymen.

It was therefore a natural, if not an inevitable, step for the Bordeaux Assembly to place the supreme executive power in the hands of Thiers. His authority was uncontested. He was the only statesman who commanded the confidence of the whole nation, or of whom it could be said that in all the parliamentary and administrative arts he towered so far above his fellows that to contest his superiority would savour of an insipid paradox. The task which lay before him was to make peace with Prussia, to repair the havoc of the war, and to give France a constitution : with a true instinct for a complex and delicate situation he saw that while the first two objects should be patiently and immediately pursued to their solution, the last should be left to ripen in the dark. The *de facto* government was republican. The peace was made in the name of the Republic, the armies obeyed the Republic, the civil servants were appointed and dismissed by the government of the Republic. On the other hand the Assembly of Bordeaux contained a large majority of royalists, and of all the political Assemblies of France none had been elected with so little official interference or under so authentic and

immediate an impression of popular emotion.   Thiers
saw that France must eventually come to the Republic,
for as he said, " It is the form of Government which
divides us least " ; but he recognized that the thing
was a delicate plant, that it was invested in a cloud of
doubts and apprehensions, that, given an opening, a
royalist assembly would unquestionably endeavour
to kill it, and that it must be allowed to insinuate
itself into the confidence of the country by the gentle
efflux of time.   All this Thiers saw, and he took a
decision of critical importance when he implored the
Assembly to devote itself to the reconstruction of
France, and gave a pledge that he would in no way
seek to prejudice the constitutional issue.[4]

In pursuance of this difficult programme the
President of the *de facto* Republic was probably
assisted by one of the most terrible calamities of
modern history.   The conduct of the defence of Paris
had more than once been embarrassed by the violent
outbreak of a mob which was convinced that sleek
bourgeois were betraying France and that a *sortie en
masse* would send the Prussians flying back to Germany.
The hardships, the excitement, the mingled tension
and lassitude of the siege had generated in the poorer
combatants a restless, angry, and bitter temper, a
kind of psychological malady, *la fièvre obsidionale.*
They had fought and had been beaten through no
fault of their own and consequently, as they argued
with fiery conviction but imperfect logic, through the
fault and treachery of their leaders.   They suspected
that Assembly of monarchists which had recently, in
patent distrust of the home of revolutions and republics,
transferred its sessions not to Paris but to Versailles.
Their honour was outraged by the terms of the peace ;

they bore with sullen rage the spectacle of a Prussian army bivouacked in the garden of the Tuileries. They were armed, idle, miserable, angry. On March 18, 1871, a fortnight after the withdrawal of the Prussian troops, the city of Paris broke out into the revolt of the Commune.

"A convulsion of famine, misery, and despair," such was Gambetta's phrase for the Commune, and in a movement so passionate and spontaneous it is vain to seek for any clear or consistent thought. Of the *communards* some were anarchists, others Jacobins, others socialists, others again foreign adventurers or escaped gaol-birds. One member of the governing assembly was a Prussian, another a tight-rope dancer, a third a lunatic, a fourth a condemned murderer. By degrees a cluster of vague aspirations was sent floating out over Paris and was accepted with varying degrees of allegiance by men who were far too busy with their rifles to attend to the furniture of their minds. Organisms were made of cells, States of communes. The miseries of society were due to centralized government and could be cured by its destruction. Republics were better than monarchies, but the Republic, one and indivisible, instead of abolishing poverty—the true end of all government— had merely lodged power and wealth in the hands of its bourgeois functionaries. France therefore should be dissolved into the cells of which it was a multiple, into independent, self-organized, self-governing communes. As in ancient times, the city was the true and only thinkable unit of democratic government. Such had been the real doctrine of Rousseau, and such was the inner spirit of the Girondin Constitution of 1793 with its elaborate provisions for a popular

referendum. A loose federation of socialistic and republican communes would be guaranteed alike against
the costly adventure of dynastic wars and the barbarous
electoral results of a clerical victory among the villages.
Much horror is often expressed at a programme
designed to procure the political dismemberment of
France; but it is proper to recognize that among the
heterogeneous ideas of the Commune there are traces
of that current of humanitarian feeling which, springing from the ideas of 1789, has ever since been a constant and melodramatic element in the republican
professions of France. The guillotine was solemnly
burned and a decree was passed for the destruction
of the Imperial Column in the Place Vendôme on the
ground that it was "a monument of barbarism, a
symptom of brute force and false glory, an affirmation
of militarism, a negation of international law, and a
permanent insult of the conqueror to the conquered."
The eighty thousand affiliated members of the Internationale dreamed that fine old dream of human
fraternity which is the prize of youth or the privilege
of inexperience, and burned to drive it home at the
point of the bayonet.[5]

All this, however, passed unappreciated in the
general horror which the Commune inspired. The
governing propensity of French politicians is timidity,
and as France welcomed the Empire, not because it
was actively enamoured of Cæsarism, but in order
to escape the Red Republic, so it was now ready to
accept a government which should undertake to cleanse
the body politic of the same malignant poison. Thiers
with his Provisional Republic performed this office.
The lively President strutted behind his troops watch-
ing through his field-glasses the success of his own

strategy with all the gusto of an expert, and the Paris Commune was crushed with inexorable severity. To prevent the spread of the inflammation in the great radical cities of the South, Thiers gave assurances that he would do nothing to endanger the establishment of a republic. The royalists of the Assembly accused him of broken pledges, and, when peace had been restored, when the Prussian indemnity had been paid and the Prussian troops cleared from the territory of France, struck down the man who had conferred these benefits on his country. Having a majority for a monarchical restoration, the deputies of the right and right centre were entitled to make their experiment, but in his caustic and perspicacious valediction (May 1873) the old man told them that three candidates could not sit on one throne, that the Republic must come, and that in the bottom of their hearts they knew it.

The only hope for the monarchy lying in a fusion of the legitimist and Orleanist sections of the Bourbon house, intrigues to this end were busily woven under the Presidency of Marshal Macmahon, himself favourable to the monarchy, but above all a plain and upright patriot. The Comte de Paris, heir to the Orleanist hopes, visited the Comte de Chambord, the head of the elder branch, and the Comte de Chambord himself paid a secret visit to Versailles. A committee of nine deputies plotted out the circumstances of the Restoration, how Henry V. was not to be subject to the indignity of a popular election or a *plébiscite*, how he was to rule in virtue of prescriptive right and grant a constitution out of the fund of his native condescension.

In the autumn of 1873 every political club and salon

in Versailles and Paris was agog with speculation. The contest would be close, the victory ambiguous, for the Republic had made converts in the Chamber and the monarchy could no longer count upon the left centre. According to one computation the monarchy had 348, the Republic 344 votes, while 36 votes were still doubtful. The fate of France, however, was not destined to be decided by a trial of parliamentary strength. It was common ground among all monarchists conversant with the political temper of the country that if the Comte de Chambord was to be invited to rule France, he must accept the tricolour flag ; but this is precisely what the Comte de Chambord refused to do. The flag was the emblem of his principle and without his principle he was merely in his own words, " a fat lame man." The old guard of the legitimist cause would, he felt, never forgive a surrender upon a point of honour. As one of them said, " Si le Comte de Chambord cède il sera peut-être mon roi, mais il n'est plus mon homme." And so, the Pope concurring, the chief of the Bourbons declined to accept the only compromise which might have brought his house back to rule over France.

However much the royalists might disguise the fact, this refusal meant the Republic. In one of the early debates at Bordeaux a deputy expressed a wish that the Republic would not come in " par la petite porte." The phrase is happy but the hope was disappointed. The Third Republic came in surreptitiously by the postern gate. The Constitution was built up piecemeal by an assembly which did not wish to build it at all, and neither in its successive parts nor in its entirety was it ever submitted to a *plébiscite* of the French nation. There was none of the old rapture as at the discovery of a new world of happiness. The Republic was accepted " faute de mieux " with the lack-lustre welcome extended to an official receiver in bankruptcy who is called in to liquidate a long course of dilapidations.   On January 30, 1875, it was carried in the Assembly by a single vote.

Meanwhile people of moderate conservative views had been steadily coming round to a solution which was already the creed of the great cities and of the departments of the north and east.   They said to themselves, " The Republic we have been afraid of is the Red Republic, the Commune ; but this has been destroyed by a government which is itself a republic in everything but name.   Between a conservative republic and a constitutional monarchy there is, as Benjamin Constant used to say, merely a difference in form.   We note that M. Laboulaye, who has been taking a prominent part in drafting the new organic laws, is a professed admirer of the English Constitution, and was himself a supporter of the Liberal Empire. Admitting that the Orleanist *régime* would be our ideal, it would almost certainly be less stable than a republic.   The legitimists would oppose it, it would not be energetically supported by a Church which day by day is becoming more ultramontane, and at any moment it might fall before a coalition of the disaffected groups.   The organic laws which have been drafted in a conservative Chamber obviate many of the objections which we have felt with regard to republican government.   In particular we are pleased that the legislature is to be bicameral, and we believe that a Senate elected by the communes of France will be a strong and salutary check upon the popular Chamber."

The character of the new Republic can find no better illustration than in the speeches of Gambetta, now conveniently published in eleven volumes by his friend and admirer, M. Joseph Reinach. If Thiers may be described as the founder of the Third Republic, Gambetta was certainly its prophet. He believed in it, he preached it up and down the country, he made it his mission to define republican ideas and to spread an enthusiasm for republican institutions. As Gambetta conceived of the Third Republic, so has the Third Republic substantially become. His appetites and repulsions, his enthusiasms and recoils are the appetites and repulsions, the enthusiasms and recoils of the political class which carries on the government of France. Imagine a small bourgeois of the Latin stock born in the south and inheriting the vivacity of the southern temperament. Give him a large, easy receptive nature, coarse, energetic faculties, a great memory, a facile tongue, a sonorous voice, an eager combative will. Throw him into the *Quartier Latin* in the middle days of the Empire when it was a rare thing for a student to descend from the seclusion of his gay, rough, reckless Bohemia into the politer quarters of Paris, when the ruling intellectual dynasty was a dynasty of revolt, its thinkers free-thinkers, its great romantic poet and novelist a proscribed exile, and remember that the atmosphere was full of the Positive Philosophy of Auguste Comte and of the grandiose democratic sentiment of Victor Hugo. It is easy to predict the kind of effect which such an environment would produce on such a young man. He believes neither in metaphysics, nor in religion nor in any kind of mystery. The Pope he regards as the enemy not only of Italian but also of human freedom. H

hates priests with the fierce, unexamining, comprehensive hatred of Garibaldi, but confides implicitly in
the " lion's marrow " of physical science as the proper
diet of energetic manhood, reads omnivorously in
French literature, and can declaim page after page of
Rabelais and Hugo. From such an apprenticeship
Gambetta went to the bar and sprang into fame as the
radical opponent of the Empire. Had he remained
a radical orator in opposition, the quality of his
politics might never have reached a high level. He
would have enunciated the same large vague principles
in the same large leonine voice, until the principles
would have become ossified and the rhetoric a vapour.
From this possible catastrophe Gambetta was saved
by the war, than which there is no school of politics
more rigorous, or less compatible with scholastic and
geometrical reasoning. He remained to the end of his
life an advocate, but he was henceforward an adaptive
advocate. He openly gloried in the fact that he had
no doctrine, but allowed his politics to be shaped by
circumstances. He regarded his inconsistencies as a
sign not of weakness but of a sage, open-eyed flexi-
bility. Before the war he roared against armaments ;
afterwards he advocated a citizen army. In oration
after oration he contended that the Bordeaux Assembly
had no constituent powers, and then he helped it to
make a constitution. Of all this he was not ashamed.
He called himself an opportunist and contrasted the
policy of opportunism with the policy of shipwreck.
Even on very fundamental questions he revised the
crude emphatic opinions of his bellicose youth. The
friend of Church disestablishment championed the Concordat, the enemy of the Second Chamber helped to
create the Senate, " the grand Council of all the com-

munes of France," and to preach its transcendent merits to a sceptical public. Again and again he protested his horror of chimeras. " There is no social question," he would say, turning his back on Utopia, " there are social questions." Such versatile obedience to the varying stress of conjuncture does not belong to the classical repertory. Gambetta was neither a red republican nor a doctrinaire republican, but a republican of a new build, less heroic but infinitely more serviceable, a republican of affairs. He represented the bourgeoisie of France, the small proprietors, tradesmen, and professional men who may be seen sipping their coffee and absinthe in the cafés and wineshops, and make the backbone of the community ; he knew the arguments which would go home to them and the kind of polity which was adapted to their needs. And as Gambetta was opportunist, so too was the Third Republic.

A great political influence cannot be built upon mere opportunism. The true statesman is like a ship which swings freely with the tides but swings at anchor. If he has no principles, he will either fix nobody's attention or earn everybody's contempt. Just as the average reader appreciates a connected paragraph, so the ordinary voter appreciates a connected politician. He is easier to read and remember, and if he is a man of real conviction, he carries through the necessary iteration of a crusade, perhaps impressively, but in any case in a fresh and tolerable way. For all his opportunism Gambetta preserved a few passionate political beliefs. He had the belief in universal suffrage and in the *scrutin de liste* as the best method of giving effect to the will of a democracy ; the belief in the sovereign efficacy of a centralized, well-conducted republican State; the belief in a complete system of free compulsory secular education " from the base to the summit of human knowledge " ; and finally the belief that " clericalism was the enemy." And this not only because the clergy of France, becoming more ultramontane day by day, supported the cause of the legitimists, but because the declared doctrine of the Papal See was adverse to the root principles of a democratic society.

So we are led to consider the ultimate antinomy which divides society in the Latin States of Europe. On the one hand there is the republican tradition dominant and established in France, evident though overmastered in Spain, partially transfused into the institutions of the national monarchy in Italy. On the other hand there is the Catholic Church, the ally of the Bourbon who rules in Spain, and of the Bourbons who can never rule in France, and the enemy and the victim of the French Revolution. The gulf is clear, the incompatibility absolute, the war truceless. The old school of Gallicans, the later school of liberal Catholics, has died out. Ultramontanism has killed it, the thing itself and the bitter ultramontane journalists of the Empire who felt the sting of the Italian wars and spread the poison through France. The syllabus of 1864 and the infallibility decree of 1870 have cut away the hazy middle ground in which many a generous and divided soul found a reconciliation for his inner discords. A French child must either be brought up a Roman Catholic or he must be brought up a Republican. There is no real alternative. In the first case he will learn that the French Revolution was the crime of crimes, that divorce is a sin, that civil marriage is a sin, that monarchy is the best form of government, that liberty is an alias for wanton pride, and that, with the exception of two brief interludes, the whole history of France since 1789 has been one ghastly aberration from the path of godly duty. And in the second case he will learn just the opposite of all this, that the Church in all ages has been the enemy of human freedom and progress, that the Civil Code is the charter of social emancipation, and that the French Revolution was the discovery of social justice upon earth. The Third Republic has captured the schools, dissolved the congregations, and disestablished the Church, but it still rules over a divided nation.[6]

CHAPTER XII

AN EXPERIMENT IN SPAIN

España es como cisne que canta in su agonía
Cuando decir podremos que España renació ?
—AGUILERA, " Ay de España," 1848

A Republican Propaganda has ceased to exist even among the Socialists.—*The Nation*, Oct. 2, 1902

IN the middle of May 1873 Charles Bradlaugh, atheist and republican, son of a solicitor's clerk and a nursery maid, born in Bacchus Walk, Hoxton, aged forty, once private in the Seventh Dragoon Guards, popular lecturer on Atheism and kindred subjects, editor of the *National Reformer*, and for all these qualities and professions held in deep aversion by the majority of his countrymen, crossed the Pyrenees in a diligence, and after suffering some molestation from Carlist bands, arrived safely in Madrid. Apart from the peculiar dangers of the time, for civil war was raging over Northern Spain, Charles Bradlaugh was not the man to travel to Madrid for pleasure. On May 11 a meeting of a remarkable character had been held in the Town Hall in Birmingham, and Bradlaugh's Spanish pilgrimage was the outcome of that gathering. He travelled as the bearer of resolutions of sympathy with the newly formed Spanish Republic, and these resolutions had been passed at an English Republican Conference containing fifty-four delegates from nearly as many English towns, and attended by some four thousand five hundred persons. The English emissary was saluted with acclamations in the Spanish capital. The newspapers devoted paragraphs to " Señor Branglong." The leaders of the republican movement entertained him at dinner. Don Emilio Castelar, the Minister of State, while carefully avoiding the indiscretion of an official reception, received him more than once in private audience, and as the burly figure of the ex-dragoon was descried on the balcony of his hotel, plaudits went up from a crowd who, had they been permitted fully to inspect the solid furniture of his mind, would have found little to attract and much to repel.[1]

The Republican Movement in England was an eddy rather than a current. Apart from the Irishmen, who are always ready to fish in troubled waters, there was a small residuum of artisans who resented the cost of the monarchy and the long retirement of the Queen from the public gaze. The republican clubs, which were formed in 1870, struggled on for a few years, gave some anxiety to Mr Gladstone, and then, other more pressing causes claiming the attention of the British workmen, perished of inanition. So far as it had roots in the past, the movement was derived from the teaching of Tom Paine, " our famous countryman, our great and only prototype," as he is described by his enthusiastic and much-persecuted editor, Richard Carlile. Through Carlile the anti-Christian and republican teaching of Paine was filtered into the undercurrents of the great English towns and affected the mind of Charles Bradlaugh. The creed of these earnest, half-educated men was very simple, very confident, and not in the least romantic. Carlile, writing twelve years before the first Reform Bill,

pleaded for a " House of real representatives, possessing a democratic ascendency renewed every year, free
from the influence or criticism of any other bodies
or establishments," and opined that such a House
would make short work of an expensive hereditary
system of monarchy. Bradlaugh was specially impressed with the shortcomings of the House of
Brunswick and with the large sums voted by the
British Parliament for the support of " small German
breast-bestarred wanderers." Given four or five more
years of political education, the country would not
tolerate a successor to Queen Victoria. It is needless
to add that Bradlaugh was as far awry in his calculation as his master Carlile, who hoped " to see the day
and witness the deed when an English Senate should
disown the divinity of the Christian religion." Queen
Victoria lived down the little republican ferment of
the seventies, as she had lived down the early unpopularity of the Prince Consort and the bitter suspicions
which clustered round the person of his adviser, Baron
Stockmar. Bradlaugh himself turned to other fields.
Advices from South America proved that presidents
were not necessarily cheap or republics necessarily
incorrupt.[2]

The Spanish Republic which aroused so much
interest and enthusiasm in the Town Hall in Birmingham, endured a short and tragic life. It was born on
February 11, 1873, and died on October 29, 1875, of a
military *pronunciamento* in the true Spanish order of
congruity. In its brief span of tortured existence it
battled with a serious cantonal insurrection in the
South, with a no less serious Carlist rising in the North,
endured four *coups d'état*, and experienced five
presidents, the first of whom dismayed the faithful by

17

secretly eloping to Paris to escape his political responsibilities. It considered, but never applied, the frame
of a federal constitution borrowed from the United
States, issued a decree emancipating the slaves of
Puerto Rico, and put out seductive schemes for the
protection of labour in factories, for industrial arbitra-
tion, and for State-paid compulsory schooling. Beautiful illusions rocked its cradle. There was to be no
more conscription, no more war : but what with the
Carlists and the Federalists, two hundred thousand
men were in arms through these two years in Spain
itself, not to speak of eighty thousand in Cuba : and,
when the last red flag had been hauled down from the
last rebel fort in Cartagena, only twenty-eight houses
in that great marine city were uninjured by the
bombardment.[3]

The story of the Spanish Revolution affords a curious
instance of the difficulty of infusing the wine of new
doctrine into a receptacle which has not been devised
to hold it. Spanish republicanism grew out of
Spanish liberalism and this in turn was a graft from
the French Revolution. In fighting the French the
leaders of the Spanish national movement learnt to
value the ideas which gave to the French armies their
peculiar momentum. The Peninsular War was a
school of politics. It taught the Spaniards that they
could live without a king ; it revived the old provincial feeling ; it led to the spread of democratic
ideas in the great towns and in the army ; it restored
the lost tradition of the Cortes, and was the means
of giving to Spain a constitution modelled upon the
latest French fashion, which, though entirely unsuited
to the political conditions of the country, served as the
battle-cry of Spanish liberalism in the age of auto-

cratic reaction. Unfortunately the sudden impulsion towards political activity was accompanied by one serious drawback. The six years of partisan warfare had revived the national taste for martial anarchy. A large population had grown up—students, smugglers, monks, soldiers—for whom conspiracy was a career and adventure an industry. They had fallen under the spell of a life, in which everything seems possible, and could not easily adjust themselves to the limiting conditions of a stable existence. The Spaniard is at once indolent and imaginative, on the one side wrapped in oriental fatalism, on the other side open to visionary prospects and Quixotic undertakings. It is difficult to rouse him at all, but he will be less easily stirred up to hoe his own garden than to caper away on Rosinante after the mirage. And quite apart from the fundamental lines of national temperament, many steadying conditions which now exist were absent in the first decades of the nineteenth century. Trade and industry were backward, and the desire to make a fortune in commerce or manufacture was, outside Catalonia, almost a negligible force in the psychology of the nation. Ambitious men did not aim at becoming captains of industry; they embarked in the exciting struggle for public employment and gambled on the rise and fall of political parties.

In this thrilling lottery, where the prizes of success were so rich and various, the army, as the most active part of the nation, was as much concerned as the civilians. The generals had become politicians, the soldiers followed the generals, and since the principal desire of the people was to escape the octroi, a military *pronunciamento* was a frequent and not ungrateful incident in the national life. By degrees a parliamentary government was forced upon the Crown, but worked in a manner peculiar to Spain. The civil governor of every province was instructed to inform the population submitted to his charge that every vote given to an opposition candidate would be requited by a rigorous exaction of taxes. Since in Spain every one is in arrears with his taxes this threat was generally sufficient to secure the desired object; but some districts were notoriously recalcitrant, and here a more drastic method, known as the *Partido de la porra* was employed with gratifying results. A party of ministerial hirelings, armed with bludgeons, assaults the inmates of an opposition quarter. An outcry is raised, the magistrate intervenes; the recalcitrant voters are taken into custody, detained until the election is over, and then released without a stain upon their characters. By these means a Cortes is obtained of which almost every member is a nominal supporter of the Government, and were the party system understood in Spain as it is in England, were Spanish politicians grouped together upon some common and established ground of principle, an energetic ministry might thus be secured in a perpetuity of office. But party government in the true sense of the term did not, and does not, exist in Spain. The members of the Cortes act for the most part for their own interest. They expect favours from the Government, and when they do not get them, they lay their heads together to procure its overthrow. A country cannot make steadfast progress when its affairs are in the hands of eloquent orators and military adventurers, and when the true spirit of constitutional government is thus persistently violated. An enlightened monarchy might have helped Spain to traverse a difficult period;

but of all monarchies in Europe the Spanish was least fitted to perform this office. It would be difficult to find a parallel for a succession of rulers so debased and unintelligent as Ferdinand VII, and the two ladies who succeeded him on the Spanish throne, Christina and Isabella II. The ancient loyalty to the Bourbon crown, divided into two conflicting allegiances by the Carlist war, outraged by the scandals of Queen Isabella's Court, spoiled by the pressure of taxes and conscription, finally broke down in 1868. The liberals had been driven into republicanism by persecution, the navy was menaced with reductions, the army honeycombed with radical propaganda. The Queen escaped into exile, and after the Crown of Spain had been hawked round Europe it was accepted by Amadeo of Savoy.

The rule of this well-meaning but alien prince was unpopular and brief. No foreigner could content Spain; no son of Victor Emmanuel could be grateful to the Church. The murder of General Prim, a man of rare power and lack of scruple, removed from Spain the successful leader of the Revolution, and from the throne its principal support. No sooner had the Duke of Aosta set foot in Madrid than the ground began to quake under his feet. The Revolution of 1868 had been the work of three parties, the Liberal Union whose ideal was the July monarchy, the progressists who were more advanced, and the democrats who secretly or openly worked for a republic. To the amazement of the Spanish conservatives the new King announced his intention to be loyal to a democratic constitution. His virtue lost him the support of one party without gaining him the confidence of the other. A Conservative Chamber was dissolved, a Radical Chamber was summoned, and the republicans, who

knew what had happened to Louis Philippe and had
never regarded the democratic monarchy as more than
a convenient portico into the shining palace of liberty
saw to it that the King's position was made intolerable.
When this happened Amadeo resigned his throne and
the orators and philosophers of the Republic had their
chance.

Save in Barcelona, where an anti-dynastic party
had existed since 1840, Republicanism was a plant
of recent growth in Spain. It had ripened rapidly
and shot up into a prominence which was a surprise
to itself. Its two most distinguished leaders, Don
Francisco Pi y Margall and Don Emilio Castelar—
the first a Catalan from Barcelona, the second an
Andalusian from Cadiz—represented types of political
conviction and sentiment which chiefly flourished in
the great coast towns and had grown up under a
plentiful aspersion of exotic doctrine. Don Francisco, a *savant* and a man of letters, was a disciple of
Hegel and Proudhon ; Don Emilio belonged to the
romantic school of Lamartine, Michelet, and Hugo
Both proclaimed themselves federalists, but while
Don Francisco held to the federal idea with the
tenacity of a philosopher and a doctrinaire, Castelar
was made of more pliant material, and in the harden
ing responsibilities of office discovered many of the
qualities of a statesman.

The arguments which led Don Francisco to the
federal solution are so characteristic of the peculiar
weakness of Spanish political reasoning at this period
that they deserve to be briefly stated. Man, said the
Catalan philosopher, is lord of himself. If one man
extends his hand over another he is guilty not only of
tyranny but of sacrilege. Between two sovereignties

there can be no bond but pacts, and out of a series of ascending pacts, pacts between individuals, families, villages, provinces, nations, the true State is ultimately built up. Federation then is the only scientific form of government, the ultimate evolution of the political idea, the only means of securing to a nation dignity, peace, and order. But federation must be distinguished from devolution. Power must come from below. The central government must receive only such attributes as those which the separate provinces and States may choose to confer on it. The federation of Spain must, therefore, begin by the constitution of the ancient Spanish provinces into organized autonomous States. The house of liberty must be built from the foundation upwards ; only so could it stand secure.

These flimsy deductions from anarchic first principles were supported by appeals to political experience. France had twice experimented with a unitary republic, and on each occasion the republic had been swallowed up by a despot. Had the French government been less completely centralized, had the control of Paris not carried with it as a necessary corollary the dominion of France, the success of the Bonapartes would have been impossible. Don Francisco and his following of Spanish republicans, taking their intellectual nutriment from France, were resolved, if possible, to avoid the double catastrophe which had befallen their brilliant and aspiring neighbour. They regarded federal autonomy as an insurance against a Bourbon restoration ; and they reasoned, not without plausibility, that the diversified genius and character of the Spanish nation rendered it peculiarly apt to the federal solution. The evils of Europe in general, and of Spain in particular, seemed to them to be largely due

to the excessive strength of governments supported
by military force.   They demanded that conscription
should be abolished ;   they protested against the
rigour of the military code, and held that federation
would cure Spain of her two most inveterate evils,
the military *pronunciamento* and the mania for public
employment.   Details were foreign to their habits,
and they had not passed beyond the vaguest and
most splendid generalities when the sudden resignation of the Savoyard King made them the arbiters
of Spain.[4]

Ever since the union of Aragon and Castile, the
spirit of separation has been strong in the Spanish
peninsula.   The old nationalities have been obliterated
neither by the imposing dignity of Castilian letters, nor
yet by the levelling action of the Castilian sovereigns.
The Basque, the Catalan, the Galician preserves his
ancient language, cherishes his ancient customs, and
views with jealous eye the ascendency and encroach-
ments of Madrid.   In the declining years of Isabella's
reign this proud and independent posture had been
encouraged by the weakness of the crown and by the
federal propaganda of the politicians.   The country
was sick of taxes, of wars, of conscription, and believed
that these plagues would disappear if only the meddlesome gentlemen from Madrid could be sent about their
business.   Active poisons mingled in the great seaport
towns with innocent hallucinations. The Internationale
was at work spreading the principles of the French
Commune broadcast among the artisans and teaching
them to clutch at every description of wild remedy
for social evils.   The consequence was that no sooner
was the republic proclaimed in Madrid than a frenzy
of revolutionary   excitement   swept   through   the

eastern and southern towns. Barcelona declared its
autonomy ; Cartagena proclaimed itself head of the
Canton of Murcia ; Seville, Cadiz, Malaga hoisted the
red flag of socialism. Don Francisco was pitiably
embarrassed. He had preached federation from below ;
and here was a spontaneous movement, federal in
name, which threatened to disrupt the Spanish nation.
He had thundered against militarism, and to save the
Republic he must send an army into Andalusia. For
a moment he cherished a belief that he could kill the
cantonal movement with rosewater ; then discovering
his mistake he resigned his office after some five weeks
of power or rather of impotence. His successor
Salmeron was equally conscientious and ineffectual.
Rather than sanction capital punishment in the army
he let go the helm and made way for Don Emilio
Castelar, in whom republican Spain at last discovered
a ruler.[5]

The new president was a great artist, the most
abundant, the most poetic, the most richly-coloured
orator of his age. Those who have heard him in the
full tide of his exuberance, filling a great hall with his
organ voice and entrancing the imagination of an
alien audience with his inexhaustible vocabulary and
splendid images, will never forget the impression.
Such men live not upon thought but upon feeling, and
the feeling which dominated Castelar was the same
romantic enthusiasm for liberty which inspired the
life of Garibaldi and the teaching of Michelet. The
intellectual lineage of the Andalusian orator came
through Rousseau and the Girondins rather than
through Voltaire and the professors of negation.
Castelar was a Christian, and believed that the Christian
ideal could only be realized on its political side in a

democratic polity. The splendours of historic S]
appealed to an imagination which was at once
sanguine, too comprehensive, and too poetic to ac
of belittling exclusions. He dreamt that Spain, w]
had long been debased by the policy of her ru.
would experience a rejuvenescence through the vig
of her people. He believed that a free Spain w(
be a great country ; that liberty being all-perva
as air, Portugal would shake off the shackles of
monarchy, and merge her political existence in ·
of her republican neighbour. He believed that
South American Republics would renew their allegia
to the parent land, and that as it was the missio
Russia to spread civilization through the Cer
Asian Steppes and the long Siberian plateau, so it
the noble destiny of the Spanish people to rec.
North Africa from barbarism and waste. All t
grandiose visions Don Emilio entertained and w·
support by prodigal displays of inexact histo:
illustration. But when the hour struck for ac
Castelar proved that he was not merely a rhetoric
He assumed powers which were practically dictatc
broke the back of the Cantonal insurrection,
showed that a theoretical belief in the virtue
federation was not inconsistent with a jealous d·
to preserve the unity of Spain.

Taxed with inconsistency he declared himse
posibilista, an opportunist desirous of a conserva
republic, reaching by an opposite route the s
conclusion as Thiers, who founded the Third Rep1
in France. The conditions of the two countries v
however, different. In Spain there was no ro
attachment in the army to the republican i(
monarchical and clerical sentiment was stronger,

the principal centres of republican feeling were those great seaport towns which had thrown themselves into the cantonal movement, the suppression of which was the first task of the new Republic in Madrid. It was not unnatural, therefore, that the new Republic should have earned unpopularity. The leaders had been professors of federation, and it was in the name of federation that town after town, and district after district, had declared its autonomy and challenged the authority of the central power. It is true that the insurrection was stamped out, but would it have burst into flame but for the agitation of the Federalists? Was not the Republic responsible for the civil war, for the five days' fighting at Seville, for the destruction of Cartagena, for the widespread desolation of the Andalusian province? Such reflections were not without justification. The course of the Republic had been starred by a succession of catastrophes—the Carlist successes in the North, the civil war in the East and the South; and the parliamentary history of the period was enlivened by one military *coup d'état*, carried out in the interest of Castelar at the expense of the Chamber in Madrid. No great prophetic gift was necessary to predict the downfall of so flimsy and unfortunate a fabric, and when, in December 1874, Martinez Campos proclaimed Alphonso XII. in Jovellar's Army of the Centre, few were much surprised or concerned. Indeed the monarchical restoration in Spain was effected with as little difficulty as the return of Charles II. of England, when once General Monk had made up his mind that the King must be brought back to his own.[6]

" The Federal Republic," says M. Cherbuliez, " was a chimera of Proudhon translated into Castilian by

M. Pi y Margall." Chimera it certainly was, for its
advocates chose the wrong moment, the wrong methods,
and the wrong arguments. The cause of federalism,
however, was not extinguished by the catastrophe of
the cantonal movement. It is still flourishing in
Catalonia, the province of its birth, and the principal
focus of republican agitation in Spain. It derives its
nutrition from elementary and permanent facts of
Spanish geography and racial distribution. It supports a literature of propaganda and prints catechisms
of belief. It has enlisted followers from the learned
and the cultured class. But the realization of the
federal ideal involves, as was seen in 1873, a number
of practical problems of great complexity. Should
the forty-nine administrative provinces be endowed
with autonomy—an arrangement which would go
very little way in satisfying the historic feeling of the
old independent nations ? Or should the Peninsula be
carved up, as was projected by the Constituent
Assembly of 1873, into thirteen States, corresponding
to the old historic groupings ? If so, would Malaga
cede pride of place to Granada, Cadiz to Seville,
Valladolid to Burgos ? These difficulties had not been
thought out by the Federal leaders of the seventies.
They made the mistake, common to unpractised and
sanguine Spaniards, of supposing that a country can
be suddenly cured of its chronic disorders by the
immediate application of a Constitutional panacea.
The federal republic became the catchword of the
hour. It would make Spain as rich as the United
States and as happy as Switzerland. It would rid her
of the costly conscript and the plaguy office-hunter and
the political Jesuit. It would stanch the running
sore of Carlism, a malady due not so much to the

cancerous germs of clericalism and legitimacy as to the obstinate provincial feeling of the Basques.

Unfortunately all the light and disordered spirits in society, everyone who nursed a grudge or a grievance, a fad or an appetite, clustered round the respectable group of political visionaries who held aloft the Federal banner. " Who gave you the right to arrest me ? " said a thief caught in the act in the streets of Madrid ; " are not we in a federal republic ? " Under the cloak of Federalism all kinds of questionable, even criminal objects were passionately pursued. Peasants broke down enclosures, arguing that by ancient right the land belonged to the community, and that the labourer was entitled to a common enjoyment of the waste or even of the harvest. The Internationale preached the dissolution of Spain into ten thousand powerless and autonomous communities. Every instrument of public order, the priest, the soldier, the policeman, was held up to opprobrium in the big seacoast cities by fevered companies of artisan politicians, who flouted patriotism as a delusion and government as a crime. So general and spontaneous an outburst of anarchy had not been seen in any European country since 1789. And when the disorder had been finally mastered, there was no surplus of energy available for the maintenance of a cause which, despite many foul accretions, embodied the purest and most enlightened spirit in Spanish politics.[7]

CHAPTER XIII

THE REPUBLICAN CAUSE

Il n'y a de bon dans l'homme que ses jeunes sentiments et ses vieilles pensées.—JOUBERT

THERE can be little question that since 1870 the cause of Republicanism has made no substantial progress in Europe. France is still the only great European republic, and the political history of France under her new *régime* has not been such as to invite imitation. The position of the monarchies, which seemed so precarious in 1848, has been considerably, indeed progressively, improved since the failure of that great and generous outburst of high but ill-calculated ideals. In part this change has been due to personal causes. The level of political intelligence among monarchs, which was very low in the generation preceding 1848, has certainly improved; and the virtues of Queen Victoria and King William I. of Prussia have had some share in dispelling the clouds of criticism which had collected round the representatives of their respective Houses. How thick those clouds were in England no student of Thackeray's " Four Georges " or of the old newspapers is likely to forget.

When George IV. died in 1830, the London *Times* wrote as follows : " The truth is—and it speaks volumes about the man—that there never was an individual less regretted by his fellow-creatures than this deceased King. What eye has wept for him? What heart has heaved one throb of unmercenary sorrow? Was there at any time a gorgeous pageant on the stage more completely forgotten than he has been, even from the day on which the heralds proclaimed his successor? If George IV. ever had a friend, a devoted friend—in any rank of life—we protest that the name of him or her has not yet reached us." [1]

Four-score years have passed since these words were written, and it is only with an effort that Englishmen can now realize that the British monarchy had, within the recollection of a single long life, fallen so low in public esteem. Thomas Carlyle, describing, in 1843, the lamentation which went up at the premature death of Prince Henry, the heir of James I., assumes that an emotion so deep and general could never again be experienced. "The sorrow of the population (as we said) is inconceivable to any population now. As yet the whole nation is like the family of one good landlord, with his loyal tenants and servants round; and here is the beautiful young Lordship and Heir-Apparent struck suddenly down! Who would not weep? We, had our time been then, should have wept as I hope; but it is too late now." [2] Such a view would not have been peculiar to Carlyle; it would have been held by most Englishmen of that generation. Yet no one can have lived in England through the last twenty years without acknowledging that a great change has been silently and insensibly accomplished by the joint influence of Queen Victoria and King Edward. The monarchy is stronger and more respected; its place in the scheme of a democratic polity is more comfortably settled, and a sphere of unchallenged utility has been discovered for the King and the royal family in the discharge of functions which lie outside the discords of parliamentary life. Nobody who witnessed the national grief in 1901, or again in 1910, can doubt but that it was general and unaffected—the grief of a people successively bereaved of two wise, familiar, and constant friends.

That the change has been mainly due to accidents of personal excellence no one could deny. The spectacle of the head of a grand and populous State punctually, prudently, and devotedly discharging his public duties inevitably excites feelings of grateful admiration among his subjects. The fact that the sovereign stands aloof from the party struggle, that he is understood to represent the whole interest of the country and not the opinion or interest of a section, greatly adds to the moral power of his office. And wherever a sovereign is endowed with public or private virtues those virtues will not be allowed to remain unperceived. Physical science, which, by planing down social and intellectual inequalities, has given us democratic civilization, supplies, by a subtle form of revenge, to persons of eminent station, a powerful engine of advertisement and a kind of automatic mechanism for the manufacture of popularity. Remote persons are difficult to know, and being difficult to know are difficult to like. But physical science enables the most remote person of all, the head of the State, to take lodgment in the feeblest and humblest imagination. The art of photography catches him at chance moments as he steps out of a train, walks after partridges, chats with a friend, or fondles a child. The cinematograph exhibits him as a spectacle in motion to crowds who have never beheld him in flesh and blood. Electricity diffuses his messages of congratulation and condolence ; steam carries him from one end of the Empire to the other. No newspaper issues from the press without a record of his doings of the guests he entertains, the sport he enjoys, the sermons he endures, the public functions he patiently performs. No detail is too trivial to be registered, and in a business age it is not unsafe to assume that the news supplied to a nation is news which a nation wishes to hear. Thus by a process of ceaseless and multitudinous attrition the image of the sovereign and his circle is stamped into the brain-stuff of the country, so that the peasant in the little thatched village carries about with him in his daily task the image of King and Queen, as beings alike splendid and familiar, whose doings in the great capital or elsewhere it is always pleasant to know and to discuss.

An even more significant change is the growing recognition of the fact that the precise form assumed by the executive is no scientific measure of political or civil liberty. Assuming that a country possesses parliamentary institutions, that the franchise is wide and the ministry responsible, the ultimate control of affairs lies with the people, whether the head of the executive be hereditary or elective. In the Constitution of Great Britain, where the Parliament is sovereign and the real conduct of affairs lies with a Minister representing the predominant party in the Lower House, the popular will acts upon the executive more swiftly and immediately than is possible under the constitution of the United States. The American President is safe for four years ; a gust of popular disfavour may, at any time, drive the British Prime Minister out of office. In the republic there is more

18

of social equality; but it is in the monarchy of the old variety that the machine of legislation and government responds most promptly to the fluctuating opinion of the mass. This, of course, is a comparatively new development. Before 1848, there was some reason for thinking that the institution of monarchy was incompatible with constitutional and economic progress. Europe was relatively poor, and weighed against the modest budgets of those days the cost of monarchy was unquestionably heavy. But while the wealth of Europe has greatly increased, the financial burden of its royal families has remained very much where it was. A nation which budgets in hundreds of millions, which spends a million on a warship and eleven millions on old age pensions, can afford to pay its King a salary exceeded by the earnings of not a few among its more prosperous merchants and manufacturers. Items of the expenditure are criticized, but with less and less of vigour and reverberation, as the true financial proportions of the transaction are more perfectly understood. Meanwhile the sphere of political liberty has been constantly expanding at the expense, not of the monarchies but of the privileged and wealthy classes of Europe. In a review of James Mill's Encyclopædia article on "Government," published in 1820, Macaulay argued that universal suffrage would upon utilitarian principles lead to "one vast spoliation," and that if it were ever carried into effect in England, "a few half-naked fishermen would divide with the owls and foxes the ruins of the greatest of European cities." Universal suffrage has come, not indeed in England, but in quarters where the intelligent prophet sixty years ago would have been least prepared to find it. It has been adopted in the elections to the Imperial Reichstag of Germany since 1871, in Spain since 1890, and in Austria since 1907. Democracy has been too busy in capturing the Parliaments to think about assaulting the crowns.

The increased urgency of social problems has tended in a similar direction. William Cobbett, who was no Republican, but on the contrary a bitter adversary of that form of government, struck the keynote of much subsequent agitation when he defined capital as " money taken from the labouring classes which, being given to army tailors and such like, enables them to keep foxhounds and to trace their descent from the Normans." [3] The question of the relations of capital and labour is in truth, and has been discovered to be, far more important than the precise form assumed by the executive in a democratic State. The artisan classes of Europe believe that it is the first duty of society to capture the unearned increment, and are not unwilling to accept hereditary monarchy as " a social-democratic institution." In the numerous programmes which are put out at Socialist congresses there is very little talk of republicanism. The French Socialist party, meeting at Tours in 1902, declared that Socialism was essentially republican, but then the French Socialists already live under a republic. The Austrians, the Germans, and the Belgians content themselves with advancing propositions which are thought to be immediately relevant to the material well-being of the lower classes, and are careful to abstain from language which might be construed as revolutionary or seditious.[4] Republican feeling may be widely diffused, but it has undergone an allopathic change. A vague, all-pervading discontent with the economic structure of society has taken the place of the simple and direct protest against the costliness of crowns and the profligacy of courts.

Three other factors have contributed to the decline of European republicanism. The first of these is the success of Bismarck's statesmanship in Germany. Finding Germany poor, weak, divided, Bismarck left it the greatest military and industrial power on the Continent. This result he achieved by blood and iron, using as the principal instrument of his purpose the force of the Prussian monarchy, and setting himself deliberately to affront all those liberal principles which enlightened Germans had derived from the political history of France or England. Those who are acquainted with the historical writings of Treitschke, the eloquent Berlin professor who spread abroad the new principles of *real Politik*, will be able to estimate the gulf which divides the German mind of 1888, from the German mind forty years before, when the Frankfort Parliament was painfully and passionately elaborating the rights of man. The atmosphere has become completely changed. Free trade has given place to protection, the spirit of liberalism to the spirit of autocracy : for the older vague, ineffectual cosmopolitanism there is now a deep and passionate national feeling, expressing itself sometimes in violent antipathy, not only to those foreign races which seem likely to thwart the historic mission of Germany, but also to the alien citizens, whether they be Jews or Poles, whose presence impairs the purity of the German race.[5]

A second factor is the growth of imperialism and " world-policy." Ask nine Englishmen out of ten to-day what they consider to be the pre-eminen value of the British monarchy, and they will reply tha the Crown keeps the Empire together. This answe would not have been given in 1837, nor yet in 1850, but it would certainly be given now. We are not called upon to consider the value of the proposition or the light which it throws upon the political psychology of the British Colonies ; the significant fact is that the proposition has become a cardinal factor in our political creed. Walter Bagehot pointed out as far back as 1865, that there must be not only useful but also dignified parts in a constitution. The taste for ritual, for playthings, for make-believe, is deeply rooted in human nature, and monarchy appeals to the deferential instincts of the ordinary human being. Overthrow the monarchy, replace the King with an elective President, and what would become of the loyalty of Australia, New Zealand, or Canada ? The British Colonists have no particular respect for the Mother of Parliaments, and a very particular and not ill-grounded aversion to the rule of Downing Street ; but they regard the Crown with feelings of simple and passionate veneration. The King, having been deprived of political power, cannot harm them ; and having little ritual themselves, they are the more fascinated by the pomp of an ancient and dignified institution which they have no means of reproducing in their several communities, but which they regard as the joint and several possession of the British race.

The argument can be reinforced from another quarter. The success of the United States proves that an elective President may rule a Continent which is geographically continuous. It does not prove that the republican system is adapted to communities so disjoined from one another by vast intervals of space as to be incapable of uniting in a common electoral system for legislative purposes. " I suppose," said

Mr Balfour on July 22, 1910, " that the community,
so far as this island is concerned, would not sink into
chaos if this was a republic and not a monarchy ;
but in my opinion the Empire would sink into chaos.
You could not have at the head of an Empire, so
peculiarly constituted as ours is, a President elected,
let us say, as the President of the United States is,
every four years—the creation, or at all events the
choice of a party, changing many times in the lifetime
of every individual, and representing the abstraction
of a Constitution and not the personal head of an
Empire.   You could never direct the Empire on that
principle simply because, if you insisted on having an
elected President in this country, he would be elected
by the electorate of this country and not by the
electorate of the Crown or of the Crown colonies."
Conversely, it may be affirmed that the cause of
monarchy in the Iberian Peninsula has been permanently weakened by the loss of the American
colonies of Spain and Portugal.

It was a widely held opinion at the time of the French
Revolution that Europe would become a federation
of republics, and that the common acceptance of the
republican form of government would secure to the
Continent of Europe the blessings of everlasting peace.
Half a century later Cobden was preaching the doctrine
that the millennium of peace would come, not through
the diffusion of republican principles but from the
common adoption of free trade.   It is now a very
general belief that the cause of European peace is
assisted by the social and family ties which subsist
between the monarchs of Europe.   The time has not
yet come to estimate with any degree of exactitude
the services which the monarchies of Europe have

rendered during the last half century to the cause of peace ; but British opinion has been profoundly impressed by the fact that the Prince Consort and Queen Victoria averted a collision between Great Britain and the United States in 1861, that the Queen helped to save France from a second war with Germany in 1875, and that the unique weight of King Edward's personal influence was steadily thrown into the scale of peace.

There can be no more signal instance of the decline of republican feeling in Europe than the action taken by Norway in 1905, upon the severance of her constitutional bond with Sweden. Of all European nations Norway is the most apt for a republic. Here is a people of peasants, merchants, fishermen, and sailors, free from those abrupt differences of wealth and station which are so painfully evident in most European States, and preserving in its geographical isolation and archaic simplicity of life the high spirit of independence appropriate to a mountain race. After a protracted and bitter constitutional struggle, Norway succeeed in severing a connexion with Sweden which had been forced upon her to suit the convenience of European diplomacy ninety-one years before. The Norwegians agitated for the creation of a Norwegian ministry of foreign affairs, for Norwegian consuls, for a Norwegian flag. The King of Sweden refused to bow to the storm, and ultimately found that he could not obtain a Norwegian ministry. The members of the Norwegian Government laid down their offices, and the Storthing declared that since the constitutional royal power had become inoperative, the union with Sweden under one King was dissolved. Having broken loose from her moorings, Norway had

the whole ocean of constitutional experiment before
her.   She might have established a republic, and there
was a party in the State led by the famous novelist,
Björnstjerne Björnson, which held republican opinions;
but whereas the republicans were divided in doctrine,
some advocating an American scheme with a strong
President, others a Constitution framed either on the
Swiss or on the French model, with a mere figurehead,
the monarchists were united.   The vacant throne was
offered first to a son of King Oscar II. of Sweden, and
afterwards, upon his refusal, to Prince Charles of
Denmark, who accepted the offer conditionally upon
its ratification by the Norwegian people.

   That the Norwegians acted with prudence at a very
difficult crisis of their national affairs will be allowed
by anyone who examines the situation.   They were
trembling on the verge of a war with Sweden, and were
unwilling to add to their embarrassments by embark-
ing upon a radical change in the Norwegian Constitution.   Such a change might precipitate a collision
on the frontier, and was certain to be the occasion of
keen internal controversy.   Besides, it had always been
their contention, not that they were averse to monarchy
in itself, but that the Constitution of the dual kingdom
was such that King Oscar II., whose personal popularity and good intentions were never in dispute, was
unable to rule as a constitutional sovereign in Norway.
The union was professedly severed, not that a republic
might be established, but that a constitutional
monarchy might be preserved.   A country therefore
which had loudly argued for a generation that its
uneasiness was caused by a neglect of the true maxims
of constitutional monarchy, could not, without losing
every shred of political self-respect, now swallow up its

ciples. It could not declare that its professed zeal
the spirit of the Constitution was not a reality but
ham ; it could not, after posing as the true con-
vative, suddenly hoist the radical colours. And
argument from consistency was justified by con-
erations of prudence. The Norwegians were given
understand that a monarchy would be more accept-
e than a republic both in England and in Germany,
1 as the future had never been less transparent, the
orthing was disposed to place a high value upon the
eem of its two great foreign neighbours. A King,
), would imply dynastic alliances, and these would
ord an additional security for peace.

A *plébiscite* of the country was taken, not upon the
iestion of a republic but upon the acceptance of
ince Charles of Denmark. A wave of loyalist
thusiasm swept Norway from end to end. The
eat republican leader Björnson advised the accept-
ice of the King. The leading newspapers commended
m. Most of the peasant members of the Storthing
)ted for him with acclamation. So striking a com-
union of enthusiasm cannot be explained by mere
onsiderations of political expediency. There is
erhaps no country in Europe where the memory of
ery ancient things is so green as it is in Norway.
:very peasant knows of the great sea-kings of far-off
imes, of Sverri, and Haakon, and Olaf ; takes the Sagas
vith his daily bread, and peoples the dales and fells
nd fiords with scenes from that simple and heroic age.
n Norway, as everywhere else, the hand of time has
voven some new patterns into the texture of the
:ommon life. Towns have risen, but they are few and
;mall. Socialism has been imported from Germany,
)ut only since 1887. The austere framework of the

mountains forbids any wide departure from the tradition of that hard and simple living which is reflected in the Sagas. The clinging illusions of the past are more potent here under the overpowering dominion of great and permanent natural forces. Mixed with a robust appetite for freedom there is a solemn and loyal reverence for the things which have been. " When a man is born under one government," remarked a Bechuana chief, " how can he be happy under another ? " The main part of the Norwegian people agreed with that African sentiment. They had always lived under kings ; they had been loyal to very bad kings ; they cherished an affectionate recollection of the days of Norwegian independence prior to 1387, when they were ruled by men of their own race. And so with the enthusiastic assent of their own famous and subtle dramatist, who has depicted the psychology of a new Norway very different from that of the ancient Sagas, the country accepted the Danish prince and rejoiced in the telegraphic assurance of President Roosevelt that the throne of Sverri, Haakon, and Olaf was once more restored.[6]

The study of history, if it does not make men wise, is at least calculated to make them sad. In the mere attrition of experience we lose something of our freshness and our hope. We see how rough a thing is government, how easily the convictions of the great become the bland and soothing make-believes of the little, and how frail and uncertain is the connexion between the professions and the practice of politicians. There are, indeed, times when large and generous ideas take possession of the air, when the tone rises and the conduct of public business is illumined by the ray of some nobler purpose ; but such times are rare, and even in the grandest crises of history the microscope discovers the familiar spectacle, old as human nature itself, of vulgar aims and low intrigue. This is so, and yet man being compounded of many elements good and bad, some gleams of idealism or sentiment may be traced even in the politics of the basest age. Creeds may stiffen into forms, forms may become shackles, but there is always somewhere or other latent in society a leaven of revolt against cant. The shape which that revolt may assume varies with every age and every people, but if it be a genuine thing and not an idle explosion of social envy or petulance, it will be found in all its varying manifestations to exhibit one fixed property, a sense of true, and an aversion from false values. The idea of a commonwealth or republic, like the idea of abstract equality or the idea of the social contract, has been a constant factor in the political consciousness of Europe, and it has exercised an extraordinary, though not unintelligible, attraction for many great and noble-minded men. Think only of the dynasty of poets who have belonged in spirit to the free republic, of Milton, Wordsworth, and Shelley, of Schiller and Freiligrath, of Alfieri and Lamartine, of Hugo (in some moods), Aguilera, and Swinburne, to exclude the ancients and to mention only a few of the more famous names among the moderns. Such a list exhibits the power and range of the republican appeal. "Give me," wrote Byron in 1813, "a republic, or a despotism of one, rather than the mixed government of one, two, or three. A republic! Look at the history of the earth,—Rome, Greece, Venice, France, Holland, America, our short (eheu) Commonwealth, and compare it with what they did under masters . . . to be the first man, not the dictator nor sultan, but the Washington, the Aristides, the leader in talent and truth, is next to the Divinity ! Franklin, Penn, and next to these either Brutus or Cassius, even Mirabeau or St Just." So ran one vein of political idealism in the first half of the nineteenth century.

The republican movement of Europe reached its zenith in 1848. The Latin world has experienced many subsequent convulsions, and the weak monarchy of Portugal has recently been overthrown. Kingship is less secure in Spain and Italy than among the Teutonic, Scandinavian, or Slavonic peoples, and it is a nice question whether the cause of monarchy is more injured by its alliance with Ultramontanism in Spain, or by its estrangement from the whole clerical connexion in Italy. Yet the Republican party in Italy is overshadowed by the Socialists ; the Republican party in Spain, discredited by its association with anarchical or federalist aims. The accepted formula of political progress seems, if we are to be guided by the recent examples of Russia and Turkey, to be constitutional monarchy rather than republicanism. The republican movement has done its work. Its ideals have been appropriated and fused with more or less of completeness into the political system of Europe, and most of the domestic programme of 1848 is now fixed and embodied in the institutions of the Continent which, save only in France, Switzerland and Portugal, retains an explicit devotion to hereditary monarchy.

" All that we have defended," says Castelar, " the Conservatives have realized. Who sustained the idea of the autonomy of Hungary ? A Republican, Kossuth. Who realized it ? A Conservative, Deák. Who advanced the idea of the abolition of serfdom in Russia? Republicans. Who realized it? An Emperor, Alexander. Who preached the unity of Italy? A Republican, Mazzini. Who realized it? A Conservative, Cavour. Who originated the idea of the Unity of Germany? The Republicans of Frankfort. Who realized it? An Imperialist, a Cæsarist, Bismarck. Who has awakened the Republican idea, three times stifled in France? A celebrated poet, Victor Hugo; a great orator, Jules Favre; another orator no less illustrious, Gambetta. Who has consolidated it? Another Conservative, Thiers." So writes the great Republican orator of Andalusia, illustrating the common truth that, with nations as with men, the colder wisdom of age uses and refines the sanguine enthusiasm of youth.[7]

NOTES

CHAPTER I

1. *De Institutione Delfini.* *Œuvres* (ed. 1858), vol. i. p. 8.
2. *Politique tirée de l'Ecriture sainte*, Bks. II. and III. *Œuvres*, vol. i. 333 ff.
3. Comparetti, *Vergilio nel medio evo*, i. 232, 235, 303-4, and see Aquinas, *De Regimine Principum*, i. 14 : " Romanam urbem Deus præviderat Christiani populi principalem sedem futuram." The interest in the history of republican Rome dates from the Renaissance. Cato, indeed, was a medieval hero, not, however, because he was a Republican, but as the reputed author of certain moral distiches. A. Graf, *Roma nella memoria e nelle imaginazione del medio evo.*
4. See Bryce, " Primitive Iceland," in *Studies in History and Jurisprudence*, vol. i. p. 312-58.
5. For the political theories of the Middle Ages, see the treatise by Dr Otto Gierke, translated, with an Introduction, by F. W. Maitland.
6. Campanella (1568-1639), *De Monarchia hispanica Discursus.*
7. Savonarola, *Discorso circa il reggimento e Governo degli Stati.*

CHAPTER II

1. Montesquieu, *Esprit des Lois*, xi. 6. An admirable account of Arnold of Brescia and of Cola di Rienzo is furnished in Bryce's *Holy Roman Empire*, c. xvi. See also Gabrielli, *Epistolario di Cola di Rienzo*, Rome, 1890. Emilio Castelar compares Arnold to Brutus, the one " the first citizen of modern Rome," the other " the last citizen of ancient Rome." *Recuerdos y Esperanzas*, ii. 40.
2. Guicciardini, *Op. Ined.*, i. 28.
3. *Ib.*
4. See a brilliant passage by J. A. Symonds, *Age of the Despots*, pp. 71-2, in answer to Sismondi. Of course the balance of genius is on the side of the republic if Florence be ranked as a republic during the veiled despotism of Lorenzo de' Medici. The comparative sterility of Genoa is one of the remarkable facts.

5. *Inferno*, xxxiv. 65-7. If Dante had read Plutarch, how different the Divine Comedy might have been !

6. The end of Boscoli is told in a narrative of extraordinary vividness by his friend Luca della Robbia, *Archivio Storico Italiano*, i. 273-309. Lorenzo's exploit and apology are given in Varchi, *Storia Fiorentina*, iii. 283-95, and Giannotti's letter in *Delizie delli eruditi bibliofili*, vii. 73. For the whole subject—Symonds, *Age of the Despots*, pp. 154-7.

7. There is a famous passage in Varchi (*Storia Fiorentina*, ii. 20), where he says that if Niccolo Machiavelli had conducted his private life with gravity and sincerity he would deserve to be compared with the intellects of antiquity.

   For the horror of the Venetian Ambassador at the silk-merchant politicians of Florence, see Alberi, *Relaz.*, 2nd Ser. i. 21. For Varchi's remark, see *Storia Fiorentina*, iii. 22.

8. Antonio Suriano, 1529, in Alberi, *Relazione*, 2nd Ser. v. 410.

9. Machiavelli, *Discorsi*, i. 55. Dante's lines on Florence (*Purg.*, vi. 145-51) are well-known :—

   "Quante volte del tempo che rimembre,
   Legge, moneta, offizio e costume
   Hai tu mutato, e rinnovato membre !
   E se ben ti ricordi, e vedi lume,
   Vedrai te simigliante a quella inferma,
   Che non può trovar posa in sulle piume,
   Ma non dar volta suo dolore scherma."

   For the instructive story of the short-lived Ambrosian Republic, see C. M. Ady, *The History of Milan under the Sforza*.

10. L. Pearsall Smith, "Life and Letters of Sir Henry Wotton." Intr. P. Paruta, a Venetian publicist who wrote in the last half of the sixteenth century, compares the heroes of his republic to the Fabricii, Marcelli, Fabii, and Scipii ; urges that though Venice had not so great an Empire as Rome, she had preserved her liberty through a longer period of time and had been less disturbed by civil discord ; and in a burst of patriotic eloquence exclaims that it was in Venice that were preserved the " last relics of the nobility of Italy." *Discorsi Politici*, i. 219, 232 ; ii. 147. The reader will not be surprised to learn that Paruta regards the Republic of Sparta as " the true example of perfect government " (*Della Perfezione della Vita Politica*, vol. iii. p. 396).

11. *Opere di Donato Giannotti*, ed. Polidori, 2 vols., Firenze, 1850.

12. Varchi estimates the number of Florentine palaces in the country at eight hundred, their average cost at 3500 gold florins. Marco Foscari, the Venetian, writing in 1527, regarded them as a great danger to the city, assuming that Florentines would always make peace with an enemy rather than sacrifice so great a treasure. Varchi, ix. 41 ; x. 29 ; Alberi, *Relazione*, 2nd Ser. i. 21.

13. Carducci was the second gonfalonier of the Second Florentine Republic and the soul of the resistance. His speeches are given in Varchi. For Burlamacchi, see *Archivio Storico Italiano*, 1st Ser., vol. x. pp. 435 ff. For the decline of learning during the Counter-Reformation, see J. A. Symonds, *The Catholic Reaction*, and Dejob, *Vie de Muret*.

San Marino, "where a hundred clowns govern a barbarous rock that no man invades" (Algernon Sidney), is the classical instance of the tiny republic, and the only Italian State spared by Napoleon.

14. The literature on Machiavelli and Guicciardini is immense. Lord Morley's two admirable essays, Villari's *Life of Machiavelli*, and L. A. Burd's learned edition of the *Principe*, will serve as introductions to the writers themselves. For Varchi's estimate of Guicciardini, *Storia Fiorentina*, x. 20.

CHAPTER III

1. See G. P. Gooch, *History of English Democratic Ideas in the Seventeenth Century* (an admirable book); E. Armstrong, *Political Theory of the Huguenots* ["English Historical Review," vol. iv., 1889]; A. Franck, *Reformateurs et Publicistes de l'Europe*, Cambridge Modern History, vol. iii. c. xxii.

Calvin's view is given, *Institutes*, iv. c. 20, § 8 (tr. Norton, 1634): "A government of the best man is the most blessed form, where liberty is framed to such moderation as it ought to be."

2. Hobbes, *Behemoth, Dialogues*; Voltaire, *Idées Républicaines*.

3. Althusius, J., *Politicæ Methodiæ Digesta*, Gröningen, 1610; and see O. Gierke, *Johannes Althusius*, 1878.

4. These debates, of extraordinary interest and importance as exhibiting the development of democratic ideas in England, are to be read in the *Clarke Papers*, ed. C. H. Firth.

5. See the full and striking account of Cromwell's hesitations in C. H. Firth's *The Last Years of the Protectorate*. Professor Firth brings evidence to show that the question was about to be reopened at the very end of·Cromwell's life.

6. For the Republican conspiracies under Charles II., see W. C. Abbott, *English Conspiracy and Dissent*, "American Historical Review," April 1909; and see Evelyn's *Diary*, 15th Jan. 1689. There was naturally a good deal of ferment at the beginning of the reign, as may be judged by the fact that Sir Roger Lestrange, the censor, destroyed editions of 600 tracts in three years.

7. A similar impression was left in English observers (as upon Æneas Sylvius in the middle of the fifteenth century) by the contrast between the "clean and cheerful" free towns of Germany, and the squalor and depopulation of the principalities. Lady Mary Wortley Montagu, *Letters*, i. 16.

19

8. Hobbes, *Leviathan*, c. 9 ; Dryden, *Prose Works*, ed. Malone, vol. iii. 266.

9. Mr Morse Stephens (*History of Portugal*) doubts whether there was ever any intention on the part of the conspiring Portuguese nobles to create a Republic in 1640 in case they should fail to persuade Duke John of Braganza to accept the throne. But see *The History of Portugal by a Person of Quality*, London, 1660 ; and also Ranke's remarks, *Die Osmanen und die Spanische Monarchie*, p. 475. That the Republic ever seemed possible in Paris rests on the authority of De Retz. A good account of the influence of Calvinism as the source of democratic ideas may be found in Charles Borgeaud, *The Rise of Democracy in Europe*.

CHAPTER IV

1. Condorcet, *Œuvres*, v. 283.

2. Montesquieu, *Esprit des Lois*, ii. 2 ; iii. 3 ; viii. 16; ix. 1-3 ; Rousseau, *Contrat Social*, iii. 7 ; Voltaire, *Idées Républicaines*. M. Aulard gives a brief and excellent summary of the opinions of the French philosophers on Republicanism in his *Histoire Politique de la Révolution Française* (Eng. tr. by B. Miall).

3. Condorcet, *Œuvres*, v. 299.

4. The enormous influence exerted by the American Revolution may be illustrated by Mably's *Observations sur le Gouvernement et les lois des États-Unis d'Amérique*, and by Condorcet's *Tableau du Progrès de l'Esprit humain* (*Œuvres*, viii. p. 266).

5. *Correspondance de Mme Roland*, ed. C. Perroud.

6. See some good remarks on the subject of the *Cahiers* in M. Émile Faguet's *Questions Politiques*, pp. 1-23 (a review of M. E. Champion's *La France d'après les Cahiers de* 1789).

7. For this and most of the succeeding paragraphs in this chapter I am indebted to M. Aulard, who has so closely studied the development of the republican party in France. It is curious to note the timidity of Robespierre. As late as July 1792, he solemnly disclaims being a Republican (Aulard, tr. Miall, i. 309 ; ii. 53). Mr L. G. Wickham Legg has printed some extracts illustrating the growth of Republicanism in his *Select Documents of the French Revolution*, vol. i. pp. 295-9.

8. Aulard (tr. Miall), i. 297.

9. For Plutarch, see Gréard, *De la Morale de Plutarque*.
      " J'étais fou de Plutarque à vingt ans, je pleurais de joie en le lisant."—Vauvenargues.
      " Je crains pour moi ces lectures-là comme la foudre."—Mirabeau.
      " Ce que Shakespeare a copié de Plutarque est bon, mais je ne saurai admirer ce qu'il a ajouté."—M. J. Chénier, 17 Feb. 1768.
      For Cicero, see Zielinski, *Cicero im Wandel der Jahrhunderte*.

Chapter V

1. Voltaire, *Idées Républicaines*, 1765.
2. The religious history of the French Revolution is now being told by a Catholic historian of great eminence, M. Pier de la Gorce.
3. Condorcet, *Œuvres*, v. 283.
4. Robespierre, April 1793. See Aulard (tr. Miall), ii. p. 177.
5. Condorcet, *Œuvres*, xviii. pp. 186-7.
6. The victims of the Terror have been estimated by Taine (*French Revolution*, Engl. tr., iii. 297) at 17,000 (probably too low a figure). Sarpi estimates the number of victims of the Inquisition in the Netherlands during the reign of Charles V. at 50,000, Grotius at 100,000. In Spain itself the figures are equally appalling. From 1480 to 1498 Torquemada is said to have burned alive 10,220 persons, and to have condemned 97,000 to perpetual imprisonment or public penitence. Symonds (quoting Llorente, i. 229), *The Catholic Reaction*, i. 194.
7. Dutard, whose excellent police reports are printed in Schmidt, *Tableaux de la Révolution Française*.

Chapter VI

1. The expectation of universal peace was not confined to Germany. Joseph Priestley and James Mackintosh both held that the triumph of reason and democracy in Europe would lead to the abandonment of colonial possessions and so greatly diminish the causes of friction between European nations. Priestley, *Letter XIV.*; Mackintosh, *Vindiciæ Gallicæ*.
2. See, for instance, Napoleon's letter to Talleyrand, 7th Oct. 1797, *Corr.* iii. no. 2292: "Vous connaissez peu ces peuples-ci. Ils ne méritent pas que l'on fasse tuer 40,000 Français pour eux. . . . Vous vous imaginez que la liberté fait faire de grandes choses à un peuple mou, superstitieux, 'pantalon' et lâche." His own attitude towards Italian parties is tersely summarised.—*Corr.* ii. p. 207, no. 1321.
3. The story of the Parthenopean Republic is told in Thiebault's *Mémoires*, vol. ii.; in Sorel, *L'Europe et la Révolution Française*, 5ième Partie; in Colletta's *History of Naples*; and by R. M. Johnston, *Napoleonic Empire in Southern Italy*.
4. For an excellent account of the effects of the French Revolution in England, see G. P. Gooch in the *Cambridge Modern History*, vol. viii. c. xxv.
5. The *locus classicus* for the history of the English democratic movement of this period is *State Trials*, vols. xxiv., xxv., where the proceedings in Rex *versus* Hardy, etc., are fully reported. Binns estimates the regular attendance at the

Corresponding Society at from 18,000 to 20,000. "The wishe and hopes of many of the members carried them to the over throw of the monarchy and the establishment of a republic' (*Recollections of J. B.*, Philadelphia). On the other hand Hardy's advice to correspondents was, "Leave monarchy democracy, and even religion entirely aside : never disput on these topics" (*State Trials*, xxiv. p. 394). And one of the characteristic features of the movement is the constan appeal to King Alfred, Magna Carta, the Bill of Rights, etc very different from the French Revolution in this respect Thus Mr Yorke, speaking at Sheffield, " enters into a com plete detail of the ancient constitution as established by Alfred, which he proved to be at this time totally defaced, i not lost " (*State Trials*, xxv. 670).

6. For Godwin's influence on Shelley, see Leslie Stephen, *Hours i a Library*, vol. iii. pp. 69-100.

CHAPTER VII

1. A good deal of information with regard to republican move ments in France from 1815-30 may be gained from G Weill, *Histoire du Parti Républicain en France*, 1900.

2. For Bentham, see Bowring's edition of his collected works, wit its great index (the most amusing in the world), and Lesl Stephen's *Utilitarians*. Goethe finds the solution for tl problems of life in free practical activity in a free land Faust seems to envy the makers of Holland, who daily batt for liberty and life.

> "Nur der verdient sich Freiheit wie das Leben
> Der täglich sie erobern muss."

3. Works, ed. Bowring, ix. pp. 127 ff.

4. *Ib.*, ii. p. 201. Shelley's Hellas was written in 1822. On Au 1, 1830, the Duke of Orleans told Lafayette that it w impossible to have spent two years in America withc regarding the American Constitution as the most perfect tl had ever existed.—Weill, *Histoire du Parti Républica* p. 43.

5. See *Cambridge Modern History*, vol. x. c. xvi.

6. E. Huyttens, *Discussions du Congrès National de Belgique*, 183c 5 vols., Brussels, 1844-5 ; and Karl Grün, *Die Sozi Bewegung in Frankreich und Belgien*, Darmstadt, 1845.

CHAPTER VIII

1. Menger thinks that some future *Kaiser* may adopt Socialism Constantine adopted Christianity.—*Neue Staatslehre*, p. 1

2. Mill, *Dissertations and Discussions*, vol. ii. p. 345. The of story, though doubtless an exaggeration, shows the sor criticism levelled against the government. Daniel St *Histoire de la Révolution de* 1848.

3. Of Lamartine it was said, "He has never read Aristophanes, he detests Rabelais, he does not understand Montaigne." De Tocqueville is even more severe—" Je ne sais si j'ai rencontré dans ce monde . . . un esprit plus vide de la pensée du bien public que le sien. . . . Il est le seul je crois, qui m'ai semblé toujours prêt à bouleverser le monde pour se distraire."—*Mémoires*, p. 164.

4. Daniel Stern (Mme Agoult) argues (*Histoire de la Révolution de 1848*) that the revolution was no accident, but the logical outcome of the philosophical movement of the age.

5. De la Normandie, *Notes et Souvenirs*.

6. De Tocqueville, *Mémoires*, p. 108.

7. Lamartine's *Trois Mois au Pouvoir* presents the authoritative apology for the Republican government.

8. See De Tocqueville's *Mémoires*, pp. 259 ff. ; and Odilon Barot, *Mémoires*, ii. pp. 215 ff.

CHAPTER IX

1. *Life and Writings of Giuseppe Mazzini*, 6 vols., London, 1864-70 ; Mazzini's Essays, tr. T. Okey, 1894 ; *Life of Giuseppe Mazzini*, by Bolton King, 1902.

2. The story of the siege of Venice is well told by W. R. Thayer, *The Dawn of Italian Independence*, 2 vols., Boston and New York, 1894.

3. See G. M. Trevelyan's brilliant *Defence of Rome by Garibaldi*. The effects of Garibaldi's life were felt far outside the borders of Italy. " ' Nothing will be done till Garibaldi comes,' was the reply of a peasant made at St Petersburg to a comrade of mine who talked to him about freedom coming."— Kropotkin, *Memoirs of a Revolutionary*, i. 51.

CHAPTER X

1. After 1830 Paris became the intellectual capital of Poland. A belief grew up and was very widely and earnestly held that Poland was the " Messiah of Nations," and that it was only through the sufferings of Poland that mankind could be regenerated. See E. Quinet, *Discours d'Ouverture*, 10th March 1848 : " Cette France du Nord, ce Christ des nations." The influence of the Polish spirit in Europe from 1830 to 1848 still awaits an historian.

2. Börne's *Briefe aus Paris* may be taken as representing the tendency prevalent among many Germans to idealise France as the home of progress and liberty. Arriving soon after the Revolution of 1830, he regards the pavement of Paris as hallowed by the blood of the martyrs of liberty, and dreams of a state of things in which France and Germany may be

united in a single polity, and governed by a national assembly sitting alternately at Frankfort and Paris. Börne wished to undo the Treaty of Verdun, just as Cecil Rhodes wished to undo the American Declaration of Independence and to have a Parliament alternately meeting in London and Washington.

3. See Laube, *Das Erste Deutsche Parlament*, and Malvida von Meysenburg, *Memoiren einer Idealisten*. Out of 370 members in the Vor-Parliament only 150 were Republicans.

4. F. Mehring, *Geschichte der Deutschen Sozialdemokratie*, vol. i. p. 49.

5. Of all the memoirs of the German Revolution in 1848, those of Carl Schurz (English) are the most illuminating and exciting.

CHAPTER XI

1. If Mr Gladstone had been a Frenchman he would have been something like M. Ollivier : exuberance, love of letters, eloquence, religious orthodoxy, political liberalism, special interest in theology are common to the English and to the French Liberal leader.

2. E. Ténot's *Histoire du Coup d'État* (1868) made a great impression. For the Republican party under the Second Empire, see Jaurès, *Histoire socialiste*, vol. x. 1 ; Tchernoff, *Le Parti républicain au Coup d'Etat et sous le Second Empire* ; G. Weill, *Histoire du Parti républicain en France de 1814 à 1870*.

3. The letters of Bakunin, Alex. Herzen, *Erinnerungen* (1907), and E. de Laveleye, *Le Socialisme contemporain*, throw light on the *Internationale*.

4. G. Hanotaux, *Histoire de la France contemporaine*.

5. Most of the philosophy of the Commune flowed from the writings of Proudhon. For the history of Anarchic ideas, see Zoccoli, *L'Anarchia*, 1907. William Morris' *Pilgrims of Hope*, a fine poem contributed to the *Commonwealth*, illustrates the sympathy felt in some quarters in England with the higher side of the Communal movement.

6. In 1852 Montalembert congratulated himself that Gallicanism was extinct. There were not four Bishops in France who would sign the Gallican articles of 1682 (Montalembert, *Des Intérêts catholiques au xix Siècle*). The divorce of the Church and the State has not, however, made for the spread of religion. See the remarkable figures given in Taine's *French Revolution*.

CHAPTER XII

1. An account of Bradlaugh's visit to Spain is given in the *Times*, June 3, 1873 ; and see *Life of Charles Bradlaugh* by Hypatia

Bradlaugh Bonner and John M. Robertson. Castelar gives a sympathetic and graphic description of Bradlaugh (his "herculean body" and the "sweet mystic vagueness of his azure eyes") in *Cartas sobre Politica Europea*, 1st ser. i. pp. 232-3.

2. For Richard Carlile (1790-1843), see *Dictionary of National Biography*. For the wave of republican feeling in 1871, Morley, *Life of Gladstone*, ii. 425-6, and Paul, *History of Modern England*, iii. 284.

3. The best history of the Spanish Revolution in English is that of E. H. Strobel (London, 1898). See also C. V. Cherbuliez, *L'Espagne Politique*, and H. Butler Clarke, *Modern Spain* (1815-98).

4. See *La República de 1873 apuntes para escribir su Historia*, por P. y Margall, Madrid, 1874, and D. Pablo Correa y Zafrilla, *La Federacion*.

5. Prince Kropotkin (*Memoirs of a Revolutionary*, ii. pp. 57, 194) says that the *Internationale* numbered eighty thousand regularly paying Spanish members—"all the active and thinking men of the population." A curious picture of the revolution is given in Saturnino Guimenez, *Cartagena*.

6. I heard Castelar speak to the students in the Sorbonne in the winter of 1889-90. His *Ricuerdos y Speranzas* give a fair picture of his opinions. There is a brilliant, though rather unsympathetic English life by Mr David Hannay.

7. The poetical side of the Spanish Republican movement can be studied in the fine lyrics of Aguilera, who watched the Italian *Risorgimento* and the movements of 1848 with passionate interest and assent. See, in particular, his *Ecos Nacionales y Cantares*, dedicated to Charles Rogier, one of the principal founders of Belgian independence. His noble advocacy of free schooling ("El Maestro que no viene"), his invocation to Pio Nono (1847), his poem against conscription ("El tributo del sangue"), his famous lyric on the five days of Milan ("En los ultimos dios de 1848"), are among the most spirited productions of modern Spanish verse. Like Castelar he dreamed that Republicanism might reunite the several members of the Iberian Peninsula.

> "Una es su lengua armoniosa
> Una su historia immortal
> En los siglos venederos
> Uno el destino será."—*Balada de Iberia*, 1869.

For the modern Catalan movement see *Lo nostre plet*, by Eveli Doria y Bonaplata, Barcelona, 1900; *Lo Catalanisme*, by V. Almirall, 2nd ed., Barcelona, 1888; *El Regionalismo*, by Alfredo Brañas, Barcelona, 1892; *Memoria en defensa de los Intereses Morales y Materiales de Cataña*, ed. 2, Barcelona, 1885.

CHAPTER XIII

1. Sidney Low, *Governance of England*, p. 278.

2. *Historical Sketches*, p. 96. [A superb piece of history]
   posthumously.]

3. Cobbett, *Political Works*, vi. 176.

4. R. C. K. Ensor, *Modern Socialism*. It may be not
   Robert Owen, the father of English Socialism, apį
   the Holy Alliance and dedicated *The Book of the N
   World* to William IV., and that Ferdinand Lasalle
   " a hereditary, monarchical, unified German Empir
   ideal of the Federal Republicans. Mehring, *Gesc.
   Deutschen Socialdemokratie*, iii. 102.

5. The estimation in which the poetry of Schiller is held
   barometer of German feeling. See Ludvig, *Schille
   Deutsche Nachwelt*.

6. I am much indebted here to information supplied ꞌ
   Kittelsen, the London representative of the N
   newspaper *Aftenposten*.

7. There were no fewer than five small republics temporaɪ
   lished in the Baltic Provinces in 1900, some of whicl
   long as two months. See Maslov, *Agrarian Qɪ
   Russia*, vol. ii. App. p. 38 (in Russian), a referencꞌ
   owe to the kindness of my omniscient friend, Profesɛ
   of Toronto. Nevertheless, ever since the brilliaɪ
   Pestel was executed in the Decembrist movemenᴉ
   there seems to have been very little republican ag
   Russia itself, though forward spirits working ɪ
   great Nicolas Muravieff (the Cecil Rhodes of Siberɪ
   of a republican federation of Siberia as a pendɑ
   Dominion of Canada. Pestel argued that Russian
   was Mongol, Russian bureaucracy German in oꞏ
   that the true spirit of Slavonic institutions was to
   in the commune, but he stood almost alone as a rꞌ
   See Castelar, *Storia del Movimiento Republicano*, ꞉
   A. Herzen, *Du Développement des Idées révolutioɪ
   Russie : Correspondance de Michel Bakounine*, ed. ꞉
   manov, tr. Stromberg ; and Kropotkin, *Mem
   Revolutionary*, vol. i. p. 198.

INDEX

A

Abjuration Act, 88
Act of Mediation, 214
Adelaide, Princess, 183
Æneas Sylvius, 289
Age of Reason, the, 142-3
Aguilera, 283, 295
Albert, *ouvrier*, 184
Albert, Prince Consort, 257, 278
Albornoz, Cardinal, 15
Alexander I. of Russia, 150
Alexander II. of Russia, 285
Alexander of Macedon, 4
Alfieri, 123, 126, 283
Algeria, 179
Alphonso XII. of Spain, 267
Alsace, 81, 238, 241
Althusius, 38
Amadeo of Savoy, 261-2
Ambrosian Republic, 22, 288
America, emigration to, 52; influence
  of, 57-8, 112, 212, 290; idealization
  of, 162-3, 292; arguments drawn
  from, 168, 191; Republican exiles
  in, 227; Presidential system of,
  273, 278; threatened collision with
  England, 279
American Colonies, 92
—— Declaration of the Rights of
  Man, 98
—— Independence, War of, 58, 142
Ancona, 115
Angelo, Michael, 28
Anjou, Duke of, 37
Antwerp, 100
Aosta, Duke of. See Amadeo of
  Savoy
Aquinas, Thomas, 17
Aragon, 7, 31
Aristogeiton, 16
Aristotle, 9, 20, 25, 38, 84
Arnold of Brescia, 14
Artois, Comte de. See Charles X.
Athens, 50
Attila, 6
Aubrey, J., 50

Augereau, 115
Augustus, 4
Aulard, F. A., 64, 77, 78, 79
Austria, 43, 81, 88, 100-2, 115, 135,
  194, 195, 230, 275
Austrian alliance, the, 80
—— Lombardy, 127
—— Netherlands, 81
Avignon, 81

B

Bacon, F., 27, 391
Baden, republican movements in, 194,
  213, 218, 223, 226
Badeners, the, 221
Bagehot, W., 277
Bakunin, 144
Balfour, A. J., 278
Barcelona, 262
Barère, 75, 107
Barras, 117
Barrot, O., 181
Barthélemy, 114, 115
Bastille, the, 66, 67, 138, 144, 147
Bazaine, 238
Beaufoys, Captain, 147
Beccaria, 125
Belfort, 156
Belgians, 100, 163-70
Belgium, 101, 115, 116, 155, 163-70,
  195
Bentham, J., 160-3, 292
Béranger, 155
Berlin, 53, 213, 217, 220
Berne, 214
Berry, Duke of, 156
Bidassoa, 156
Bill of Rights, 137, 138
Binns, John, 139, 291-2
Birmingham, 255
Bishops (French), election of, 98
Bismarck, 102, 219, 276, 285
Björnson, B., 280
Blanc, Louis, 172, 177, 180, 184, 186,
  187, 213, 227

Blum, Robert, 213
Bodin, 39
Bohemia, insurrection in, 193
Boissy d'Anglas, 112
Bonaparte, L. See Napoleon III.
Bonaparte, N. See Napoleon I.
Bonapartists, 154-5, 156-7
Bonn, 225
Bonnamy, General, 130
Bordeaux, Assembly of, 240, 243-5, 248, 251
Borgia, Cesare, 31, 123
Boscoli, 17
Bossuet, 1, 2, 49, 95
Bourbons, 80, 123, 151-2, 247-8, 253
Bradlaugh, Charles, 255-7
Brissot, 69, 70, 85, 151
Broglie, 66, 73
Brumaire, 121
Brunswick, Duke of, 70, 83, 148
—— Duchy of, 163, 215
Brussels, 163, 166
Brutus, 17, 85, 86, 284
Buchez, 176
Buddhism, 102
Bugeaud, Marshal, 183
Bunyan, J., 239
Burke, E., 89, 137-9, 142-3
Burlamacchi, 29, 289
Burleigh, Lord, 57
Byron, 283
Byzantium, 5, 13, 88

C

Cabet, 176
Cabinet Government, English, 137-8 ; French, 153
Cadiz, 265, 268
Cæsar, Julius, 85
Cahiers, the, 60
Cahors, 235
Calabria, 132
Calas, 93
Caligula, 18, 86
Calvin, 35, 289
Campagna, the, 56
Campanella, 9, 287
Campo Formio, 115
Campos, Martinez, 267
Canada, 58
Cannæ, 85
Cantonal movement, 264-5, 266
Capponi N., 20, 28
Carbonari, the, 134, 156, 196, 202, 229

Carducci, 29, 289
Carlile, R., 256-7
Carlists, 255, 257, 258
Carlyle, Thomas, 271
Carnot, 114, 115
Cartagena, 258, 265, 267
Casimir Périer, 179
Cassius, 17, 184
Castelar, Emilio, 256, 262, 265-6, 284-5, 295
Castlereagh, Lord, 164
Catalonia, 52, 259, 268, 295
Catharine II. of Russia, 53
Catiline, 84
Catilinarians, 17
Cato, 85, 287
Cavaignac, G., 158-9, 188
Cavalier Parliament, 48
Cavour, Count, 285
Cayenne, 115
Chambord, Comte de, 247-8
Champ de Mars, 72
Champion, E., 60
Championnet, 129-31
Chansons de Geste, 5
Charbonnerie, 156
Charlemagne, 6
Charles I. of England, 36, 40
Charles II. of England, 46, 48, 267
Charles VII. of France, 119
Charles VIII. of France, 21
Charles X. of France, 156-9, 241
Charles III. of Savoy, 51
Charles III. of Spain, 53
Charles IV. of Spain, 101
Charles Albert of Piedmont, 203-4
Charles, Prince of Denmark, 280, 281
Charter, the, 153
Chartist movement, 213
Chartreuse, 147
Chateaubriand, 151, 157
Chaumette, 107
Cherbuliez, 267
Christina of Spain, 261
Cicero, 4, 17, 84
Cisalpine Republic, 116, 127, 128, 134
Civil Constitution of the Clergy, 97
—— List, 274
—— Marriage, 97, 122
Clarendon Code, 48
Classics, influence of, 19-20, 50-1
Cloots, A., 78
Cobbett, W., 275
Cobden, R., 278
Coblentz, 110
Coke, Sir E., 40
Coleridge, S. T., 142, 145

Colletta, 132, 134
Colmar, 156
Cologne, 223
Committee of General Security, 107
—— of Public Safety, 106, 107, 109, 114
Commonwealth, the English, 40-51, 88, 91, 283
Commune of 1792, 74, 107, 113
—— of 1871, 213, 241, 244-7, 294
Comte, A., 174, 251
Concordat, the, 122, 251
Constant, B., 249
Constantine, 4
Constituent Assembly, the, 61, 63, 72, 90, 91, 94-7, 109, 112
Constitutional Code (Bentham's), 160-3
Consulate, the, 109, 122
Convention, the, 74, 77-9, 83, 107, 109, 111
Conway, Dr M., 142
Corresponding Society, 292
Coup d'État of 1851, 227, 228, 233, 234
Cracow, Republic of, 213
Crimean War, 229
Cromwell, Oliver, 41, 42, 46, 88, 91
Cuba, 258
Custozza, 204

D

Dandolo, E., 208
Dante, 5, 8, 17, 23, 201, 288
Danton, 73, 79, 101, 109
Deák, F., 284
Decazes, 157
Declaration of the Rights of Man, 98
De la Normandie, 182
De Maistre, 118, 150-1
Denmark, 217, 222, 225, 229
Des Brosses, 123
De Serre, 157
Desmoulins, C., 93
De Zoude, 168
Diocletian, 115
Directory, 112, 131, 132
Discourses on Government (Sidney's), 49, 50
Divorce, 97, 122
Dryden, J., 51
Du Camp, Maxime, 181
Dumouriez, 83, 238
Dupont de l'Eure, 185
Düsseldorf, 223

Dutch Independence, 91
—— points of conflict with the Belgians, 164-6
—— Republic, 2, 36-9, 46, 49-50, 51, 57, 88
Duvernier, 176

E

Eccelin da Romano, 16
Éducation Sentimentale (Flaubert), 181
Edward VII., 271-2, 279
Eikon Basilike, 44
Elizabeth, Queen, 39, 52
Emden, 38
Émigrés, 98
Empire, Roman, 4
—— medieval, 7, 8, 13
Empires, succession of, 9
England, 7, 8, 9, 40, 52, 58, 100, 101, 104, 136, 141
Eugénie, Empress, 228, 241

F

Faust, 160, 292
Favre, J., 236, 237, 285
Federalism (Spanish) 262-5, 268-9
Ferdinand II. of Austria, 195
Ferdinand IV. of Naples, 129, 134, 135
Ferdinand VII. of Spain, 261
Ferdinand of Aragon, 31
Ferrucci, 20
Ferry, Jules, 104
Filanghieri, 125
Flaubert, G., 181
Florence, 9, 17, 19, 20-33, 206, 287, 288
Foscari, M., 288
Fourier, C., 175-7
Fox, Charles, 138
Foy, General, 215
France, heresies of, 9, 11
—— influence of America on, 58-9, 112
—— monarchy of, 2, 49
—— rise of republicanism in, 52-118
—— Second Republic in, 171-92
—— succession to the throne in, 3
—— Third Republic in, 228-54
Francis I., 33
Francis II. of Austria, 82

Frankfort, Parliament of, 216-7, 221-3, 226, 276
Frederick II., Emperor, 16
Frederick II. of Prussia, 53
Frederick William II. of Prussia, 81
Frederick William IV. of Prussia, 195, 217, 218, 223
Freiligrath, 224, 283
French Revolution—
  Antecedents of, 53-63
  At war with Europe, 81-3
  Oratory and journalism of, 84-7
  Political philosophy of, 89-91
    Anti-Clericalism of, 91-8, 253-4
    Individualism of, 173
    Later course of, 106-18
    Retrospect of, 171-2
    Spirit of propaganda of, 99-102
Frisia, estates of, 38
Fronde, the, 52
Fructidor, 114
Fructidorians, 115, 116

G

Gaeta, 205
Gambetta, L., 104, 234, 235-7, 239, 240, 245, 250-3
Gardiner, S., 144
Garibaldi, 128, 207-9, 265, 285, 293
Geneva, 51-2, 84
Genoa, 13, 47, 124, 128, 135, 206, 287
Gensonné, 76
George III., 136, 137, 139, 140, 141, 162
George IV., 270, 271
Germany, autocratic spirit in, 276
——— confessional frontiers of, 39
——— conservatism of, 120
——— epics of, 5
——— free cities of, 3, 30
——— political condition of, 210-1
——— Revolution of 1848 in, 210-27
——— Tacitus on, 5
——— threatened war with France, 279
——— universal suffrage in, 275
Gerousia, the, 85
Giacomoni, 182
Gianotti, Donato, 17, 24-7, 32
Giovane Italia, 202
Girondins, the, 82, 109
——— Lamartine on, 180
Gladstone, W. E., 256
Godwin, W., 142, 143-4

Goethe, 83, 123, 160-1, 292
Goldoni, 123, 124
Greece, sympathy with, 155, 195
Grégoire, 79
Guadet, 76
Guelph and Ghibelline, 14, 15
Guicciardini, 15, 16, 28, 29, 31-3
Guizot, 144, 180, 182
Gustavus III., 55

H

Haakon, King, 282
Hanover, rising in, 163, 215
Hapsburgs, 38, 50, 123
Hardy, T., 140, 141, 291, 292
Harold the Fair Haired, 6
Harrington, Sir James, 44-5, 50, 136
Hébert, 109
Hecker, F., 218-9, 221-2, 227
Hegel, 262
Heidelberg, 220
Helvetian Republic, 214, 215
Henry III., 8
Henry of Navarre (Henry IV.), 36, 110, 119
Henry, Prince, 271
Hérault de Séchelles, 105
Hervegh, 222
Hesse-Cassel, rising in, 164, 215
Hobbes, Thomas, 36, 50, 200
Holland, 37, 52, 100, 155, 164
Hollis, T., 142
Holstein, 222
Hugo, Victor, 14, 116, 250, 251, 262, 283, 285
Hundred Days, concessions of, 172, 232
Hungary, 193, 284

I

Iceland, 6, 7
Illyrian Kingdom, 193
Imperialism, 276-7
Index, 29
Inferno (Dante's), 17
Innocent XI., 2
Instrument of government, the, 41, 42
Inquisition, the, 11, 106, 123, 291
Internationale, the, 234, 246, 264, 269, 294, 295
Ionian Islands, 115
Ireland, 141
Ireton, H., 41, 42

INDEX

Isabella of Spain, 261
Italy, despotisms of, 16
—— French sympathy with, 155
—— influence of Revolution and Empire on, 135-6
—— Napoleon's campaign in, 126-7
—— Napoleon I.'s plans for, 172
—— Napoleon III. and, 229
—— Napoleonic Kingdom of, 134
—— republics of, 15
—— Revolution of 1848 in, 192-210
—— Risorgimento in, 125
—— Spanish influence in, 29, 30

J

Jacobin Club, 69, 72, 159
Jacobins, the, 105, 107, 118, 145
Jamaica, 43
James I., 271
James II., 48
Jansenists, the, 93, 94
Jesuits, Order of, 29, 48
—— the, 93
Joan of Arc, 119
Johnson, Dr, 141
Judas Iscariot, 17
June, days of, 188-9, 241
Justinian, 125

K

Kant, 119, 151
Kellermann, 83
Kinkel, Professor, 226, 227
Knox, J., 35
Kossuth, L., 227, 284

L

Laboulaye, E., 249
Lacedemon, 23
La Farina, 210
Lafayette, 67, 155, 160
La France Libre, 93
Lamartine, 172, 180, 183, 186, 191, 262, 283, 293
Lamennais, 201
Landor, W., 142, 146
Lasalle, F., 234, 296
Laud, 40
Ledru-Rollin, 180, 187
Legations, the, 127

Leghorn, 206
Legislative Assembly, the, 72, 73, 82, 112
Leipzig, 213, 223
Lelius, 51
Leopold II., 53, 81, 82
Léroux, Pierre, 174
Les Misérables, 116
Leviathan, the, 50
Lewes, Song of, 8
Liberals, the French, 155-6, 231-3
Lilburne, J., 44
Lille, 115
—— Registers of, 37
Lisbon, 52
Livy, 4, 19, 50
Locke, J., 103
Lombardy, aristocracy of 13
—— Austrian government of, 197
—— fusion with Piedmont, 203
—— political state of, 123
—— towns of, 13
London, city of, 137
Long Parliament, the, 40, 45
Longwy, 76
Louis VI., 119
Louis IX., 2, 119
Louis XI., 119
Louis XIV., 1, 2, 39, 48
Louis XVI., 65-74, 80, 83
Louis XVII., 76, 80, 110
Louis XVIII., 67, 110, 111, 152, 156, 171, 178
Louis Philippe, 159-60, 169, 178-84, 195, 241, 262
Louvet, 84
Lucan, 4
Lucca, 135
Luther, 12, 34
Lycurgus, 86, 238
Lyons, 106, 107, 233

M

Macaulay, Lord, 274
Macaulay, Mrs, 141
Machiavelli, 22, 23, 26, 29, 30-1, 35, 123, 288
Macdonald, Marshal, 133
Mack, General, 129
Macmahon, Marshal, 247
Madrid, 80, 255, 264
Mainz, 82
Mallet du Pan, 108
Malmesbury, Lord, 115
Malmoë, 222

Mamiani, 206
Manchester, 141
Manin, D., 204, 210
Manuel, 155, 215
Marathon, 85
Marcia, 85
Marengo, 134
Margall, Pi y, 262-5, 268
Marianne, the, 216
Maria Theresa, 53
Marie Antoinette, 66, 68
Marie Caroline of Naples, 129, 133, 134, 135
Marmont, Marshal, 159
Marrast, 184
Martignac, 157
Marx, K., 216-9, 224, 225, 234
Massinissa, 51
Mazzini, 9, 196, 197-202, 207, 210, 227, 285
Medici, Alessandro de', 16, 17, 18
Medici, Catherine, de', 35
Medici, Cosimo de', 27
Medici, expulsion and restoration of, 21, 24-29
Medici, Giuliano de', 17
Medici, Lorenzo de', 17, 30
Medici, Lorenzo de' (Lorenzaccio), 17-9
Medici, Lorenzo de' (the Great), 16, 28, 30
Metternich, 102, 151, 194
Menger, Anton, 178
Mercure de France, 108
—— Nationale, 64
Mérimée, Prosper, 243
Metz, 108
Mexican campaign, 229, 241
Meysenburg, Malvida von, 221
Michelet, Jules, 262, 265
Milan, 22, 128, 193, 203
Mill, James, 274
Mill, J. S., 103, 145, 178
Milton, John, 35, 43, 46, 47, 50, 88, 136, 149
Minos, 86
Mirabeau, 61, 67, 84, 284
Molé, Count, 182
Monarchy, Bentham on, 161-3
—— Bossuet on, 2, 3
—— contractual theory of, 8
—— discussed in Brussels, 167-70
—— Huguenot theories of, 35, 36
—— increased popularity of among Teutons, 270-2
—— least secure in Latin countries, 151, 284

Monarchy, Medieval, 7
—— pressed on Cromwell, 42, 43
—— Savonarola on, 9, 10
—— Sidney on, 49
Montaigne, 51
Montesquieu, 15, 55, 56, 98
Mountain, the, 113
Muretus, 29, 289

N

Nantes, 107
Naples, 52, 53, 80, 123, 128-35, 151, 156, 196, 197
Napoleon I., 102, 114, 115, 122, 126-7, 134-6, 141, 149, 154, 172, 214, 232
Napoleon III., 192, 207, 227, 228-36
Napoleonic legend, 172, 241
Narbonne, Comte de, 101
Naseby, 40
Nationale, le, 183
National Reformer, the, 255
—— workshops, 177, 186, 188
Nationalist aspirations, 155
Necker, 66
Nelson, 129, 133
Nero, 18, 86
Netherlands, the, 102
Neue Rheinische Zeitung, 224, 225
New model army, 41
Nice, 230
Niebelunglied, 120
Normandy, 90
North, Lord, 137, 138
Northomb, 168
Norway, rupture with Sweden, 279-82

O

Oates, Titus, 48
Oceana, 45
Offenburg, 220
Olaf, King, 281, 282
Ollivier, Émile, 232
O'Meara, Dr, 141
Orange, Prince of, 28
Organisation du Travail, 177
Orleans, Duke of. See Louis Philippe
Orleans, Helena, Duchess of, 183-4
Oscar II. of Sweden, 280
Oudinot, General, 207
Owen, Robert, 296
Oxenstiern, 57

P

Palais Royal, 62
Palatinate, 218
Palermo, 193
Palestine, 229
Papacy, 7, 8, 28, 29, 205-9, 229, 253-4
Papal States, 197, 229
Paris, 52, 66, 67-70, 73-4, 78, 82, 93, 110, 115, 181-4, 229, 233, 239, 244-7
Paris, Comte de, 247
Parma, 80
Parthenopœan Republic, 128-34
Paruta, P., 288
Patriote Français, 69, 70
Peninsular War, 258, 259
Penn, W., 284
Père Duchesne, 108
Pericles, 86
Pestel, Colonel, 296
Peter the Great, 53
Petrarch, 14, 29
Phalaris, 18
Philadelphia, 139
—— Convention, 63
Philip Augustus, 119
Philip II. of Spain, 37
Philippe Égalité, 110
Philosophy, influence on French Revolution, 59, 60
Piedmont, 123, 156, 203, 229, 230
Piedmontese, 229
Pillnitz, 81, 82
Pio Nono, 205-6
Pisa, 16
Pistoia, 16
Pitt, William, 140
Plutarch, 4, 17, 47, 59, 84, 288, 290
Poland, Castelar on future of, 266
—— kingship in, 169
—— Napoleon I. and, 172
—— Napoleon III. and, 229
—— revolutionary influence of, 212-13
—— risings in, 163, 222
—— sympathy with, 155, 188, 225
Polignac, Duc de, 158
Politicæ methodiæ Digesta (Althusius), 38
Political Justice, Inquiry concerning (Godwin's), 144
Polybius, 19, 51
Portugal, 52, 160, 278, 284, 290, 295
Prairial, 111
Prato, 24
Prelude, the (Wordsworth's), 146-8
Presidential system, 190-2, 273, 278

Price, Dr, 139
Prim, General, 261
Prince, the (Machiavelli's), 30, 31
Proudhon, 262, 267, 294
Provence, Count of. See Louis XVIII.
Provincial Government of 1848, 185-6
Prussia, 43, 81, 83, 101, 114, 223, 230, 241
Prynne, W., 40
Purgatory (Dante's), 8, 23

Q

Quiberon, 111
Quinet, 200
Quirinal, the, 205

R

Rabelais, 251
Radicalism, 103
Rastadt, 223, 227
Ready and Easy Way (Milton's), 46, 47
Reflexions on the French Revolution, 139, 142
Reform, Parliamentary (England), 142 ; (France), 180-1
Réforme, la, 183
Restoration monarchy in France, 152-60
Rhine frontier, 101, 102, 179
Rhodes, Cecil, 294, 296
Richelieu, 119
Rienzo, Cola di, 14, 15, 125, 287
Risorgimento, 125
Robert, M. and Mme., 64
Robespierre, 84, 100, 108, 109, 110, 112, 113, 149, 290
Rochefort, Henri de, 233
Roland, 6
Roland, Mme., 59, 60, 85
Romagna, 22, 31, 197
Rome, example of, 50, 84
—— French Church and, 95
—— French Republic in, 128
—— Mazzini on, 200
—— medieval republics in, 13-15
—— Republic of, 205-9
—— Senate of, 88
Roosevelt, T., 282
Rossi, Count, 205
Rota Club, 44
Rouen, 67, 91

Rousseau, 38, 56, 62, 84, 86, 87, 245, 265
Ruffo, Cardinal, 133
Rüge, A., 216
Russia, 53, 160, 225

S

Sadowa, 241
Saguntum, 28
St André, Jean Bon, 116
St Bartholomew, massacre of, 35
St Cloud, 68, 121
St Germain, palace of, 49
St Helena, 141, 172, 232
St Just, 85
St Mark, convent of, 27
—— Republic of. See Venice
St Simon, Count of, 174-6
Salasco, 204
Salmasius, 35, 43
Salmeron, 265
Sand, Georges, 192
San Marino, 30, 135, 289
Saumur, 156
Savonarola, 9, 21, 24, 29, 30
Savoy, 230
Saxony, 163, 215
Scheldt, 100, 165
Schiller, F., 221, 224, 283, 296
Schleswig, 222
Schurz, 225-7
Scipio, 51
Second Empire, 172, 192, 228-36, 241
—— Chambers, 63, 113, 190, 238, 249, 251
Sedan, 236, 241
September massacres, 148
—— Revolution, 236-7
Seron, 167
Seville, 265, 267, 268
Shaftesbury, Earl of, 48
Shakespeare, 59
Shelley, 14, 142, 144, 283
Sicily, 7, 123, 129
Sidney, Algernon, 40, 41, 48-50, 136
Sieyès, 70, 79
Sinamary, 115
Slav power, 218
Slave trade, abolition of, 148
Socialism, 173-4, 216, 234-5, 265, 275-6, 281, 285, 296
Socialistic writers, 174-8, 234-5
Soderini, 21
Solon, 238
Sonderbund, war of, 179, 214-5

Southey, 142, 145
Souvaroff, 133
Spain, 9, 53, 151, 156, 160, 164, 275, 278, 284
Spanish marriages, 179
Spanish Republic of 1873, 255-69
—— Republics of South America, 158, 170, 195, 266
Sparta, 50
Spartacus, 189
Spencer, Herbert, 176
Stockholm, 53
Stockmar, Baron, 257
Sully, 57
Suriano, A., 21
Surinam, 115
Sverri, King, 282, 283
Sweden, 53, 279-82
Swinburne, A., 283
Swiss cities, 30
—— Confederation, 3, 39, 50, 56, 88, 168, 214-5
Switzerland, 115, 149, 179

T

Tacitus, 4, 5, 19, 29, 134
Talleyrand, 101
Tarquins, the, 85
Temple, the, 110, 148
Terror, the, 74, 75, 109, 114, 116-7, 291
Thackeray, W. M., 270
Theodoric, 6
The Rights of Man (Paine), 142, 143
Thierry, A., 174
Thiers, A., 159, 240-47, 250, 266, 285
Thionville, 70
Thompson, J., 59
Thoughts on the Present Discontents, 137
Timoleon, 17
Tocqueville, A. de, 181, 184, 187, 189-91
Toleration, doctrine of, 39
Tolstoian system, 102
Tolstoy, 144
Tooke, Horne, 140, 141
Toulon, 156
Toussaint l'Ouverture, 149
Treitschke, H. von, 276
Tricolour, party of, 154-5
Trier, 82
Tuileries, attack on, in 1792, 74, 148
—— attack on, in 1848, 183
Turgot, 54-5, 57, 103

Tuscany, Grand Duchy of, 124, 206
—— cities of, 14
Tyndale, W., 35
Tyrannicide, 17-19
Tyranny, doctrine of resistance to, 35-6, 39

U

Ultramontanism, 253-4, 284
United Netherlands, Kingdom of, 163-70
—— Provinces. See Dutch Republic
—— States. See America
Universal suffrage, 77, 187, 192, 231, 235, 274-5
Utrecht, Treaty of, 123

V

Valmy, 78, 83-4
Valtelline, 127
Vane, Sir H., 43, 44
Varchi, 17, 18, 20, 28
Varennes, 68, 71
Victoria, Queen, 257, 270, 271-2, 279
Voltaire, 36
Volterra, 16
Vendée, the, 106, 111
Venetia, 127, 197, 203

Venetian Republic, extinguished by Bonaparte, 127, 149
Venice, 2, 13, 22-4, 29, 45, 47, 88, 124, 135, 193, 204-5, 288
Verdun, 76
Vergniaud, 75-6
Versailles, 65, 94, 125, 244
—— Peace of, 56
Vico, 125
Victor, Emmanuel, 210, 261
Vienna, 53, 217-8, 220
—— Congress of, 150, 151
Vieux Cordelier, the, 108
Villèle, 157
Vindiciæ contra tyrannos, 35
Virgil, 5
Voltaire, 56, 57, 59, 62, 93, 94, 101, 108
Von Struve, 218-9, 221
Voyage en Icarie, 176

W

Waterloo, 154
Weimar, 160
Westphalia, Treaty of, 39
Wilkes, J., 137
William I., King of the United Netherlands, 165-6
William I., King of Prussia, 270
William of Orange, 37
Wordsworth, W., 142, 145-9
Wyclif, 12

Lightning Source UK Ltd.
Milton Keynes UK
UKHW011443240219
337804UK00009B/1599/P